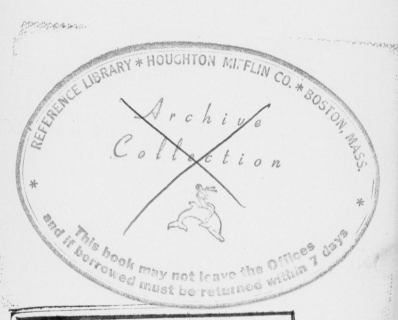

JOURNALS

OF

RALPH WALDO EMERSON

1820–1872

VOL. II

Madam Emerson

JOURNALS
OF
RALPH WALDO EMERSON

WITH ANNOTATIONS

EDITED BY

EDWARD WALDO EMERSON

AND

WALDO EMERSON FORBES

1824–1832

BOSTON AND NEW YORK
HOUGHTON MIFFLIN COMPANY
The Riverside Press Cambridge
1909

CONTENTS

TEACHER AND DIVINITY STUDENT

JOURNAL XV

1824

JOURNAL XVI

1825

JOURNAL XVII
1826

THE YOUNG MINISTER

JOURNAL XVIII

1827

JOURNAL XIX

1828

MINISTER OF THE SECOND CHURCH OF BOSTON

JOURNAL XX
1829

JOURNAL XXI
1830

CONTENTS

JOURNAL XXII

1831

CONTENTS

Obedience conquers. Shame of ignorance. Verses,
on *Death;* Γνῶθι Σεαυτόν. President Monroe. Morals
and Intellect. Point of View. Law. The blessed
Nineteenth Century. The right word; test of good
writing; poems; Shakspeare; Wordsworth; the old
English writers. He invents who proves; the discerning eye. The Solitude of the Soul among friends.
God in us. Education. Love and Death. Phi Beta
Kappa. Longing for friendship. Thoughts that set one
aglow; friends capable of such; Ellen. Thin disguises. Right use of riches. The real power; Napoleon, Cromwell, Andrew Jackson. Misrepresenting
God. Trust reason; The Oversoul; God's door.
Right and wrong way to make Christ loved. Quotations from Bacon. Threads tie the Universe.
Campbell. Justified books. Reputation. Adams's Eulogy
on Monroe. Temperance. Silence; Speech; Poverty.
Education. Coming Death. Who Knoweth? Origin of
Sunday Schools. Everyman's gauge. Miracles. Com-
pensation. Elevated and clear writing. Pestalozzi on
effect of surroundings. The moral law infinite. Verses,
The Mines of Truth. Non-resistance; Judge each by
his law. Creeds or Commandments; Calvinism;
Heaven here. Quotations; Schelling, Landor, Cicero,
Shakespeare's Sonnets. Formal and polemic Worship;
Calvinism and Unitarianism; the Soul's worship. Derry
Academy; limitations; trust your instincts. Abide your
time. Your Future here. Exchanges of pulpit. Robert
Burns, Wordsworth, praise and criticism. Madam
Emerson's remark. Mayhew School-Committee.
Prayer should be entrance into God's mind. Origin

JOURNAL XXIII

1832

CONTENTS

ILLUSTRATIONS

JOURNAL XV

(The last half of 1824, from "XV," "XVI," and "XVIII," 2d)

[FOR the next few years, Mr. Emerson kept several journals or note-books, the distinction between which is not strictly followed, with entries of dates covering several years. Therefore it seems better to avoid confusion by grouping the selections by years, rather than by separate note-books. It will be specified from what manuscript book the selections for each year were taken.

It must be understood, then, that, in this part of the work, the heading for each year given by the editors, Journal ——, does not signify a separate manuscript, but a combination; and yet, unfortunately, three of the journals that are here drawn upon have the Roman numerals xv, xvi, and xviii, 2d, given by Mr. Emerson.]

R. W. E. TO MISS EMERSON

(From "XVIII")

July 26, 1824.

. . . I suppose it jarred no chord in the Vale [1] when Byron died, a man of dreadful history, who left no brighter genius behind him than is gone, and no such blasphemer of heaven or pander to sensuality. But the light of sublimer existence was on his cheek, even in his sarcastic beastliness and coarse sneers, nor seemed less than archangel ruined, and the excess of glory obscured. It is one of the hardest errors to get rid of, — the admiration of intellectual excellence though depraved, and one cause is, there seems to be no reason why a spirit should be finely touched for such poor issues. One is glad of eternity, when we find so much to learn. But it is melancholy to have your well dry up, your fountain stopped from whence you were wont to look for an unfailing supply. Men marvel at Scott's never-ending traditions, but they set no bounds to their expectation from Byron's creative genius. Wit, argument, history,

1 "The Vale" (Waterford, Maine) was the name of the Haskins farm, in which Miss Emerson had some rights, and which was long her place of residence.

rhapsody, the extremes of good and ill,—everything was to be expected from his extraordinary invention. He might have added one more wonder to his life—its own redemption. And now he is dead, and is seeing the secrets his paramount genius dared to brave. It is terrible in example to presume as he has done, it is a risque not many are willing to run, but it is less mean and no worse thus to face the things unseen, and shake hands with Lucifer, than to commit the deed, and love the lust, and shake at the contumely of being over-good, and refuse to speak out all the time out of fear of being struck dead.

[BOOKS OF THE CENTURIES]
(From " XVI ")

October, 1824.

" By books," says the gentle Shepherd, " I crack with kings." 'T is a godlike invention which thus annihilates to all purposes of mental improvement both space and time, and suffers the solitary scholar by these silent interpreters to converse with minds who illuminated the beginnings of the world. My memory goes back to a past immortality, and I almost realize the perfection of a spiritual intercourse which gains all the good, and lacks all the inconvenience and disgust of close society of imperfect beings. We are then likest to the image of God, for in this grateful rapidity of thought a thousand years become one day. Providence has equitably distributed the highest order of minds along successive periods of time, and not clustered them all into one fortunate age. Hereby their potent influence enlightens the dark and cheers the gloom of barbarism. But an evil consequence ensues, that they are deprived of that splendid enjoyment which their equal society would afford them. But, as they everywhere rise above the sinking mass in which they stand, the eye of the distant historian associates them together, as in a distant prospect the vast intervening lowlands vanish and the mountains tower above them, seeming to come together in solemn and sublime society.

[A MAN]

I am partial to one sort of portrait. . . . I like the image my fancy presents me of a wise man, well bred to a vast variety of sound learning, carrying through sun and rain, through his rambles and business, and animal refections and filthy occupations, through visits of ceremony, and all the attitudes into which the versatile scene of life may throw him, — his *soul*, that rich world of thought; that subtle and elegant arrangement of conceptions, ripe for communication so soon as another spirit is presented. I like an unity of purpose in a man like the oft repeated warning of Cato, "It is also my opinion that Carthage should be destroyed." Scipio also. Mr. Wilberforce never speaks in British Parliament but for slaves. Mr. Everett is the expounder of a certain practical philosophy which always breaks forth incidentally, or in the plan of all his productions. In Voltaire, they who have vainly sought for any unity of character or object have been reduced to fix it in the absolute disregard of all character, object and truth. Anacreon tried to sing of heroes, but his lyre responded only Love; Byron's lyre returned but one sublime note, and it was *hatred*. He dreamed by day and by night but one dream, himself. He hated all others and also himself.

[EACH AND ALL]

In God's system, the virtue pervades the whole world, and none so poor as not to partake: if not opulent, he may impart of his wisdom; if foolish, of his strength, and so thoroughly *social* is our constitution that scarce an infant or idiot exists who cannot somehow or other contribute to the well-being of the universe. All are inevitably amenable to the Author of their power for the right use of it, and chiefly, or in the highest degree, those who have most liberally received. Are you then chief among ten thousand in the rarest endowments of genius, of wealth, of power, of accomplishments? You are but the wider channels through which the streams of his goodness flow. It was a noble saying of a Stoic that wise men are the perpetual priests of the gods.

Tiberius forbade they should consult the Sybilline books about the Inundation "*perinde divina humanaque obtegens . . . ut callidum ejus ingenium, ita anxium judicium.*" The Spanish Philips have been Tiberii. Austria today is Tiberian. 'T is so true and common and so bad a combination of real human elements that Tacitus might have wrought it up, as Xenophon did the character of Cyrus, *exempli causa.*

Candidus insuetum miratur limen Olympi,
 Sub pedibusque videt nubes et sidera Daphnis.
Apud LEIBNITZ, *de Bayle.*

[QUESTIONINGS]

(Continued from "XV")[1]

October 8, 1824.

It is a striking feature in our condition that we so hardly arrive at truth. . . . The final cause of this is, no doubt, found in the doctrine that we were not sent into this world for the discovery of truth, but for the education of our minds, and our faculties are best exercised by doubts, not by facts. The immediate consequence of this arrangement, like all other parts of human nature, has its admixture of evil. It is productive of that scepticism which throughout the world combats the advancement of truth. What you say is probable, says the Pyrrhonian, but the interval is always infinite between the highest probability and certainty. I will not renounce my old opinion for what may be an error. Prove it true, and I will be converted.

In opposition to this scepticism, in science, reason fights with truth; in religion [with] conscience. When a pure creed is proposed and

[1] The young literary man pleased himself by putting a large part of the journal from which the next pages are taken into the form of a publication like the *Spectator* or *Rambler*, though without serious thought of its ever appearing in print : it was purely for pleasure and practice.

accepted by the multitude, in whom the force
of truth and conscience ordinarily overbalances
the ambition of doubting, the infidelity of the
wise, who alone are privy to the full force of
objections, is commonly kept a secret among
themselves. That the number of avowed infidels
is small must not be esteemed decisive on the
success of Christianity. On the contrary, there
are few men who cannot number in the small
circle of their acquaintance one or more sceptics.
There are few Christians indeed who have not
nourished, if they don't now nourish, a latent
scepticism as to some portions of their system. . . .

When one considers that such is the constitution of the human mind that physical truth,
even when established by experiments of invariable success, is forced to encounter innumera-
able obstacles from vulgar prejudice, as in the
instance of vaccination, of Czar Peter's canals,
of Harvey's blood-circulation, and the like, and
since great force is added to the apprehension
that a metaphysical theological creed will not
prosper but against infinite odds, a doubt may
very naturally arise whether God would leave his
dispensation of such immeasurable moment to
his creatures, to struggle against this mighty bias

with so small chances of success. The more this objection is weighed, the more its force will be felt. We are so much the creatures of education that we find it hard to put ourselves in the place of those who lived under the imperfect religions of paganism. Christianity is so much adapted to the course of human feelings that it requires more discrimination than we are perhaps masters of to separate its fruits from the native promptings of humanity. There are moments in the life of every reflecting man wherein he seems to see farthest into the intellectual world, when his convictions of the existence of God and his own relations to him rise upon his mind with far greater force than they are accustomed to exert. But it is by no means certain that the mind of the old idolaters ached for any inspiration, or accused philosophy and nature with any emphasis for their scanty revelations.

Providence supports, but does not spoil its children. We are called sons, not darlings, of the Deity. There is ever good in store for those who love it; knowledge for those who seek it; and if we do evil, we suffer the consequences of evil. Throughout the administration of the world there is the same aspect of stern kindness; of good against your will; good against your good; ten thousand channels of active beneficence, but all flowing with the same regard to general, not particular, profit. . . .

And to such an extent is this great statute policy of God carried, that many, nay, most of the great blessings of humanity require cycles of a thousand years to bring them to their height. . . . The arts which do exalt and lengthen life by carrying on the old landmarks of thought to new stations, make a vast difference in the existence of the 1st and the 60th Century. Yet all these truths, of such vast consequence to our improvement, lay hid. The Compass, Press, Steam Engine; Astronomy, Mathematics, Politics, have scarce begun to exist till within a thousand years. Yet the principles of which they are results are surely in our nature. " Nature," said Burke, " is never more truly herself than in her grandest forms. The Apollo Belvidere is as much in Nature as any figure from the pencil of Rembrandt, or any clown in the rustic revels of Teniers." It is our nature to eat bread, yet the making of this substance is a very artificial process. " Man has no natural food," but was expected to convert inedible to edible substances. Thus, too, God has done with the religious education of men ; he has sowed truth in

the world, but has let them arrive at it by the
slow instrumentality of human research. Such
is the wise remark of Origen. . . .

[BOOKS AND MEN]

The great library of books that is in the
world, instead of making all mankind wiser and
better, is addressed for the most part to a very
small minority of men, to the learned alone. In
so great a mass of works, doubtless every appetite must be suited, and so we find a portion
which seems specially intended for coxcombs
and deficient persons. To this department belong the greatest part of Novels and Romances,
and all that part of the English Drama which
is called Living Plays. . . . But the third class
of men, the great body of society who make up
nations and conduct the business of the world,
these are least consulted in the composition of
books. The immense importance of this order
of men makes them indeed the subject of authors ; they form the groundwork of their reasonings, and from them illustrations are quoted.
But the books written on them are not written to them. Authors write to authors. And
as this Order (to use a local term), this Mid-
dling Interest of mankind, are immersed in daily

labours for daily bread, they seldom have the will or power to take up the pen in their turn. The consequence often is that they utter the same complaint as the Lion in the fable, that "if they were painters," etc.

[WRITING FOR AMERICANS]

Now this oversight of the greatest human interests might be excused by those political imperfections which were its cause as long as they lasted. It cannot now be excused. That portion of the community which all over Europe is called the Third Estate, has righted itself, by God's aid, in America, and has absorbed into itself the old distinctions of nobility and office. We have plucked down Fortune and set up Nature in his room. Consider who are the patrons of my muse. Not a frivolous dowager queen, not an imbecile baby, born, forsooth, in a royal bed, is now to be flattered in florid prose or lying rhyme —then I had been silent, — but to ad   a great nation risen from the dust and sitting in absolute judgment on the merits of men, ready to hear if any one offers good counsel, may rouse the ambition and exercise the understanding of a man. It is fit that something besides newspapers should be put into the hands of the people. It were well if short practical treatises on a hundred topics, all of primary importance, could make them prize what all the world covets. In the Capital of New England are many individuals who both serve and adorn their country. I have waited to hear them speak, but they are silent ; the hours are passing that should complete our education, the moment of instilling wholesome principles may not return. I shall therefore attempt in a series of papers to discuss, in a popular manner, some of those practical questions of daily recurrence, moral, political and literary, which best deserve the attention of my countrymen.

It is now a hundred years since the *Spectator* was found duly laid on every plate in the coffee houses and palaces of London. It was a book daily read by near fifty thousand people of every condition, and being a book of faultless persuasive morality and a sharp censor of fashionable vices, it operated with great force on the side of virtue. The common accounts say that 14,000, sometimes 20,000 *Spectators* were sold in a day. Supposing that four persons read each copy (and though some were no doubt read by less, others were read by many more), we shall have each of those moral lessons read by more than 50,000 persons. Since, the number has been indefinitely multiplied.

Sometimes, as seasons and circumstances change, I shall smile; sometimes I shall laugh, and that heartily; but my readers may expect that my garrulous humour may get the upper hand of my moral turn, and vent itself in anecdotes of myself and my friends, living and dead, in this and every age. And that which I reckon my chief recommendation is the confidence my reader may entertain of finding me his friend. I shall appear every evening at his tea-table, always speaking to him in the frankness of love, and communicating to him my choicest observations on men and manners. He who reflects what numbers are made miserable by the unhappiness of missing those offices of kindness 't is a friend's duty to perform, and who considers that the best and most consolatory use of friendship is the unreserved communication of thoughts, will not lightly esteem this overture I have made in the sincere desire of soothing discontent and sweetening solitude.

I have ever been noted for my fondness for children, and children are always fond of me. Nature has so vigilantly provided for the care of children in the affections of parents that, at a certain season of life, these irrepressible feelings break forth in bachelors also and secure a thousand endearments for the child that comes in their way. 'T is like, my brother used to tell me, the strong instinct of sea-shells which accompany the hoarse murmur of their native Ocean, though far removed from its social abodes and though withered and dried up in cabinets. . . .

And if ever, in administering to the wants of one class of my readers, I should offend another, I must ask their charity beforehand for my case, answering, as I must, such different demands; and it becomes me, like the old lady who worshipped the picture of St. Michael, while I hold up one candle to the Saint, to hold another to the dragon. I shall also allow myself such a latitude as to relate to my younger readers occasionally certain old stories which I heard in Germany touching the Trollfolk and the Elf gentry that yet lurk in some corners of that ancient empire, for I spit at the scepticism of the moderns.

. . . .

CIVILIZATION, MORAL.

. . . If we fulfil the expectations of mankind, we flatter ourselves we have fulfilled the demand of duty. Especially are we liable to this self-deception when the tone of feeling in society runs with any strong current towards the natural obligations of conscience. And now when Virtue has *éclat*, and Fashion itself has taken the Cross, there is indeed danger lest we mistake our conformity to this prevalent correct taste for the fruits of severe and ineradicable principles. Those sacred rules of life, companions of its sorrow and its well-being, companions and elements of its eternity, the objects of its present probation, the ties by which 't is to be bound to the Universe of Good beings, are not thus easily put on and off, with the succession of insignificant opinions and the customs of high life. They are slowly formed by many sacrifices of self, by many victories over the rebellion of fashion, and their genuineness is ever to be suspected when of hasty growth. . . .

It is perilous for Religion to be a fashion, as it is apt to lead men to errors both in the *nature* and in the *degree* of their virtue. . . .

SOCIETY OR SOLITUDE?

I propose to write presently on the use of our powers and passions, on abstinence and action, on hermits and men of affairs.[1] I propose to remember that 't is one thing to stifle and another to direct a propensity. I propose to look philosophically at the conduct of life; to remember [that] to the course of the meanest all the high rules of the theorist can be applied; and [to write] of the acceptance that sedulous action will find on high beside shiftless contemplation, and infer a law whether either life be embraced, or a golden mean preserved. Admit the exception of possibility of sublime virtue in absolute inaction, when inaction is martyrdom, but scrupulously exclude the claim of conceited or deceived indolence. A fine train of final Causes in the rewards attached to action. (Eichhorn — relatively and absolutely.)

1 L'étendue des connoissances dans les temps modernes ne fait qu'affoiblir le caractère quand il n'est pas fortifié par l'habitude des affaires et l'exercice de la volonté. Tout voir et tout comprendre est une grande raison d'incertitude ; et l'energie de l'action ne se développe que dans ces contrées libres et puissantes où les sentiments patriotiques sont dans l'âme, comme le sang dans les veines, et ne se glacent qu'avec la vie. — Mme. de Staël's *Germany*. (R. W. E.)

FINAL CAUSES

Ignorance is not a malady contracted on the earth, nor an incidental defect foreign to the purpose of our existence, but is an original want with which we were created, and which it is a chief business of life to supply. As hunger stimulates us to procure the food appointed for our sustenance, ignorance is but an appetite which God made us to gratify. . . .

[METHOD IN STUDY]

December 1, 1824.

I may digress, where all is digression, to utter a wish not altogether fruitless, that there might be an order introduced into the mass of reading that occupies or impends over me. It was a reasonable advice that a scholar gave me to *build* in the studies of a day; to begin with solid labour at Hebrew and Greek; theological criticism, moral philosophy and laborious writing should succeed; then history; then elegant letters — that species of books which is at once the most elevated amusement and the most productive suggester of thought, of which the instant specimens are the bulk of Johnson's

works, as Lives of Poets, Rambler, etc., Pope's
Moral Essays, and conspicuously Montaigne's
Essays. Thus much for the day. But what arrangement in priority of subjects? When shall
I read Greek, when Roman, when Austrian,
when Ecclesiastical, when American history?
Whilst we deliberate, time escapes. A poor plan
is better than none, as a poor law. I propose,
therefore, every morning before breakfast to
read a chapter in Greek Testament with its
Commentary. Afterwards, if time serve, *Le
Clerc;* or my reading and writing for disserta-
tions; then Mitford (all history is Ecclesiastical,
and all reasonings go back to Greece), and the
day end with Milton, Shakspere, Cicero or
Everett, Burke, Mackintosh, Playfair, Stewart,
Scott, Pope, Dryden. . . .

TIME

December 10.

I confess I am a little cynical on some topics,
and when a whole nation is roaring Patriotism
at the top of its voice, I am fain to explore the
cleanness of its hands and purity of its heart. I
have generally found the gravest and most useful
citizens are not the easiest provoked to swell
the noise, though they may be punctual at the

polls. And I have sometimes thought the election an individual makes between right and wrong more important than his choice between rival statesmen, and that the loss of a novel train of thought was ill paid by a considerable pecuniary gain. It is pleasant to know what is doing in the world, and why should a world go on if it does no good? The man whom your vote supports is to govern some millions — and it would be laughable not to know the issue of the naval battle. In ten years this great competition will be very stale, and a few words will inform you the result which cost you so many columns of the newsprints, so many anxious conjectures. Your soul will last longer than the ship; and will value its just and philosophical associations long after the memory has spurned all obtrusive and burdensome contents. . . .

[FRAGMENT FOR USE IN A SERMON]

A celebrated English preacher, whose praise is in your churches, closed his discourse with a bold appeal which the fervour of his eloquence permitted, to the passions and imaginations of his hearers. He pointed their minds' eyes to the Recording Angel who waited on the wing

in the midst of the assembly to write down some
name of all that multitude in his book of Life.
" And shall he wait in vain?" he said, "and will
you let him take his departure for heaven without making him the witness of a single soul converted from his sins?" My friends, we know
that his sentiment was but a flight of oratory,
natural enough to a fervid spirit, and which the
urgency of the occasion might excuse. My
friends, no Recording Angel that we know of
hovers over our assembly, but a greater than
An Angel is here. There is one in the midst of
us, though your eyes see him not, who is not a
fictitious or an imaginary being, but who is too
great and too glorious for our eyes to bear.
There is one here, imparting to us the life and
sense we at this moment exercise, whose tremendous power set yonder sun in the firmament, and upholds him and us. You cannot
discern him by the gross orbs of sight, but can
you not feel the weight of his presence sinking
on your heart; does no conscious feeling stir in
your bosoms under the eye of your Author and
God, who is here? What doth he here? and how
shall we acknowledge the almighty mind? . . .

IMAGINATION

I propose to write an Essay on the Evils of Imagination, which, after such a panegyrick on this beautiful faculty as it easily shall admit, may treat of those egregious errors that, growing out of some favourite fancy, have shot up into whole systems of philosophy or bodies of divinity, and have obstructed truth for thousands of years. The Essay should exemplify its statement by some of the most signal instances of this capacity in which the imagination has held the Reason of Man.[1] Thus the picturesque dogma of a *ruined world* has had a most pernicious fascination over nations of believers. It was an error locked with their life. They gave up the ghost for the love of this lye. And it clings, to this day, in the high places of know-

[1] "Man," says Brown, "loves what is simple much, but he loves what is mysterious more. 'I am persuaded,' said Fontenelle, 'that, if the majority of mankind could be made to see the order of the universe such as it is, as they would not remark in it any virtues attached to certain numbers, nor any properties inherent in certain planets, nor fatalities in certain times and revolutions of these, they would not be able to restrain themselves on the sight of this admirable regularity and beauty from crying out with astonishment, "What! is this all?"'" — Brown's *Philosophy* (R. W. E.).

ledge and refinement. Hence the avidity with which tales of wonder are caught and propagated. Hence Gibbon's remark that men of imagination are dogmatic. See, on this subject, one of Stewart's Introductory Chapters in the Philosophy. See Mr. Hume's remarks on the agreeableness of the feelings engaged.—Chapter on Miracles, and some of the fables anciently recounted touching Memnon's marble harp, renowned of old, and the oracles of Dodona and Delphos, and the histories of enchanters, ghosts and stars. Le Saurin called Earth the "scaffold of divine Vengeance";[1] also, e. g., "Nature abhors a vacuum." . . . On this head, consult the Introductory Lectures of Brown's Philosophy. Quietists, Essenes, Quakers, Swedenborgians. *Vide* Prideaux. For Proselytism and Missions see Vattel, p. 219.

Christ came not unforeseen by the ancient prophets, whose eyes had caught a glimpse of blessed light across the cloud of futurity. A thousand years brooded over the prophecy ere the event was matured.

[1] Origen, conforming himself to the extravagancies of his time, shews the necessity of 4 gospels, from 4 winds, 4 pillars of a house, and ransacks nature and nonsense for resemblances of the Cross. (R. W. E.)

PROVIDENCE

Another remark which belongs to the Econ-omy of Providence is the cheapness (if the ex-pression may be used) with which its operations are performed. A man conversant in books of history must often have deplored the immense expense of wit, of time, that are incurred by us to promote any designs of considerable extent. If a legislator would relieve the necessities of a thousand paupers he has the task of life, and of all his abilities, and of many more lives and minds than his own. Much of his labour is mere experiment, and much therefore of his labour is lost. Private and public subscriptions which searched the charity and taxed the means of a whole nation may leave the evil as bad or worse than it was found. . . . Does Providence botch up its broken or disordered machinery with the same awkwardness, miscalculation and prodigal expense? Look a little at its vast and serene policy, and see how it answers the same end which we have seen human wisdom toiling to gain. As if to delight itself with the exhibition of its contrivance, it brings all men into life pau-pers. Not destitute of wealth alone, but in the destitution of all faculties of action and capacities of thought and enjoyment, without virtue, affection, knowledge or passion. This deplorable poverty it is the proposed problem to relieve, and it may furnish amusement to many hours of Idleness in him that once thought life wearisome, to detect the beauty and simplicity of the means whereby it is done. (Read Rousseau's *Émile*, — Rousseau the unrivalled observer of infantile development, — and Buffon, the ingenious and benevolent describer of the growth and habits of animals.)

Faith is a telescope.

[Here follows part of a letter which Miss Emerson, stirred by some daring heterodoxy in his (lost) letter, wrote to her nephew, now on the eve of entering the Cambridge Divinity School.]

(From "XVIII," 2d)

WATERFORD, MAINE,
December 6, 1824.

He talks of the Holy Ghost. God of Mercy what a subject! Holy Ghost given to every man in Eden; it was lost in the great contest going on in the vast universe; it was lost, stifled; it was regiven, embodied in the assumed humanity of the Son of God, and since — the reward of prayer, agony, self-immolation! Dost not like the faith and the means? Take thy own — or rather the dictates of fashion. Let those who love the voice of uncorrupt nature seek for supernal aid — for an alliance with the most powerful of spirits — the Holy Ghost. Such was the ambition of Paul — of holy martyrs — it burnt up every earthly element, and would not stoop to ask an angel's record nor an angel's wreath. Would to God thou wert more ambitious — respected thyself more and the world less. Thou wouldst not to Cambridge. True they use the name "*Christo*," but that venerable institution, it is thought, has become but a feeble, ornamented arch in the great temple which the Christian world maintains to the honour of his name. It is but a garnished sepulchre where may be found some relics of the body of Jesus — some grosser parts which he took not at his ascent, and which [the College] will be forgotten and buried forever beneath the flowrets of genius and learning, if the master spirits of such as Appleton, Chalmers and Stewart and the consecrated Channing do not rescue it by a crusade of faith and lofty devotion. The nature and limits of human virtue, its dangers, its origin — "questions an-

swered at Cambridge — easily " God forgive thy
child his levity!—subjects veiled with something of Thine own awful incomprehensibility,
soothed only by the faith which reason loves,
but can never describe, which rests in solemn
delight on Him who not once calculated it for
any earthly emolument.

This was written with the pen taken for the
old almanacks at the moment of reading yours
of antediluvian date. Then you do not go to
Stewart [at Andover]. You might like him,
though he makes mouths at the heartless . . .
kindnesses which tickle, not benefit, the weak
world. He thinks a man in pursuit of greatness
feels no little wants. Why did you not study
under the wing of Channing which was never
pruned at Cambridge? If he advised Cambridge;
. . . Alas that you are there! There is a tide in
the affairs of men who connect the soul to the
future, which, taken at the moment, bears on to
fortune; omitted, the rest may be shallows. Do
we repine that so much is dependent on mortal
life? The reason we can't determine, yet that
this dread responsibility is not extended, is not
lengthened to the unknown world, is matter of
constant gratitude to those who find terrors in
the divine law and government, and in His natu-

ral attributes. Were this protection to be extended, as the liberal believe, to those who have heard of the gospel — of what reason was that astonishing apparatus given? Did not Christianity — even as much as the good Ware allows (which seems to leave more difficulties, though not so frightful as Calvin and the improvements of Woods) — imply much war with human nature, why do its professed disciples run into Atheism so often, rather than deism? Diluted as it is, it demands too much lofty and serious virtue, and, as humanitarianism opens the door to conclusions most forbidden, they make them. Price, so eminent, yet so flouted, says Christianity cannot be credible on Lardner's scheme; rather does it seem more so if necessarily connected with the Trinitarian. Blessed be God for the history, whether the penmen were inspired or not, of primitive religion in the Old and New Testaments. A descended being, the Companion of God before time, living and suffering as he did — giving not an intimation that he provided for any earthly comfort to his disciples, leaving if but a few of the precepts and engagements which he did, contains enow to demand constant martyrdom of speculation or interest — gives and does enable its devoted children to look at death and hell with sovereignty, to call God, though so tremendously holy, to witness that while he sustains their fulfilment of his conditions, while they love him thus, He himself can do nothing against them. This deep and high theology will prevail, and German madness may be cured. The public ear, weary of the artifices of eloquence, will ask for the wants of the soul to be satisfied. May you be among others who will prove a Pharos to your country and times. But I wander, because it is a penance, from the design of writing. It is to say that the years of levity and pride &c. &c. [which render me unworthy to speak of the heights of religion] I cannot but think were, in some measure, owing to the atmosphere of theology; to my own speculation, to what is worse and certain, the sore of human nature — could years of penitence restore me the last twenty years! It was pretty, it seemed best, to tell children how good they were [1] — the time of illusion and childhood is past, and you will find mysteries in man which baffle genius. . . . May the God of your fathers bless you beyond your progen-

[1] She blames herself for having fostered the (uncalvinistic) good opinion of themselves of the Emerson boys in their childhood, which has unfitted them for belief in original sin.

itors to the utmost bounds of your undying existence.

[The following is probably an extract from the nephew's answer to the foregoing.]

December 17, 1824.

I am blind, I fear, to the truth of a theology which I can't but respect for the eloquence it begets, and for the heroic life of its modern, and the heroic death of its ancient defenders. I acknowledge it tempts the imagination with a high epic (and better than epic) magnificence; but it sounds like mysticism in the ear of understanding. The finite and flitting kingdoms of this world may forget in the course of ages their maxims of government, and annul today the edict of a thousand years. And none would be surprised if the Rome of the Popes should vary in policy from the Rome of the Consuls. But that the administration of eternity is fickle; that the God of Revelation hath seen cause to repent and botch up the ordinances of the God of Nature—I hold it not irreverent, but impious in us to assume. Yet Paley's deity and Calvin's deity are plainly two beings, both sublime existences, but one a friend and the other a foe to

that capacity of order and right, to that understanding which is made in us arbiter of things
seen, the prophet of things unseen. When I see
wise and good of all [ages] consenting to a
single creed that taught the infinite perfections
and paternal character of God, and the account-
ableness of man, I cannot help acknowledging
the first and invariable fruit of those means of
information that are put in all hands. I cannot
help revolting from the double deity, gross
Gothic offspring of some Genevan school. I
suppose you'll think me so dazzled by a flambeau that I can't see the sun when I say that
the liberality of the age, though it stray into
licentiousness and deism, &c. &c. [The rest is
missing.]

["FOREFATHERS' DAY"]

("From XVI")

December 22.

Whose is the bark that comes over the deep
And lags on the waters while winds are asleep?
The salt foam scarce whitens the wake of its keel,
Scarce a motion of air can its loose sail reveal;
No gay streamers aloft on its main-top are hung,
No ensign declares whence its mariners sprung.
Unconvoyed the dull vessel sails and forlorn,
Her masts have been racked and her canvas is torn.

Whose is this bark, and what doth she here
By this winter-bound coast in the night of the year?
War is not the errand this traveller brings,
For her sides are not armed with the thunders of kings;
Nor for Commerce she visits yon barbarous shore,
Which the ship of the stranger ne'er greeted before.
Heave gently, dark Ocean, thou bear'st on thy breast
The hope of mankind to its home in the West.
If the tempest should bury that ship in the deep,
The fortunes of nations beside it should sleep,
For she brings through the vast solitudes of the sea
The pride of Old England, the . . .

AUTHORS OR BOOKS QUOTED OR REFERRED TO IN JOURNALS OF 1824

Bible;

Homer; Anacreon; Euripides;

Horace; Tacitus, *Annales;* Juvenal; Origen; Boethius;

Calvin; Montaigne, *Essays;* Hobbes, *Leviathan;*

Shakspeare; Bacon, *Essays, Henry VII;*

Milton, *Comus, Paradise Lost, Il Penseroso, Prose Works;*

Pascal; Cudworth; Locke;

Newton, *Maclaurin's Life of;*

Leibnitz, *Letters;* Le Clerc; Prideaux; Wollaston, *Religion of Nature;* Massillon;

Lardner (Rev. Nathaniel?); Addison; Saurin; Young; Butler, *Analogy*;

Pope, *Essays*, and *Poems*; Montesquieu, *Esprit des Loix*;

Hume, *History*, *Essays*; Vattell, *Law of Nations* (?); Goldsmith, *Retaliation*, and *Deserted Village*;

Burke, *Economic Reform*; Paley, *Natural Theology*; Gibbon; Playfair; Pitt, and Fox, *Speeches*;

Franklin, *Ephemeris*, etc.; Dugald Stewart, *Philosophical Essays*, *Introduction to the Encyclopædia*;

De Staël, *French Revolution*; Mackintosh; Thomas Brown, *Philosophy of the Human Mind*;

Byron, *Childe Harold*; Scott; Hogg; Wordsworth, *Excursion*;

Canning, *The Pilot that weathered the Storm*; *Mother Goose.*

JOURNAL XVI

1825

(From "XV," "XVI," and "XVIII," 2d)

[REFLECTIONS]

(From "XV")

Roxbury, *January* 4, 1825.

I have closed my school. I have begun a new
year. I have begun my studies, and this day a
moment of indolence engendered in me phan-
tasms and feelings that struggled to find vent in
rhyme. I thought of the passage of my years,
of their even and eventless tenor, and of the crisis
which is but a little way before, when a month
will determine the dark or bright dye they must
assume forever. I turn now to my lamp and my
tomes. I have nothing to do with society. My
unpleasing boyhood is past, my youth wanes into
the age of man, and what are the unsuppressed
glee, the cheering games, the golden hair and
shining eyes of youth unto me? I withdraw myself from their spell. A solemn voice commands
me to retire. And if in those scenes my blood
and brow have been cold, if my tongue has

stammered where fashion and gaiety were voluble, and I have had no grace amid the influences of Beauty and the festivities of Grandeur, I shall not hastily conclude my soul ignobly born and its horoscope fully cast. I will not yet believe that because it has lain so tranquil, great argument could not make it stir. I will not believe because I cannot unite dignity, as many can, to folly, that I am not born to fill the eye of great expectation, to speak when the people listen, nor to cast my mite into the great treasury of morals and intellect. I will not quite despair, nor quench my flambeau in the dust of " Easy live and quiet die."

Those men to whom the muse has vouchsafed her inspirations, fail, when they fail, by their own fault. They have an instrument in their hands that discourses music by which the multitude cannot choose but be moved. Yet the player has sometimes so many freaks, or such indolence, as to waste his life. If you have found any defect in your sympathies that puts a bar between you and others, go and study to find those views and feelings in which you come nearest to other men. Go and school your pride and thaw your icy benevolence, and nurse somewhere in your soul a spark of pure and heroic enthusiasm. Ambition and curiosity — they will prompt you to prove by experiments the affections and faculties you possess. You will bind yourself in friendship; you will obey the strong necessity of nature and knit yourself to woman in love,[1] and the exercise of those affections will open your apprehension to a more common feeling and closer kindred with men. You will explore your connexion with the world of spirits, and happy will you be if the flame of ardent piety toward the Infinite Spirit shall be taught to glow in your breast. . . .

(From "XVI")

O what have I to do
With merriment and jollities, —
Youth, golden hair and sparkling eyes,
And deafening games that children prize?

I am not made to tune a lute,
Nor amble in a soft saloon;
Nor mine the grace of kind salute
To mien of pride and heart of stone.
My pulse is slow, my blood is cold,
My stammering tongue is rudely turned.

. . . . .

1 "No thought infirm altered his cheek." (R. W. E.)

Man to his work, the merry to their wine,
Friend to his friend, folly to festivals,
All hopes and humors to their several ends,
Sages to schools, young Passion to its love,
Ambition to its task, and me to mine.
I am not charged with dallying messages
That thus I mingle in this glittering crowd,
Seeing with strange eyes their buffooneries.
I am not tangled in the cobweb net
That wanton Beauty weaves for youth so knit
To some fair maid he follows with his eye.
A sterner errand to the silken troop
Has quenched the uneasy blush that warmed my cheek;
I am commissioned in my day of joy
To leave my woods and streams, and the sweet sloth
Of prayer and song that were my dear delight;
To leave the rudeness of my woodland life,
Sweet twilight walks and midnight solitude
And kind acquaintance with the morning stars,
And the glad heyday of my household hours, —
The innocent mirth which sweetens daily bread,
Railing in love at those who rail again,
By mind's industry sharpening the love of life.
Books, Muses, study, fireside, friends, and love,
I loved ye with true love, so fare ye well.

I was a boy; boyhood slid gaily by,
And the impatient years that trod on it
Taught me new lessons in the lore of life.

I've learned the sum of that sad history
All woman-born do know, that hoped for days,
Days that come dancing on fraught with delights
Dash our blown hopes as they limp heavily by.
But I — the bantling of a country Muse —
Abandon all those toys with speed, to obey
The King whose meek ambassador I go.

(From "XV")

[MUST PROSPERITY REST ON ARMS?]

. . . .

Pray in your multifarious reading, look out for an instance to disprove Bacon's and the common opinion that the armed nation is a prosperous one. Can ye not find in the extent of time one people, one hour, when a conquered, unambitious community surpassed the Victor in comfort, in intelligence, in real enjoyment? It concerns the weal of mankind that the position be denied. . . .

[EDITORIAL CONFIDENCES]

When, some . . . pages back, my communicative mood was on me, and I was fain to take captive in print, not, as before, one or two compassionate eyes whom accident brought to my page, but the whole world of hearts, I attempted to bespeak some kindness for my fortunes by promising to make the reader acquainted with my friends, my habits and my worldly lot, I frankly told him that I spurned the vanity of external greatness, and had no sympathy with the effeminate soul that was cheated by the unmeaning names of Grace and Majesty. For me, I had as lief be the simple Cobbler of Agawam as the lineal Bourbon of the House of Capet; and a thousand times rather receive my immortal life from Sophroniscus, the stone-cutter, and his plain spouse, the midwife, so that I should be to future times the godlike mind, the Liberator of the Understanding who sprung from them, than be any Porphyrogenet of them all. I shall have future occasion to give a reason of my dissent from the universal prejudice to which no man can succumb and be wise. I return to my purpose of describing my connexions.

It is my own humor to despise pedigree. I was educated to prize it. The kind Aunt whose cares instructed my youth (and whom may God reward), told me oft the virtues of her and mine ancestors. They have been clergymen for many generations, and the piety of all and the eloquence of many is yet praised in the Churches. But the dead sleep in their moonless night; my business is with the living. The Genius that keeps me, to correct the ínequalities of my understanding, did not make me brother to clods of the same shape and texture as myself, but to my contraries. Thus, one of my house is a person of squared and methodical Conduct.[1] Another, on whose virtues I shall chiefly insist,[2] is an accomplished gentleman of a restless, worldly ambition who will not let me dream out

[1] William, the eldest, on whom from his early teens a large share of the burden of family affairs had fallen. While studying in Germany, doubts begotten by his philosophic instruction arose; so, at the bidding of conscience, though otherwise advised by Goethe, whose counsel the youth sought in a special pilgrimage to Weimar, he abandoned the hereditary profession and came home to study law. He practised honourably and successfully in New York for many years, in spite of constant ill-health, the result of his early asceticism on the family's behalf, and of unremitting work. He was a gentleman of great probity and courtesy, and an accomplished scholar.

[2] Edward Bliss, two years younger than Waldo, handsome, eloquent, and a brilliant scholar. He was destined for the law, and studied in Daniel Webster's office and was tutor to his sons; but his early promise was blighted by disease, and after years of broken health, he died in Porto Rico in 1834. Emerson in his "Dirge" (see *Poems*) mourns his

" Brother of the brief but blazing star."

For accounts of Edward see Cabot's and Holmes's Memoirs of Emerson.

my fine-spun reveries, but ever and anon jogs me and laughs aloud at my metaphysical sloth. In the acquaintance I propose to form with my readers I shall insist on my brothers' opinions as often as my own, and without knowing or caring whence spring the differences in character between equals in education, or whence fall the seed of virtues and abilities into the child which were not seen in the sire, I shall yet try to clothe him to the reader's eye in those attractions and dignities wherein he appears to my own. The day is gone by with me — such are the connexions into which Providence has thrown me — the day has gone by, when the useless and the frivolous should command my respect. I know very well that the great brotherhood of folly in the world, the idlers, the maniacs and the fools in society, exercise an influence over the daily course of events as vast and intimate as that of men of study and soul. Since it is not truth, but bread, that men seek, and when bread is procured, the exercise of their faculties delights them not so much as love and pride, it follows that very different agents enter into the offices of life from those of which wise men would compose their ideal Commonwealths. A fair skin, a bank-note, a fashionable dress, a tapestried parlor, a granite house, cause more steps and acts each day and keep more eyelids open by night than all the theories of the French Academy, or all the lofty images of *Paradise Lost*. If one of those silly angels that writers sometimes feign, to help them out of their difficulties, should be stationed at the corner of Court Street to inquire of every passenger the business he was upon, no doubt he would marvel much for what ends this world was made. For not one in a thousand could inform him of any mental or moral concern he had in hand. Every one, whatever bait attract him, whatever associates accompany him, picks out his own course, forgets in his own engrossing occupations the infinite multitude that bustles round him. It slips his memory that there are six hundred times ten hundred thousand persons on the planet: set aside the score of people with whom he has habits of familiar connexion, and the one or two hundred more with whom he has occasional intercourse, and the rest are of as little consequence to his life and his death as if they were the tenants of another globe. No information transmitted from one man to another can be more interesting than the accurate description of this little world in which he lies; and I shall deserve the thanks of every knowing reader, if I shall shew him the colour, orbit, and composition of my particular star.

[EVERETT'S PLYMOUTH ORATION, etc.]

Jack Cade was not more inclined to proscribe Grammar from his domains, than I method from mine. I had a freak three days ago to describe Tom, Dick and Harry, but my freak is clean gone by. I have been at an Ordination, hearing maxims on eloquence till I burned to speak. I have been reading Everett's rich strains at Plymouth,—gazing at the Sun till my eyes are blurred. This consenting declamation from every quarter on the auspicious promise of the times; this anxious and affectionate watching of the elder brothers over the painful birth of new nations in South America, Asia, Africa, (this " transfusion of youthful blood into aged veins" in Greece), is an authentic testimony to the reality of the good, or at least to a degree of it. It is infinitely better than that ill-omened cry of warning and fear that in the Middle Age bemoaned an enormous present degeneracy and the destruction of the world drawing nigh. Men congregated together in processions, fasts, penances, *miserecordias*, impressed by the sympathies of fear. The tremblers saw nothing in nature but symptoms of decay; nothing in the heavens but the torches that should light the conflagration. . . .

It is better to go to the house of feasting than to such a house of mourning as that. Sympathy with the wassailers is twice as easy and clever. But for my part, I am sorry that they could not have remembered the only thing worth remembering in those pall-holders, namely, their devotion. In their tribulation they kneeled to God, and acknowledged him as the sender of the adversity which overpowered them. But when, as the Hebrew bard would say, God repented of the evil which he thought to do, men, in their prosperity, forget the salutary lessons of an uniform and ancient experience, forget how the heart has always grown giddy and proud and blasphemous with what ought to make it thankful, and now, forsooth, in congratulating each other on their prosperity, they pronounce themselves *fortunate*; the advancement of knowledge, the acknowledgement of popular rights, *fortunate*; and the settlement at Plymouth (the most conspicuous interposition of God's Providence in these latter days) *fortunate*.[1] I mourn at the

[1] "That any thing happens by chance," said Bishop Butler, "every thinking man knows is absurd." (R. W. E.)

scepticism of prosperity, the scepticism of knowledge, the darkness of light. I love to trace the unambiguous workings of a greater hand than ours. Poetry had better drink at immortal fountains. Eloquence is best inspired by an Infinite cause. It is always an agreeable picture to the human imagination, the allusions to the strength of seeming weakness. No eye was ever offended at the tiny violet peeping out in fresh bloom on cold autumnal days, when the leaves are fallen and the oak is bare. None are disgusted at the fable of the bending willow which outlived the storm that tore down the monarchs of the forest. Yet such a power of meek sublimity is detected all along the course of human events, (among men, not of men), impelling and immortalizing the salutary principles of nature.

PRACTICAL POETRY

January 23, 1825.

Poetry, wise women have said, hath a noble inutility, and is loved, as the flowers of the field, because not the necessaries, but the luxuries of life; yet I observe it has sometimes deigned to mix in the most important influences that act on society. The revolutionary spirit in this cold and prudential country, it is said, was kept alive

and energized in 1776 by the seasonable aid of
patriotic songs and satirical ballads pointing at
well-known names and acts. Of Tyrtæus and his
conquering elegies who has not heard? And
Greek history has another more extraordinary
instance to the purpose. When Lycurgus medi-
tated the introduction into Sparta of his unpre-
cedented political model, he prevailed on Thales,
whom he met as he travelled in Asia Minor, to
pass to Laconia and compose poems there of
such a character as to prepare the minds of his
countrymen for the novel schemes of the Reformer.[1]

"KEEPING"

He that searches analogies in arts and life will
discern something akin to what in painting is
called *keeping*, in many corners where 't is un-
looked for. For though mine ear is untaught
by nature or art in the mysteries of music, yet I
have found my guess that such performance was
good or bad, on more than one occasion borne

[1] The most remarkable instance of the power of mere literature is Dean Swift, a modern Tyrtæus, who turned the tide
of political opinions in the British nation, ruined Marlborough,
and denounced Wood's half-pence by pamphlets. Nothing
fell from his pen in vain, says Johnson. Idolized by the Irish,
and proud of his influence. See *Lives of the Poets*. (R. W. E.)

out by competent hearers when my only means
of forming a judgment was the observation that
there were abrupt transitions from loud to soft
sounds without the just degrees which might be
termed the *keeping* of music. A skilful critic will
readily see the justice of the application of this
figure to any composition, also whether in verse
or prose. (Though I admit the propriety of certain exceptions in all the applications of the rule;
as when in Haydn's *Creation*, an explosion of
sound announces the change from darkness to
light; or in Dryden's *Ode on Cecilia's Day*,
violent transition of subject and manner is
permitted.)

SOLITUDE

ROXBURY, *January* 29, 1825.

["But when it pleased God, who separated me from my
mother's womb, and called *me* by his grace, to reveal his Son
in me, that I might preach him among the heathen; immediately I conferred not with flesh and blood: neither went I up
to Jerusalem to them which were apostles before me: but I
went into Arabia, and returned again unto Damascus."]

Galatians, chap. i. 15, 16, 17.

. . . You will be told that it is wholly a fanciful scheme, such as boys all have in their turn
and all sound minds outgrow — thus to talk of
divorcing yourself from society and making

yourself a haughty alien from flesh and blood
and its vulgar concerns, in the conceit of giving
your life to books, prayers, and barren meditations, and when you have been taunted as a friar,
grave sophists will accost you and tell you, under
the sanction of great names, that man is born by
the side of his father, and therefore should remain a social being; that it is deducible from
the laws of political economy that we should be
social, and many of the human faculties have no
use in solitude, which is the strong voice of nature pronouncing you fool. They will tell you
that Newton and Bacon and Shakspeare were
nursed and bred in crowds. Nay, veteran reformers may go a step or two beyond, and tell you in
a learned whisper that Religion has been mere
Reason of State ever since Numa's time, and always will be: that, though men of sense and spirit
are seen in *public* worship, 't is merely as they
countenance the constables; and that by no accident did any eye in earth or Heaven ever detect them in *private*. So 't were better you did
not set your judgment against the whole world's,
and so ruin a promising youth by falling into
disesteem and opprobrium. Against this consenting witness, or more, against this lofty derision, what Stoic can stand? You judge it best to

leave the ground you took, and rather than be
persuaded twice, O son of the ill-advised Adam,
pluck the fruit that others have plucked, and
rush into the great, foolish procession that goes
through the world drawing all men into its train,
and none know whence they come or where
they go. " O for a warning voice which He that
saw the Apocalypse heard cry in heaven aloud,
Woe to the inhabitants of earth." And you too
will enter, you who should have been prophet
and rescuer to a thousand of your brothers.
You will submit that hopeful character to these
depraved influences and be ground down to the
same base level. Meantime though you have
let it go, there *is* a good, solid and eternal, in
casting off the dishonest fetters of opinion and
nursing your solitary faculties into a self-exist-
ence so that your thoughts and actions shall be
in a degree your own. I commend no absurd
sacrifices. I praise no wolfish misanthropy that
retreats to thickets from cheerful towns, and
scrapes the ground for roots and acorns, either
out of a grovelling soul, or a hunger for glory
that has mistaken grimace for philosophy. It is
not the solitude of place, but the solitude of
soul which is so inestimable to us. . . .

. . . The Parnassian nag I rode, I perceive has thrown me, and I have been bestriding a hobby. It was my design, and must be the topic of a true discussion of this nature, to commend study, meditation, the preference of moral and intellectual things to appetites for outward things; and as far as Solitude can be a generalization of these things it may be admitted as the cardinal topic. But in this light 't were foolish to admit Newton, Bacon and Shakspeare as counter instances, or at all as exceptions. For all that made them great, is my very argument, the very stuff I praise, and all that subtracted from their respective worth is the very object of my invective sarcasm, admonition, rebuke, irony, satire, derision, assault,—O ye words! I have no breath to utter 'em. The philanthropist will perchance throw in the teeth of the anchorite the verse of Milton:—

" The Mind is it's own place, and in itself
　Can make a heaven of hell, a hell of heaven —
　What matter where, if I be still the same ? "

I only propose to let that mind be unswaddled, unchained, and there is no danger of any excess in the practice of this doctrine.

"So forcible within our hearts we feel
　The bond of nature draw us to our own."

Nature vindicates her rights, and society is more delicious to the occasional absentee. Besides, though I recommend the wilderness, I only enforce the doctrine of stated or frequent and habitual closetings. Men may be read, as well as books, too much. . . .

HENRY CLAY

February 6.

And if Henry Clay is dead, another great spirit has gone, like Byron's, over the unvoyageable gulf, another contemner of moral distinctions, to the award of the Divinity who set those distinctions, and not the less created the genius which defied them. Man feels a property in the eloquence, as in the poetry, of his fellows, or rather owes allegiance to those who exercise lordship over his noblest and dearest capacities, and so the public loss is mourned as when a sovereign dies. But it is a paradox that is again and again forced on our wonder, how those who act a part so important in its influences on the world should be permitted to give their genius to the worst passions, to cast the children's bread before the dogs. That ancient doctrine that a human soul is but a larger or less emanation from the Infinite soul is so agreeable to our imagination that something like this has always been a cherished part of popular belief. . . . Man is but the poor organ through which the breath of Him is blown; a pipe on which stops are sounded of strange music. A torch not lighted for itself. Yet these, such is the mystery of Free Will, turn on the hand that feeds them, dishonour the energy that inspires them, blaspheme the spirit that in them blasphemes. Byron, who partook richest of Divinity, foully ridicules the virtues practised to obey Him. Clay scorns the laws which bind all God's creatures.

February 8.

He is not dead. The story of the duel was false. Alas! for mine ejaculations.

REFLECTIONS

ROXBURY, 1825.

It is the evening of February eighth, which was never renowned that I know. But, be that as it may, 't is the last evening I spend in Canterbury. I go to my College Chamber to-morrow a little changed for better or worse since I left it in 1821. I have learned a few more names and dates, additional facility of expression, the gauge of my own ignorance, its sounding-places

" But to sit idle on the household hearth
A burdenous drone ; to visitants a gaze
Or pitied object."

Samson Agonistes.

" Short is the date of all immoderate fame.
It looks as heav'n our ruin had designed
And durst not trust thy fortune and thy mind."

Absalom and Achitophel.

" Dim as the borrowed beam of moon and stars
To lonely, weary, wandering travellers
Is reason to the soul ; and as on high
Those rolling fires discover but the sky,
Not light us here ; so reason's glimmering ray
Was lent, not to assure our doubtful way,
But guide us upward to a better day ;
And as," etc.

Religio Laici.

BIBLE

" This only doctrine does our lusts oppose
Unfed by nature's soil, in which it grows."

Religio Laici.

" Scripture was scarce and, as the market went,
Poor laymen took salvation on content,
As needy men take money, good or bad ;
God's word they had not, but the priest's they had."

Religio Laici.

As much as you men of the world acknowledge good and noble is all derived from religion,
from the principles of nature to which I appeal,
as your honour, etc.

[THE MINISTRY OF THE DAY]

What have we to say worth the attention of
men, when we put on, in these latter days, the
profession of the sacred teacher? We remember
with pride and gratitude the venerable men who,
in all past time, have instructed humanity, from
those Oriental sages who gave the first direction
to the understanding, down to the accomplished
orators whose accents yet ring in the ear of this
generation. And have they left anything unsaid? Is this a science of discoveries? What
contribution in your hand, what hope have you
in heart? Theology, which in pagan lands was
only one part of Ethics, the revolution of events
has enriched with noble parts. Theology, since
Revelation, has become the great science of man,
the only object here known worth the sole engagement of the intellect. Ethics is a secondary — a branch of this first philosophy. A correspondent change affects its professors. To be
the curious speculators on the contradictory
phenomena of thought, to be the humble ad-

visers to courses of conduct least dark, where all was doubtful, — this was the ambition, this the merit of the heathen sages. The ordinations of the Divinity respecting this world have put that office on different foundations. Those men who assume the charge of directing the devotions and duties of society are now the immediate representatives of the Deity, the organs through which he speaks to his creatures; the vicars, as the ambitious have said with a profane secular import, of God. Ah! what? Has Nature broke her marble silence? Has the spell of weary centuries dissolved and the Deity disclosed himself to men? Has the Most High opened his sublime abodes and come down on his sorrowing children with healing in his wings? Speak! How came he? What is he? What said he? and what is to come? Here we sat in the world waiting; admiring what could be the design of the appointments we seemed to be fulfilling, enduring as we could the pangs we met, desiring joy, but embracing evil with heavy hearts, sickening and alway dying, to the eve of our short day which went down in darkness, and especially moved with a sad curiosity and foreboding as to what should befall us after death. We saw in the world that some Mind had wrought, or now per-

chance consummated its active will with inex-
pressible might, and we waited when at last he
should break out into audible declaration of himself to our ears. But in vain we waited, who died
before the sight. Say what he hath said. This is
the language the eager stoic should utter to us
when restored to consciousness.

SOLITUDE OR SOCIETY (*continued*)

There can be no doubt that, in the disposition of human affairs which Providence has
made, there are great natural advantages proper to the social state. But it is equally conformable to divine dispensations that these
should be blended and balanced by disadvan-
tages. It is the part of wisdom, therefore, to
choose that safe middle path which shall avail
itself of the good and escape as much of the
evil as is possible. . . .

No man can examine the connexions and de-
pendencies of men in society without being struck
with the harmony and value of the whole design.
That infinity of relationships which spring from
parentage, from marriage, is a singular advantage
of the present order of things. If the world
should be conceived to be peopled in any other
mode, the innumerable connexions that tie soci-

ety together being taken away, would take off a mighty check from the bad passions.

It is pleasant to see in society two strangers introduced. True to the social principles of nature, they begin to feel round on the ordinary topics of conversation, until they find where they can nearest meet and sympathize. And you can hardly make two countrymen acquainted who will not frequently find some name with which both are connected by nature, affection or acquaintance; so far do the roots of families extend.

It is an ignoble and ungrateful part, in a man who rightly considers the goods of existence, to submit to be only born to this heritage, to be a passive recipient of life, or to lay a light and sloven hand on the generous bequests of Nature and Providence. It manifests a noble spirit, in harmony with the liberal giver, to come eagerly into the enjoyment to which we are invited, instead of skulking to a mouthful in the dark. We would not be the parasites of God's bounty, hungry for the good, but too mean and selfish to be capable of gratitude. We would rather be forgiven for a noble daring, for an ambition to see all, to know all, to use all. We would fain try the virtue of these powers, we would grapple with what is great, we would follow what flies, take hold on truth and imprison pleasure. We would go boldly on our adventurous quest and risk something to acquire a light on the nature, extent and end of our condition. In short, we would feel that it is action which exalts our nature above the slothful clod.

There is reason in Action. The good that is borne to us is not sharpened by our sluggishness. There is no indication in the fearful whirl of the rolling Universe that we should squat down unprofitable quietists in its lap. Besides the strong presumption there is, that by pushing these energies to their utmost we may even *deserve* something, may earn *merit*, instead of being a charge on the Universe.

[RICHES [1]]

Hae ye seen the caterpillar
Foully warking in his nest?
'T is the puir man getting siller;
Without cleanness, without rest.

1 Mr. Emerson copied these verses into his "Verse book," in a slightly modified form, which would show that, in spite of their Scottish dress, they were his own, and, as such, they are included in the Centenary Edition of the *Poems* (page 374).

Hae ye seen the butterfly
In braw claithing drest?
'T is the puir man gotten rich
With rings and painted vest.

The puir man crawls in web of rags
And sair beset with woes,
But when he flees on riches' wings
He laugheth at his foes.

R. W. E. TO MISS EMERSON
(From "XVIII," 2d)

March, 1825.

Anthropomorphism is, or has been, a bug-bear of a word, and yet it wraps up in its long syllables a sound and noble doctrine. So simple is the deduction of Reason, or so inevitable the inborn propensity to believe in God, that the Sadducee is solitary in his cheerless creed. In the excess, as it seems to me, of the same faith, we find human faces in the clouds, hear human voices in the roaring of the storms, and shake at spectres that surround us in the dark. The frivolous mythologies that are heard of in history pass and repass in the eyes of men, but take a firm root nowhere. Religion, like metaphysics or physics, hath its string of old wives' tales, told to its dishonour in every country; one tissue in Assyria, another at Memphis, another in Gaul, another by the Baltic, but probably there was no single spot and no one moment when legitimate notions of the First Cause did not find place along with this contemporary nonsense. For the sober divinity of common sense is no aristocrat. He dwells in high and humble places, he is no recent revelation, but is of Greek and Babylonian, nay, of antediluvian antiquity. And the grounds of proof are not more new. The eye, proverbially called the cure for Atheism; the hand, a machine of as exquisite and undeniable design; the mind, that busy deducer of causes from effects, itself the strongest and most evasive of all phenomena; the great globe itself and all mighty connexion that bind together its vast innumerable species —all these things subsisted in their entire force, bare all their testimony to the mind of Adam, as to mine. . . .

The life of a man is the epitome of the life of a body of men. "A single house will show whatever is done or suffered in the world," [said] Juvenal. The effects of circumstances on the individual are wonderfully analogous to the same effects on a state. And those final causes, whose harmony strikes the eye with more grandeur on the vaster theatre, are as conspicuous and as conclusive evidence to the wisdom which arranged them in the individual as in the nation. Yet the foolish folk of the ancient time are represented, with the solitary exception of here and there an Aristotle or two, as bowing down to an ox, to an onion, to a block, and devoutly believing in the divinity of the poor baggages. Now I put the question, whether in the course of your life (which, pardon me, I do not mean is long) you have not known at least half a dozen persons who, without being Aristotles, have yet had dogged sense enow to have disbelieved, to have scouted all that mythological flummery as soon as they came to years of discretion? And if so be that you have known six or seven, and each other explorer of mankind six or seven more, why, we shall very soon be able to acquit our pagan forefathers of being such absolute bears as the learned, in their lampoons, will have them to be. There is no doubt something very imposing in an ancient establishment that has intertwined its roots with government, property, art and poetry; but there is something also revolting in the gross superstition to correct the seduction; and moreover there are scenes and hours of redemption Nature hath provided for her children (or some of her children), when she sends down upon them the night in its beauty, and takes off the veil of garish day from the glowing, adorning firmament. These sights stir the strong principles afresh in the soul; and I do not think it is in the Understanding of man, when he stands in *that* temple, to ascribe the *whole* matter to a cat or crocodile, or yet to a sorry society, like the Olympian banditti. In fine, I do not so disparage Reason, God's elder Revelation, as to think 't would leave men entirely in the lurch in their greatest concernment; nor swallow such fables as to admit the firmness with which I see society amid all her institutions stood, without ascribing to men's conscience the same wholesome and sublime authority it exerts now.

[LATER COMMENTS]

But our author should remember that there are some things so absolutely impossible as not to be found by the most curious and microscopic eye, "for what never was will not easily be found, not even by the most curious." Public prosperity was content in old times in old nations with very gradual advances. She made many pauses and some retrocessions, but latterly she has mended her pace and has called in art to her aid; she travels the land in railroads and steam coaches; she sweeps the sea with a pressure of a thousand pounds, and all sails spread; and sends her parachute through the air like a cloud. There are some men whose minds misgive them, when they see the prodigious rate at which they are borne in the public vessel. They cannot help but be giddy and out of breath at the accelerated velocity of their motion. A Sabbath day's journey would be a safer jog.

.   .   .   .

[THE EDUCATED MIND]

Choose a sensible man to a responsible place rather than a man versed in the particular art which is to be taught, inasmuch as a method of acquiring truth is better than the truth it has already ascertained. Let your discipline liberalize the mind of a boy rather than teach him sciences, that he may have means, more than results.

The Indian will give his bow for the knife with which it was made.

Books to Read

Philippe de Commines;
Machiavel;
Cardinal de Retz;
Montaigne's *Essays*;
Plato's *Dialogues*;
Isocrates' *Panegyric*;
Constitution of the United States;
Adam Smith, *Works*.

[The last two entries, following the letter to Miss Emerson, are written in a large, straggling hand, the writer evidently not looking on his page. There are no more journal entries in 1825. Emerson's family letters of this time showed that his health failed rapidly after he moved to Divinity Hall. His eyes gave out completely, and he had a "stricture of the chest," and a very lame hip. He was obliged to give up his studies and go to visit his Uncle Ladd, who lived in Newton. He staid there until summer, helping as he could on the farm, and his health improved. Madam Emerson had taken a house on North Avenue (near Jarvis Field) to be near her sons, for Edward was teaching and studying law in Daniel Webster's office, and Charles in College.

Waldo took some private pupils during the summer, and taught a school in Chelmsford in the autumn. Some recollections of their schoolmaster by pupils at Chelmsford are given in *Emerson in Concord*, p. 32.]

JOURNAL XVII

(From "XV," "XVI," "XVIII," 2d, and Cabot's
Q and R)

[SOMEWHAT improved in health, Emerson came
to Roxbury at the beginning of the year to take,
for a time, a school which Edward's health had
obliged him to give up. He taught there during
the winter, and in April rejoined his mother in
Cambridge, in the "Mellen House" on North
Avenue, which afforded a schoolroom. There
he gathered his last school, which he taught until
the end of the summer. Among his scholars were
Richard Henry Dana and John Holmes. (See
Morse's life of Richard Henry Dana, page 5,
and Holmes's life of Emerson, page 50.)]

(From "XV")

January 8, 1826.

I come with mended eyes to my ancient friend
and consoler. Has the interval of silence made
the writer wiser? Does his mind teem with well
weighed judgments? The moral and intellectual universe has not halted because the eye of
the observer was closed. Compensation has been

woven to want, loss to gain, good to evil, and good to good, with the same industry, and the same concealment of an intelligent cause. And in my joy to write and read again I will not pester my imagination with what is done unseen, with the burden that is put in the contrary scale, with the sowing of the death-seed in the place of the nettle that was rooted up. I am a more cheerful philosopher, and am rather anxious to thank Oromasdes than to fear Ahriman.

Since I wrote before, I know something more of the grounds of hope and fear of what is to come. But if my knowledge is greater, so is my courage. I know that I *know* next to nothing, but I know too that the amount of probabilities is vast, both in mind and in morals. It is not certain that God exists, but that he does not is a most bewildering and improbable chimæra.

I rejoice that I live when the world is so old. There is the same difference between living with Adam and living with me as in going into a new house unfinished, damp and empty, and going into a long occupied house where the time and taste of its inhabitants has accumulated a thousand useful contrivances, has furnished the chambers, stocked the cellars, and filled the library. In the new house every comer must do all for himself. In the old mansion there are butlers, cooks, grooms and valets. In the new house all must work, and work with the hands. In the old one there are poets who sing, actors who play and ladies who dress and smile. O ye lovers of the past, judge between my houses. I would not be elsewhere than I am.

COMPENSATION

All things are double one against another, said Solomon. The whole of what we know is a system of compensations. Every defect in one manner is made up in another. Every suffering is rewarded; every sacrifice is made up; every debt is paid.

The history of retributions is a strange and awful story; it will confirm the faith that wavers, and, more than any other moral feature, is perhaps susceptible of examination and analysis, and, more than any other, fit to establish the doctrine of Divine Providence. . . .

I have seen — all men in the common circumstances of society may see — the thrift, cold-blooded and hard-hearted thrift, that has wrought out for itself its own reward, men and women that set out to be rich, that sold their body, its strength, its grace, its health, its sleep; yea, and sold their soul, its peace, its affections, its time, its education, its religion, its eternity, for gold. They have paid the price and by the laws of Providence they shall receive their purchase. But by the laws of Providence they shall receive nothing more. They have not bought any immunity from bodily pain, any grace from the elements, any courtesy from the diseases; they made no mention with their dealers of gentle affections, and asked no more of the Intellectual Principle than how to cast their drivelling balances of loss and gain. Health, knowledge, friendship, God, — these were no parties to their contract, no guarantees against disaster. These were defrauded of the just debt which each human being owes them, to scrape together the means by which wealth was to be bought. But these are creditors that will not let them pass unchallenged. They have asked no protection against the evils of life, and God has left them naked to them. . . .

Ignorance shall curse them with a leaden cloud on their understandings, their hours shall drag by in stupid darkness, unvisited by Thought, the daughter of God, denounced, forgot, unrecognized by the great brotherhood of intelligent minds who are penetrating into the obscure on every side and adding new provinces to the kingdom of Knowledge. . . .

But all who sell themselves do not sell for wealth. There are many dupes of many passions. Nor are the compensations that God ordains confined to a single class of moral agents. To come nearer to my design, I will venture to assert that whilst all moral reasonings of necessity refer to a whole existence, to a vaster system of things than is here disclosed, there are, nevertheless, strong presumptions here exhibited that perfect compensations do hold, that very much is done in this world to adjust the uneven balance of condition and character.

There are certain great and obvious illustrations of this doctrine which lie on the outside of life and have therefore been always noted: that prodigality makes haste to want; that riot introduces disease; that fearful crimes are hunted by fearful remorse; that the love of money is punished by the care of money; that honest indigence is cheerful; that in fertile climates the air breathes pestilence, and in healthy zones there is an iron soil; that whilst the mind is in ignorant infancy, the body is supple and strong; when the mind is informed and powerful the body decays,— these and all this most important class of facts lie at the foundation of our faith in God's being and providence. . . .

I say that sin is ignorance, that the thief steals from himself; that he who practices fraud is himself the dupe of the fraud he practices, that whoso borrows runs in his own debt; and whoso gives to another benefits himself to the same amount.

Our nature has a twofold aspect, towards self and towards society; and the good or evil, the riches or poverty of a man, is to be measured, of course, by its relation to these two.

And in the view of individual, unconnected character, as a moral being having duties to fulfil and a character to earn in the sight of God, am I impoverished that I have given my goods to feed the poor, that I have hazarded half my estate in the hands of my friend in yielding to calls of moral sentiment which made a part of my highest nature? Am I the richer in my own just estimation that I have unjustly taken or withheld from my fellow man his good name, his rights, or his property? Am I the richer that I have tied up my own purse and borrowed for my needs of the treasure of my friends? Shall I count myself richer that I have received an hundred favours and rendered none? Myself

— the man within the breast — am the sole judge of this question and there is no appeal from the decisive negative. The daily mistake of thousands and tens of thousands who jump to make any pitiful advantage of their neighbour must not be quoted against this tribunal. . . . It is not the true estimate of a man's actual value that is made from the balance of figures that stands in his favour on his ledger. This is to be corrected from the book of Life within him. . . . If it is the reward of honest industry and skill, to which, said the ancient philosopher, the gods have sold all things, his estimate is correct, his doings are respected in heaven and in earth. Each man knows . . . what is his just standing, whether he is indebted or whether he has rendered others rich and happy.

We have, we trust, made it apparent, that in the aspect of *self*, our doctrine that nothing in the intercourse of men can be *given*, is sound. The doctrine is no less true, no less important in its respect to our social nature. If a man steals, is it not known? If he borrows, is it not known? If he receives gifts, is it not known? If I accept important benefits from another, in secret or in public, there arises of course from the deed a secret acknowledgment of benefit on his part and of debt on mine, or, in other words, of superiority and of inferiority.

(From Cabot's Q)

LETTER TO MISS EMERSON

January, 1826.

The name of Hume, I fancy, has hardly gathered all its fame. His Essays are now found all over Europe and will take place doubtless in all Pyrrhonian bosoms of all other freethinkers of England or France. German theology will prop itself on him, and suggest to its lovers a sort of apology and consolation in his mild and plausible epicureanism. He is one of those great limitary angels to whom power is given for a season over the minds and history of men, not so much to mislead as to cast another weight into the *contrary scale* in that vast and complex adjustment of good and evil to which our understandings are accommodated and through which they are to escape by the fine clue of moral perception. For me, I hold fast to my old faith, that to each soul is a solitary law, a several universe. The colours to our eyes may be different, your red may be my green. My innocence, to one of more opportunity, shall be guilt. To one age, in like manner, Christianity is a stern dogmatical and ritual religion, but it answers their prayers and does also fulfil its Divine purposes. To the next generation it is a gentle and intellectual faith, for its disciples are men of minds and manners, and it likewise doth God's will to them. New England is now the most reading community in the world, and, of course, has the love of knowledge, and lust of change. In the supposed case of the external evidences being shaken down of Christianity, will there be any hope beyond the experiment of the morals of Seneca and Antonine on an improved age? Shall we not be safer for Butler's "Analogy"? Suppose we could lose our hold on the foundations of Christianity, would there be nothing satisfying in esteeming it also a great permitted engine of most exact and benign adaptation to the wants of many past ages, and so, yielding to an offensive aphorism, that what is absolutely false may be relatively true? Judgment must be measured to a man of Bagdad on a compound regard to the law of Conscience and the law of Mahomet. If the secrets of external nature were disclosed, there were no science to discipline our minds. If every candle were a sun, we should be blind. If every doubt were solved, we should be listless clods. Presently the door will be unbolted at which we daily knock, and some of us shudder.

[GREATNESS]

It is doleful consolation to those who aspire in vain, to see how imperfect is greatness;— Buonaparte finding his greatest felicity in bed, *in a bed*; Byron attributing his poetic inspiration to gin; Charles XII dozing and boasting away an insignificant manhood in the provinces of Turkey. Richard III is respectable when he says,

> "Slave, I have set my life upon a cast,
> And I will stand the hazard of the die!"

> Whoso, alas! is young,
> And being young is wise
> And deaf to saws of gray Advice,
> Hath listened when the Muses sung
> And heard with joy when on the wind the shell of
> Clio rung.[1]

[1] The last two lines, in different form, occur among later poetical fragments, apropos of the greater charms History had for the youth than Metaphysics:—

> Slighted Minerva's learned tongue,
> But leaped for joy when on the wind
> The shell of Clio rung.

THE SABBATH

. . . The Sabbath is a respite from the importunacy of passion, from the dangerous empire of human anxieties; a pious armistice in the warfare of the world, a point of elevation like the Pisgah of the man of God, an observatory whence we measure backward the wilderness we have traversed, and forward the interval that is yet to be trodden by us ere the solemn shadows descend upon our path, beyond which the magnificence of other worlds is towering into the distance.

SLAVE TRADE

To stop the slave traffic the nations should league themselves in indissoluble bands, should link the thunderbolts of national power to demolish this debtor to all Justice human and divine.

VERSES [1]

Ah Fate! Cannot a man
Be wise without a beard?
From east to west, from Beersheba to Dan,
Pray was it never heard

1 These verses, amended in several lines by the Author, but never published by him, appear, with an additional stanza, in the Appendix to the *Poems*, in the Riverside and Centenary Editions.

That wisdom might in youth be gotten,
Or wit be ripe before 't was rotten?

He pays too high a price
For knowledge and for fame
Who sells his sinews to be wise,
His teeth and bones to buy a name,
And crawls half-dead, a paralytic,
To earn the praise of bard and critick.

Is it not better done
To dine and sleep through forty years,
Be loved by few, be feared by none,
Laugh life away, have wine for tears,
And take the mortal leap undaunted,
Content that all we asked was granted?

But Fate will not permit
The seed of gods to die,
Nor suffer Sense to win from Wit
Its guerdon in the sky,
Nor let us hide, whate'er our pleasure,
The World's light underneath a measure.

[RULERS]

. . . Who are the real sovereigns of Britain and France? Not surely the simple gentlemen that are kept in the palaces and produced on state occasions with gaudy frocks and baubles on their heads, or in their hands, and saluted with the smooth old title of King. Surely these are not they who act most powerfully on the fortunes and the minds of the British and the French. But Scott and Mackintosh and Jeffrey and Laplace, these are the true *de facto* sovereigns, who rule in those countries. They never affect the airs, nor assume the trappings of vulgar majesty, but they receive the secret and open homage of all classes, they command feelings, determinations and actions.

Pulchrum est laudari a laudato viro. Newton said of Cotes, " If he had lived, we should have known something."

FITNESS

I am pleased with every token, however slight, in nature, in institutions, in arts, of progressive adaptation to wants. The men of Switzerland cover their houses with shingles of the larch tree, which in a little time give out their pitch to the sun and fill up every joint so that the roof is impervious to rain.

[THE WIND]

The Wind, who is the great poet of the world, sings softer measures on summer eves in groves and gardens, and hoarser and sublimer music in mountains and on the desolate sea.[1]

R. W. E. TO MISS EMERSON

Madam,

You have received the boding letter I writ from Cambridge concerning German faith. I am anxious to have sight enow to study theology in this regard. The objections the German scholars have proposed attack the foundations of external evidence, and so give up the internal to historical speculators and pleasant doubters. The eager appetite for novelty that rages among us undieted, uncloyed by religious establishments and venerable abuses, will not stand on ceremony with any name or form or fact, by whatsoever men or prejudices hallowed, when its genuineness is denied. There will be to good men henceforward a horrid anticipation when the majestic vision that has, for ages, kept a commanding check upon the dangerous passions of men — has rivetted the social bonds and brought forward so many noble spirits and prodigious benefits to the

1 For Mr. Emerson's delight in the song of the wind see, in the *Poems*, the " Wood Notes II," where it sings through the pine ; also " The Harp " and " Maiden Song of the Æolian Harp."

help of struggling humanity—shall roll away, and let in the ghastly reality of things. Regard it as a possible event, and it is the prospect of a dark and disastrous tragedy. These great Eleusinian Mysteries which have hoarded comfort from age to age for human sufferings,—the august Founder, the twelve self-denying heroes of a pious renown, distancing in moral sublimity all those primeval benefactors whom ancient gratitude deified; the apostles, whose desiring eyes saw little lustre on earth, and no consolation but in extending the victories, the moral victories of the Cross; the martyrs, who had found after so many sensual ages, in a faith for things unseen, in a moral intellection, more than a compensation for the lust of the world, and the pride of life; and after all these, and better even than all these, the boundless aggregate of hearts and deeds which the genius of Christianity touched and inspired; the violence of fiery dispositions to which it has whispered peace; the antidote it has administered to remorse and despair; the Samaritan oil it has poured into wounded hearts; the costly sacrifices and unpurchaseable devotion to the cause of God and man it has now for eighteen centuries inspired—all these must now pass away and become ridiculous. They have been the sum of what was most precious on earth. They must now pass into the rhetoric of scoffer and atheist as the significant testimonies of human folly, and every drunkard in his cups, and every voluptuary in his brothel will roll out his tongue at the Resurrection from the dead; at the acts, the martyrdoms, the unassailable virtues and the legendary greatness of Christianity. God forbid. It were base treason in his servants tamely to surrender his cause. The gates of hell will not prevail against it. But it were vile and supine to sit and be astonished without exploring the strength of the enemy. If heaven gives me sight, I will dedicate it to this cause.

Patriots turn pale when some paper privilege, some national punctilio, is withheld or disputed to their country, and Christians should not sit still when the honour of their Order (no transient institution of one age or one realm, but the Chivalry of the Universe) is trampled in the dust. For the love of truth and good send me your sentiments on this subject. . . .

[REASON]

To the times preceding Christianity, Mind and its works was a luxury; to the times subsequent, it has been a solemn instrument of truth and goodness.

March 27, 1826.

My years are passing away. Infirmities are already stealing on me that may be the deadly enemies that are to dissolve me to dirt, and little is yet done to establish my consideration among my contemporaries, and less to get a memory when I am gone. I confess the foolish ambition to be valued, with qualification. I do not want to be known by them that know me not, but where my name is mentioned I would have it respected. My recollections of early life are not very pleasant. I find or imagine in it a meanness, a character of unfounded pride cleaving to certain passages, which might come to many ears that death has not yet shut. I would have the echoes of a good name come to the same ears to remove such imputation. . . .

BYRON

Lord Byron calls Circumstance, that unspiritual god and miscreator; and what thing is there in the world he has not marred or misplaced by his unwise agency?

AGE OF CHIVALRY

[After speaking of its glamour, and its dark side.] I can faintly hear some tremendous tones in the clang of the Conqueror's Curfew as it is borne to my ear over the distance of centuries, and I am glad to be relieved by any images, however imperfect, of valour and virtue of the same times, so that I own I love the flourish of the silver trumpet of Chivalry, for it speaks to me of prevented oppression and vindicated innocence in a forlorn and benighted time. But all I wish to say is an opinion I am proud to owe to my youngest brother, and not to Bacon. It runs somewhat in this wise:—Let the fictions of Chivalry alone. Fictions, whether of the theorist or poet, have their value as ornaments; but when they intrude into the place of facts, they do infinite injury, inasmuch as it is only by the perception and comparison of Truth that we can perceive and enjoy the harmonies of the system of human destinies which the Deity is accomplishing from age to age.

[THE WORLD OUR TEACHER: HISTORY]

I have heard of monks who had grown so silly and deficient under their Rule that they

shut their eyes,—the lean, cowled coxcombs—
shut their eyes, when their mothers and sisters
came to see them. We too shall be monks of a
more renowned canon of Folly, of Dulness, if
we can without shame take station at our grated
window, which commands a prospect of the universe and the great unmarshalled crowd of all its
agents, and shut our eyes upon the eminent and
the amiable, on what might please and what
might warn us.

Why else this complex machinery, these dependent agencies of mind and matter, conspiring
to bring about the useful effect,—to teach us
something of other men,—running backward to
the beginnings of our race? Why the active curiosity which in us corresponds to these contrivances out of us for intelligence? Why, but that
it behoved us to know what had been done, that
we might acknowledge and exercise the moral
affinities which time and space do not affect, that
we might sympathize with the eldest and feel that
we set an example to the latest man. This is the
only unity, the only accord into which the diver-
sities of human condition can be blended. In
the error and the rectitude, in the agreeable and
distressing events, in the education and degeneracy of so many nations of minds, there runs

through all the same human principle in which our hearts are constrained to find a consanguinity, and so to make the registers of history a rule of life. In this way Moses and Solomon, Alcibiades and Bonaparte have existed for me; the fortunes of Assyria, of Athens and of Rome have not become a dead letter — have not fulfilled their effect in the universe, till they have taught me and you, and all men to whose ears these names may come, all the lessons of manners, of political and religious causes, and of a high paramount Providence which the great scripture of a nation's history contains. This is the immortality of moral truth, which is not a vague name, a trumpet flourish, but a thing of incessant activity from age to age; and the errors and successes of Cicero become impelling motives to thousands of men though now, for nineteen centuries, his tongue has been dumb.

It is an important observation that though our perception of moral truth is instinctive, and we do not owe to education our approbation of truth or our abhorrence of ingratitude, yet we are not born to any image of perfect virtue. We recognize with faithful readiness the virtue and the vice of action presented to us, but we need a learned experience to enumerate all the partic-

ulars that make the whole of virtue. And many
a mind after studying men and books for twenty
or thirty years has found in the story of an ancient hero a quality or colour of moral worth
which he adds to this image, this growing God-
head within him. . . .

I am answerable for whatever wisdom I can
glean from the wisdom of Rome; for whatever
counsel I can extract from the death of so many
heroes and the decline of so many nations. This
should shame pedantry.

TO MY CORRESPONDENT IN WATERFORD[1]

April 10, 1826.

'Tis a curious measure to see what a fragment,
what a span of time, our intellectual history
would subtract from life. The oil and wine of
existence, the moral and intellectual nature, are
grudgingly dealt out by the atom, at long intervals of dull sensual pain and comfort. And what
reason to suppose it will be otherwise when we
get rid of the clay, now that our ancient traditions are tottering to ruin around us? To what
good purpose this cumbrous apparatus of good
and evil? Sages of all sects answer, 'Tis a discipline. These are the gymnastics in which the

1 Miss Emerson.

youth of the universe are reared. Aye, but 't is plain that the bigger part of mankind die in a state of little comparative preparation for high event, for moral sacrifice, for intercourse with angels and "ardours," and that all come very far short of their own conception of suitableness to die. Of course, the light of nature countenances the notion of a proper Purgatory, of an island between evil and good where the poor tempest-driven sufferers must perform sad quarantine to purge out the sores of human nature that might infect or offend the society of heaven. I do not apprehend the grounds, if they exist, of believing we shall launch at once into any free and pure element of thought, in which it will be indefinitely quickened in its processes and exalted in its tone. For this must come from within, not from without. What external help can be afforded, I have no doubt will be afforded, and this chiefly in two ways, — an increased facility of locomotion, and of social intercourse, and this at once removes the chief impediments that in this world obstruct our education. When therefore we escape from life, we shall not perchance escape from disappointment, from indolence and the punishment of indolence — *ennui* — from the frequent sense of incapacity and of immense inferiority. Hope has a thousand times cheated us here, and we may find reasons, now too subtle for our apprehension, to be dissatisfied, even with the immense advancement promised us in that uncertain and silent infinity. The whole of truth (it has been nobly said) will not probably be found injurious to the whole of virtue. They will be found to be seal and print. It is the necessary consequence of this doctrine, that a great progress of knowledge — and nothing on earth has a title to the name — will be a great progress in goodness. But happiness, we know, belongs only to the last. It follows, that periods of study, long courses of initiation in the colleges of heaven, may waste away before the soul of a man in heaven may begin to be happy. Is it then a false association that, among men, from the rise of this great doctrine of the Reformation, has coupled the ideas of heaven and happiness? If riches cannot confer this excellence in earth, neither can knowledge (except remotely, as explained) confer it in heaven.

PUBLIC PRAYER

CAMBRIDGE, *April* 12, 1826.

Most men, who have given their attention to the prayers publicly offered in a Christian con-

gregation, have felt in the institution an un-
suitableness to their feelings. They have found
themselves ready, in their own exculpation, to
accuse a certain stubbornness of sympathy in
their natural disposition, or else their past lives
of such discontinuance of the offices of piety as
has issued in a total incapacity of joining their
fellowmen in this venerable service. Disuse has
made their contemplations of their Creator cold
and ungrateful to their understandings. The man
who prays is in quite another mood from the
man who hears, and tones and language which
we have once become accustomed to regard with
suspicion, or at best with admiration, it will be
long ere we learn to listen to them with sympathy. The truth is, public prayer is rather the
offspring of our notions of what *ought* to be,
than of what *is*. It has grown out of the sentiment of a few, rather than the reason of many.
Indeed we have said all, — and I am sorry to
say it, — in characterizing it as an appeal to our
veneration, instead of our sympathy.

That it is right to ask God's blessing on us
is certainly reasonable. That it is right to enumerate our wants, our sins, even our sentiments,
in addresses to this unseen Idea, seems just and
natural. And it may probably be averred with

safety that there has been no man who never prayed. That persons whom like circumstances and like feelings assimilate, that a family, that a picked society of friends, should unite in this service, does not, I conceive, violate any precept of just reason. It certainly is a question of more difficult solution whether a promiscuous assemblage, such as is contained in houses of public worship, and collected by such motives, can unite with propriety to advantage in any petition such as is usually offered by one man.

PROGRESS OF AN INDIVIDUAL IN KNOWLEDGE

April.

Every cultivated man observes, in his past years, intervals of mentality — and is accustomed to consider the present state of his mind as the result rather of many periods of singular intenseness of thought and feeling than of a perpetual and equable expansion. Corn grows by jumps. The ordinary growth of mind, especially till the old age of man, depends on aliment procured from without. But this aliment for which we search the bosoms of other men, or their books, or the face of external nature, will be got in larger or less amounts according to circumstances quite as often without as within our controul.

Whoever explores his recollection of those periods, will find that by some casualty or some study he had arrived at one of those general ideas which not only epitomize whole trains of thought, but cast a flood of new light upon things inscrutable before; after waiting mostly in the vestibule, had picked up unawares the Master Key, whose wards and springs open every door, and the surprised adventurer goes on astonished from cell to cell, from chamber to chamber, gratified, but overawed at the unexplored extent and opulence of his own possessions.[1]

May 20.

Any degree of profoundest consideration is due to the least action before it is performed, and afterwards the least.

" We are purified by terror and pity."

[ARISTOTLE?]

FRIENDSHIP

CAMBRIDGE, *May* 28.

Friendship is something very delicious to my understanding. Yet the friends that occupy my

---

1 Compare the third paragraph in " Education," *Works,* vol. x ; also in *Poems,* Appendix, Centenary Edition, p. 357, lines beginning,

" With the Key of the Secret he marches faster," etc.

thoughts are not men, but certain phantoms clothed in the form and face and apparel of men by whom they were suggested and to whom they bear a resemblance. The gods gave life to Prometheus's ivory statue, and the revolution of events may one day give me the men for the prototypes.

You love your friend for your sake, not for his own, might say Hobbists and wolves, for you would not have that good fortune befall him that should raise him above your reach and your society. I please myself that I can dimly see how it would gratify me to promote that very good fortune of my friend.[1] In God's name what is in this topic? It encourages, exhilarates, inspires me. I feel that the affections of the soul are sublimer than the faculties of the intellect. I *feel* immortal. And the evidence of immortality comes better from consciousness than from reason.

STYLE

A man's *style* is his intellectual voice, only in part under his controul. It has its own proper

[1] Have I a lover
     Who is noble and free?
     I would he were nobler
     Than to love me.
          Poems, "The Sphinx."

tone and manner, which, when he is not thinking of it, it will always assume. He can mimic the voices of others, he can modulate it with the occasion and the passion, but it has its own individual nature.

[HINTS OF HISTORY]

Ballads, *bon mots*, anecdotes, give us better insight into the depths of past centuries than grave and voluminous chronicles. "A Straw," says Selden, "thrown up into the air will show how the wind sits, which cannot be learned by casting up a stone."

(From "XVIII," 2d)

June, 1826.

I pursue my speculations with confidence and, though I can discern no remoter conclusion, I doubt not the train I commence extends farther than I see, as the first artificer of glass did not know he was instructing men in astronomy, and restoring sight to those from whom nature had taken it. There is no thought which is not seed as well as fruit. It spawns like fish.

When success exalts thy lot
God for thy virtue lays a plot ;

And all thy life is for thy own,
Then for mankind's instruction shewn;
And, tho' thy knees were never bent,
To heaven thy hourly prayers are sent,
And whether formed for good or ill,
Are registered and answered still.[1]

Proverbs, chapter 2, 18. The Jewish philosopher did not know that the soul survived the body, yet there seemed to him a peculiar sympathy and conjunction between vice and death, and the idea was natural, and suggests the evidence we have from nature of the immortality of the soul. The intellections of the mind are scarcely discriminated from the sensations which occasion them. They end in themselves and do not imply the notions of merit and reward. But moral actions seem not a mere

1 The last four lines had this origin : The summer before, when Emerson had gone to his Uncle Ladd's in Newton to restore his health, he was talking with his companion, a Methodist labourer, named Tarbox, as they worked in the hay-field. Tarbox said, that *men were always praying*, and that *their prayers were answered*. On these two heads the young divine wrote his first sermon, adding the comment, *Then men must be careful what they pray for*. This was the sermon preached in Waltham, October 15, 1826. Next day, in the stage-coach, a farmer said to him, "Young man, you'll never preach a better sermon than that."

bundle of facts, but of relations, relations to something unseen, and because thus related to something to which the body was not, possess for themselves a principle of life in which the body had no share. Since Virtue was imperishable, every act contrary to it would seem to tend to the destruction of the agent. Vice is the soul's suicide.

R. W. E. TO MISS EMERSON

CAMBRIDGE, *June* 15, 1826.

I rejoice in the prospect of better sight and better health. Seasons and calendars have little to do with him who distinctly sees eternity writ upon his dial, but on earth his impatience is irrepressible, who finds his years increasing, whilst his means of acquisition are withdrawn. Loss of eyes is not exactly one of Socrates's superfluities. How many things do I not want. For when I came back to books, I felt like Columbus on the new shore. The value of this art (of reading), when remembered as man's addition to his wealth, is the best argument of perfectibility, and is a sound one. Alas for Adam ! — not Milton's nor Moses', — but the first adventurer that was accomplished only with his own perfections; the noble savage whom poets extol, the wretch whom philosophers pity. Alas for his joyless hours, though in powers and dispositions perfectly moulded, and in understanding profound as a god, the better his understanding of good, the keener his perception of surrounding evil. We should be glad if the next periods of our existence were only so much an improvement on this as the man of the 60th century is a being of greater powers and resources than the man of the first. Yet Campbell does not lament the loss of the sun, because all the arts

> " And triumphs that beneath thee sprang
>   Healed not a passion or a pang
>   Entailed on human hearts."

All which I am fain to call sublime lying. For 't is the noble and exhilarating discovery of modern grand juries, and the more noble that it is more trite, that educated men are never brought to the bar for felonious crimes, and that the all but immedicable crimes of drunkenness and indolence have found their antidote in the love of reading.

I have not forgiven Everett one speculative doctrine of the Φ B K oration, the more disagreeable, that I have found some reason to think it true, — to wit, that geniuses are the organs, mouthpieces of their age; do not speak their own words, nor think their own thoughts. It has occurred to me that, though we think Shakspeare so singularly grand as to be a hermit in the fields of thought where he travels, yet we bind up in his volumes four or five plays of which the authorship is disputed betwixt him and certain unknown contemporaries. Other productions modern criticism has quoted from his time, bearing very respectable comparison with his own. So that the time, not the man, gave birth to this empyrean conceit.

'T is not in man to thank the philosopher that merges his selfish in the social nature. 'T was a foolish vanity in the Stoic to talk in this wise. It suggested or else grew out of that primeval dogma of the Mundane Soul. No man loves it; the meanest loses more than he gains by parting with his identity to make an integral atom of the Whole. Nor perhaps need we dread anything. If any one feeling is positive, it is personal accountability. I know that I exist, but the age and the Universe are alike abstractions of my own mind, and have no pretensions to the same definitive certainty. One can some-

times feel pretty clearly where these fancies originate, when we observe the grouping together
of men into generations and countries, and the
dismally gregarious manner in which they walk
and talk and think. If men were like Phœnixes,
and only at long secular intervals the world tra-
vailed with this noble progeny, we should feel
more secure of ourselves both now and hereafter. But this fulsome generation, this redundant prodigality of being, whereby they are cast
out, clean and unclean, heroes and underlings,
by millions, — begets a doubt whether the
riches of eternity can be as prodigally spent, and
whether such immense resources as each one
feels his own capacities crave can be furnished
from the storehouses of God to every one of
the individuals of these inconceivable numbers
of systems of life. It is indeed pleasing to the
mind, as she sits serene in her own firmament,
to find from her nature that these doubts have
no force, that the physical limit to physical increase is a humble law of material nature which
does not taint her majesty. Speedily she expects
a divorce from her gross mate, who, because he
hungers and thirsts, makes her forsake her
celestial musings to find out where he may go
to be fat and where to be warm. But when this

dissolution shall have taken place, no incongru-
ity is seen in the project of an immeasurable
multiplication of sentient individuals. There is
no bankruptcy in the commerce of thought to
be occasioned from an overdoing of its craft.
Mind has no relation that we know to space.
All the analogies of matter are, in this regard,
inapplicable to the intensity of the enjoyment
(though hard to analyze, or at any moment to
say "It is now") which we, in this world, extract from friendship, and to which we continually see the "Miscreator Circumstance"[1] to be
an insuperable bar, estranging us from characters to which we feel an affinity, and separating
us from those to whom we are already allied.
This great element, the social principle, instructs
us in the mystery of future happiness by suggesting the noble and endless entertainment that
a free access to innumerable minds out of clay,
and skiey influences is of itself able to furnish.
But all men feel their incompetency to uncover
the secret employments of the emancipated
spirit, and the silly conceit of singers and children about the psalm-singing of the other world
is not more inadequate perhaps than the conception of a passive receiver or channel through

1 Byron's expression.

which flows forever the stream of immortal thought. We can determine something in this, as in all general speculations, by consulting the whole of our nature, and we find ourselves emasculated by a description that leaves out our active faculties. Yet the appropriate objects of our action we shall not easily ascertain. All our action here is material, and that to such an extent as to have induced a metaphysical doubt whether action is predicable of mind. Almost all suffering, exercising the soul's fortitude, is of the body. Indeed, I would submit whether a philosopher subjecting his griefs to rigid analysis will not find them all to be ultimately related to body, unless it be the apprehension of the disesteem of others, and of annihilation. Now action and sufferance go hand in hand. " None can aspire to act greatly but those who are of force greatly to suffer," said Burke. And it would seem all our action and passion are of the body. I do not say the mind does not act when, for example, it prefers honesty to guilty wealth, but it is clear the things about which it is concerned are of body, not of mind, — as whether the hand, foot or tongue shall move in a certain way. Nor can we conceive of virtuous action in the soul ending in the soul. Yet we

should be very loth to add to modern vagaries
the dogma that matter was essential to virtue.
We know better. We know that all speculation
of this sort pushed to any extreme is inconclusive
and idle, for the nature of matter, as of mind, is
buried in inscrutable night; and that we are fools
to fear Matter when we do not know that there
is any such thing. What, then, do we know? I
know that I exist, and that a part of me, as
essential as Memory or Reason, is a desire that
another being exist. If I am not an anomaly,
but was made, and what is within was made,
with reference to what is without, then there is
another Being who made me. And having such
intuitions, such golden rudiments whereof to
frame my history, I can look unappalled at the
future, and welcome the coming on of my
untried Being.

R. W. E. TO MISS EMERSON (?)

CAMBRIDGE, *June* 30, 1826.

In all the vagaries I have troubled you with,
not much has been said of poetry, though a subject near to us both. I should be glad to see
your thoughts on its general nature and value.
Does the continuation of your own speculations
shew its fairy web to be superficial, or wrought

into the grain of man? Is it left behind as we advance, or is it more perfect in the Archangel than in the child? And for the professors of the art, can they not err by excess of relish for the same? It would seem that the genuine bard must be one in whom the extremes of human genius meet; that his judgment must be as exact and level with life as his imagination is discursive and incalculable. It would seem as if abundant erudition, foreign travel, and gymnastic exercises must be annexed to his awful imagination and fervent piety to finish Milton. That the boisterous childhood, careless of criticism and poetry, the association of vulgar and unclean companions, were necessary to balance the towering spirit of Shakspeare, and that Mr. Wordsworth has failed of pleasing by being too much a *poet*.

A man may propose a course of exercises designed to strengthen his arm with such indiscreet zeal as to paralyze it. A boy enamoured of the beauty of a butterfly chases and clutches it with such eagerness that he finds his hand full of dirt and blood. I can't read this poet's mystic and unmeaning verses without feeling that if he had cultivated poetry less, and learning and society more, he would have gained more favour at the hands of the Muses, who must be courted, not taken by violence. 'T is sufficient proof of a man's aberration to know that he is writing verses on a theory; that he has agreed with two or three antics more to bring the public over to a new taste in poetry.

It would seem there was some kindred between this new philosophy of poetry and the undisciplined enterprizes of intellect in the middle age. The geniuses of that era, all on fire with that curiosity which is, in every age, inextinguishable, to break the marble silence of Nature and open some intercourse between man and that divinity with which it seems instinct, struggled to grasp the principles of things, to extort from the spheres in the firmament some intimations of the present or some commentary on the past. They were impatient of their straitened dominion over nature, and were eager to explore the secrets of her own laboratory, that they might refine clay and iron into gold, might lengthen life and deduce formulas for the solution of all those mysteries that besiege the human adventurer. Not otherwise this modern poet, by natural humour an ardent lover of all the enchantments of wood and river and seduced by an overweening confidence in the force of his own genius, has discarded that modesty under whose influence all his great precursors have resorted to external nature sparingly for illustration and ornament, and have forborne to tamper with the secret and metaphysical nature of what they borrowed. He has been foolishly inquisitive about the essence and body of what pleased him, of what all sensible men feel to be, in its nature, evanescent. He can't be satisfied with feeling the general beauty of a moonlight evening, or of a rose. He would pick them to pieces and pounce on the pleasurable element he is sure is in them, like the little boy who cut open his drum to see what made the noise. The worthy gentleman gloats over a bulrush, moralizes on the irregularity of one of its fibres, and suspects a connexion between an excrescence of the plant and its own immortality. Is it not much more conformable to that golden middle line in which all that is good and wise of life lies, to let what Heaven made small and casual remain the objects of a notice small and casual, and husband our admiration for images of grandeur in matter or in mind? But I should not worry myself with abusing Mr. Wordsworth, not even for his serene egotism, whereby he seems at every turn thunderstruck to see to what a prodigious height

human genius has headed up in *him*, but that
he has occasionally written lines which I think
truly noble. He would be unworthy your notice but that now and then comes from him a
flash of divine light and makes you uneasy that
he should be such an earthen vessel. He has
nobly embodied a sentiment, which, I know not
why, has always seemed congenial to humanity,
that the soul has come to us from a preëxist-
ence in God; that we have a property in the
past which we do not ourselves recognize, and a
title to the future for which we should be a little thankful.[1] Wait a little, says this venerable
faith, and this feverish being for which you are
so anxious will be whelmed in a vaster being to
which it is only subsidiary; but let the glory and
virtue of other worlds be as they may, in parting with our identity we part with happiness.

Every age, as it augments the number of the
successful experiments of genius, whilst it should
seem to furnish that large induction from whence
we can ascertain the true extent and nature of

[1] It may be interesting to refer in this connection to what
Mr. Emerson said later of Wordsworth; of his personality
and his poetry in *English Traits*, chapters i, xiv, and xvii,
and also in the papers from the *Dial*, " Modern Literature "
and " Europe and European Books," in volume xii of the
Works.

poetry, has rather appeared to carry its title into new empires, and annex an import yet more vague and universal to the word. What is poetry? It is philosophy, it is humour, it is a chime of two or three syllables, it is a relation of thought to things, or of language to thought. It converses with all science and all imagination, with all accidents and objects, from the grandest that are accessible to the senses, and grander than those, to the coarsest parts of life. And I would go to the farthest verge of the green earth to learn what it was or was not. If the spirit of him who paced the Academe and had this virtue in his soul, though he feigned to disparage it in his philosophy, or the laurelled lovers of the British Muse, harp in hand, sit on your misty mount, or soothe their majesties by the margin of your lakes, conjure them, I beseech you, to announce this secret that the wit of humanity has been so long in vain toiling to unriddle. It shall be reverently received, and cautiously dispensed, and shall add a rich item to the scanty stock of truth of which your friend is the humble master.

(From Cabot's Q)

CAMBRIDGE, *July* 28, 1826.

There is but one meaning can be put upon the term happiness consistent with what our experience has shewn. It consists in reliefs, not in enjoyments; and unhappiness is an uneasiness, a useful uneasiness in the body or mind prompting to the attainment of some good agreeable to its nature. That is to say, All unhappiness tends to happiness.

(From " XVIII," 2d)

LETTER TO MISS EMERSON

1 *August,* 1826.

T is a droll life, and the only humour proper to it seems quiet astonishment. Others laugh, weep, sell or proselyte. I admire.[1] There are, I take it, in each man's history insignificant passages which he feels to him not to be insignificant; little coincidences in little things, which touch all the springs of wonder and startle the sleeper Conscience in the deepest cell of his repose, — the Mind with all her faculties rushing out in alarm, suspicious of a Presence which it

1 Probably suggested by St. Augustine's exclamation, " Wrangle who will, I will wonder."

greatly behooves her to respect — touched not more with awe than with curiosity, if perhaps some secret revelation is not about to be vouchsafed; or doubtful if some moral epoch is not just now fulfilled in its history, and the tocsin just now struck that severs and tolls out an irreparable Past.

These are not the stale reasons by which we can enforce the burdensome doctrine of Deity on the world, but make often, I apprehend, the body of evidence on which private conviction is built. In solitude and in silence Memory visits her inmost chambers to produce these treasured tokens of connexion and immortality. Much of what is subtle and mysterious in our intervals of mentality is more flattering and more favoured than the ordinary acquisitions in the general progress of the soul, and — but what congratulation ought to be heard in the earth from theist and patriot when God, in these eminent instances of these our latter days, departs from the ancient inviolable sternness of an unrespecting Providence to harmonize the order of nature with the moral exigencies of humanity. Arise from the dust, put on thy beautiful clothing, oh thou that wast despised for depravity, want and presumption! Human nature will go daft in our time, like the Grecian father who embraced two Olympian victors in one day.

(From Cabot's Q)

CAMBRIDGE, *August* 3, 1826.

Yesterday I attended the funeral solemnities in Faneuil Hall in honour of John Adams and Thomas Jefferson. The oration of Mr. Webster was worthy of his fame, and what is much more, was worthy of the august occasion. Never, I think, were the awful charms of person, manners and voice outdone. For though in the beginning unpromising, and in other parts imperfect, in what was truly grand he fully realized the boldest conception of eloquence.

(From "XVIII," 2d)

TO HIS BROTHER, EDWARD BLISS EMERSON[1]

August 12.

Eyes so rich will atone for many petty uneasinesses; for hands that are poor, and (a little while) for hopes deferred and affections fasting for their food. In the long run, in the great existence, they will vindicate their paramount importance and hold at a cheap rate the disappoint-

1 Then travelling in Europe for his health.

ment or even blight of a particular affection. For the wealth of the eye passes into the mind, elevating its tone, nourishing its strength, enlarging its proportions; and this godlike Inhabitant is always a favourite, and can create for itself new attachments whensoever and where it chooses. Blood is a dear tie, and old love is not easily forgotten, but this sort of feeling is but a rag of wretched humanity, low itself and dwelling in low places and striving to link its necessities to lofty sentiment. But the soul sternly assures us that there are affinities dearer and truer, that these are perishing, but those eternal.

(From Cabot's R)

QUIDDLE

Excessive love of order denominated quiddle. Apparent why it should be the mark of a weak mind, because proximity of time and place being the simplest of associations, a violation of it in a mind where higher relations do not enter must produce painful confusion.

TWO SORTS OF PEOPLE : ——

(1) Who find themselves in life, and content themselves with looking at the great show they

find around them, and (2) who like the game
and enter into it with spirit.

September 10, 1826.

The days blow me onward into the desarts
of Eternity; I live a few strong moments, in
the course, perhaps, of each day; I observe a
little the ways of man, and in them accumulated,
the ways of God. I act a little. I shape my fortunes, as it seems to me, not at all. For in all
my life I obey a strong necessity, and all that
sacrifice of time and inclination which certain
of my fond friends regard as virtue, I see and
confess to be only a passive deference to the
course of events. For, in reference to those passages of my life which please their moral sense,
I could not have done otherwise without doing
violence to my own or my neighbour's feelings.
There was, in those instances, in the very likely
supposition that I had disliked to play the martyr, no nook, no pretence such as commonly
falls to other people, under cover of which I
might plausibly decline the assured alternative
of inconvenience and loss. It is melancholy to
suffer on account of others without any appeal
to our own self-devotion as the cause. It is low
and ridiculous to be the football of vulgar cir-

cumstances and never by force of character to have surmounted them. And yet, inasmuch as the course of events in the world appears to consent to virtue, these regretted evils may be ennobled by being a portion of the sublime necessity which links all agents and events together under an omnipotent jurisdiction. Be the theories as they may, it suits my humour to sit and speculate, a civil philosopher, mild and composed in the presence of little and of majestic minds; without contempt of reptiles, and, as the stoics say, without being afraid of gods.

"GROWTH OF THE MIND" [1]

Our American press does not often issue such productions as Sampson Reed's observations on the Growth of the Mind, a book of such a character as I am conscious betrays some pretension even to praise. It has to my mind the aspect of a revelation, such is the wealth and such is the

1 A young man, an apothecary in Boston, had just written a book with this title, which Emerson valued highly, and which first interested him in Swedenborg and his teachings. In a letter written to Rev. James Freeman Clarke in 1834, Mr. Emerson said, "Have you read Sampson Reed's *Growth of the Mind*? I rejoice to be contemporary with that man, and cannot wholly despair of the society in which he lives. There must be some oxygen yet."

novelty of the truth unfolded in it. It is remarkable for the unity into which it has resolved the various powers, feelings and vocations of men, suggesting to the mind that harmony, which it has always a propensity to seek, of action and design in the order of Providence in the world.

September 23.

Health, action, happiness. How they ebb from me! Poor Sisyphus saw his stone stop once, at least, when Orpheus chaunted. I must roll mine up and up and up how high a hill! But hark, I can hear on the eastern wind almost the harp of my coming Orpheus. He sets his sail and flees over the grim flood.[1] Breathe soft the winds, and shine warmly on him, the autumnal sun. It may be, a contrary destiny will be too strong on me for the help of his hand. But speed his bark, for his heart is noble and his hand is strong, and the good of others is given into his hand.

It would give me very great pleasure to be well. It is mournful, the expectation of ceasing to be an object of hope, that we may become objects of compassion, and then go gloomily to nothing, in the eye of this world, before we have

1 Edward was on his return voyage from Europe.

had one opportunity of turning to the sun what we know is our best side. But there have existed on earth noble thoughts, and souls that gave them free entertainment, which sentiments were designed as counterpoises to these very sorrows, and consolation to worse distresses. What is stoicism? what is Christianity? They are for nothing (that is to say, the human mind at its best estate and the Divine mind in its communication with the human, are for nothing), if they cannot set the soul on an equilibrium, when it leans to the earth under the pressure of calamity. I bless God, there *is* virtue in them. The warlike soul that has put on this armour has come off conqueror. Little vexations that eat into the hearts of meaner men were to them that were of the household of this faith dust and smoke; . . . they met with undaunted eye and even temper. They felt the slow wasting of disease which seems to consume the powers of resistance whilst it augments the force of the attack. The fires, that hope had kindled up in the firmament within, were seen to wane in their light, and, star by star, were slowly extinguished ; but there was that in them of robust virtue, that derived a blameless triumph from contrasting the health of the soul with the decay of its house; the eternity of the universe with the transition of its parts; the grandeur of the ends, themselves were pursuing, with the puny weakness of the instruments; the immortal life, the great, the immeasurable, the overwhelming progression of the Mind, with the little passing cloud of tears, decline and death with which it was afflicted on earth. These things they thought on and were comforted. These were the good angels that gathered before them on the holy mount of their hope, and beckoned them to walk boldly forward in the vallies of life, proof to temptation, and not afraid of trial, overlooking the crosses and accidents of the way, for their bright and burning eye was fixed steadfastly on the future.

Thus much must serve me for a consolatory soliloquy now; or for a sermon by and by, if I prosper better than I at this present apprehend. These that have been said, are the stated, the official consolations. There is another key on which vulgar understandings are sometimes to better purpose addressed. Up, up! faint heart never won fair lady.

> No, there's a necessity in fate
> Why still the brave, bold man is fortunate!

Die? What should you die for? Maladies? What maladies? Dost not know that Nature has her course as well as Disease? that Nature has not only helps and facilities for all beneficial operations, but fangs and weapons for her enemies also? Die? pale face, lily liver! go about your business, and when it comes to the point, then die like a gentleman.

Christianity . . . in its purified and primitive state, makes one with the moral code. They cast mutual light and honour on each other. The doctrine of immortality, the grand revelation of Christianity, illuminates and ennobles the existence of man.

This solves the question concerning the existence of evil. For if man is immortal, this world is his place of discipline and the value of pain is then disclosed. . . .

The most absurd and frivolous superstitions have been defended as the most precious doctrines which Jesus Christ came into the world to teach. These insane tenets have been sanctioned by Councils and sealed by the blood of martyrs. An age went by; a revolution in men's minds took place, and these famous dogmas are pleasantly quoted to amuse an idle hour and speedily are forgotten. And now, it may be, another set of opinions is taught in Councils, and illustrated in pulpits; but what security is there that these are more genuine than those that went before, or that another age may not treat them with the same irreverence? And in this shifting spectacle, is not a doubt thrown upon the gospel itself, which is thus represented to different ages in such contradictory lights?

Poison, poison, poison; the poison of vanity, the poison of fear, the poison of testimony. "Poison expels poison, and vices are expelled by pride."

"The ænigma of ourselves swallows up, like the Sphinx, thousands of systems which pretend to the glory of having guessed its meaning."   DE STAËL.

(From "XVIII," 2d)

R. W. E. TO MISS EMERSON

September 28, 1826.

Hume, all grimace apart, you honour as a genuine scholar, as an exact and powerful philosopher, without a single word of dulness, and with this single qualification of praise, that because of the novelty of the ground he had taken, he was seduced from the grand view of human nature which he ought to have taken, into a consideration, too partial and minute, of the defective nature of our reasoning; and this, entering into all his habits of thinking, chilled and belittled (compared with a true, with a religious wisdom) all his philosophy. In the history of metaphysics and ethics, however, the advantage is of course great. The experiment might not have been tried under better auspices, and every experiment must once be made. Of his friend Gibbon, I think there can be but one idea among people of good feeling and sense. He was a sort of Alcibiades whom all the instructions of Socrates might adorn, but could not purify. Then Shakspeare and Burke. The old poet is crushed under his laurels, and you would hardly withdraw a leaf, but for the indecency of the old stage. It was queer; a sort of representation of humanity, that the truest of all bards should be permitted thus to mix the highest and vilest. Heroism, virtue, devotion thrown into these brothel associations. But the words of Brutus in *Julius Cæsar* will search out a sympathy in the purest heart that ever turned a severe eye on the spotted web of human intellect. But why maul the old idol? We think alike of him. Then we can have no quarrel about Burke, an improved Cicero; improved precisely in the proportion of the advanced age. . . . As to what is met from our American press, I can't but think the glowing epithets that come down from the mountains are a full echo of the applause of the valleys. I think of our orators. For one's reputation's sake 't is always well to stick in a word to qualify admiration, and you should have heard us tax, in Everett, the want of an abounding, delicate philosophy not at all compensated by the dazzle of the imagery. Moreover, there is in many minds a certain dulness to perceive God; not so quick a habit of detecting and confederating final causes, whence He is inferred. But for diligence, rectitude, fancy and sense we reckon Edward Everett chief among ten thousand.

Next, it seems I am cold, and when shall I kindle? I was born cold. My bodily habit is cold. I shiver in and out; don't heat to the good purposes called enthusiasm a quarter so quick and kindly as my neighbours. Yet, so depraved is self-conceit, that I sometimes imagined this very seed of wrath to be one of my gifts, though not graces. " Poor mortals do themselves beguile."

TO THE SAME

October.

But what, in the name of all the fairies, is the reason you don't like Sampson Reed? What swart star has looked sparely on him? Can anything be more greatly, more wisely writ? Has any modern hand touched the harp of great nature so rarely? Has any looked so shrewdly into the subtile and concealed connexion of man and nature, of earth and heaven? Has any, in short, produced such curiosity to see the farther progress, the remoter results, of the caste of intellect to which he belongs? I speak for myself, and not for another. I believe he must have admirers, but I have not seen any. The Sabbath after it came out, Dr. Channing delivered a discourse obviously founded upon it. And, as to his sect, you know they exult in the independent testimony of poor Wordsworth, to the same truths which they get from Swedenborg. Lo! what confirmations to what I said about sentiment ruling the roast in these our matchless times. What holiday the easy satirist might hold in pleasant observance of the fickle world, but for the iron fate that levels the destiny of each with the destiny of all, and afflicts the observer with the same evil and folly which he analyzes.

[On October 10, the young divinity student, having, though irregularly, studied what seemed to the authorities enough to make such action on their part safe, had been "approbated to preach" by the Middlesex Association of Ministers. He had, even a month or two before this, preached his first sermon in his Uncle Ripley's pulpit in Waltham; and after his approbation preached in his father's, the First Church, in Boston.]

(From Cabot's R)

" Le triomphe de la raison c'est de bien vivre avec ceux qui n'en ont pas." VOLTAIRE.[1]

HOUSE OF HAVE AND HOUSE OF WANT

See the 68th number of the *Quarterly Review* for some prodigiously fine remarks at the close of the Geological article.

Rombold's opinion, who died on the Rye House plot, quoted by Jefferson: — men sad-

---

1 In the fragmentary verses in the Appendix to Emerson's *Poems*, this saying is versified thus : —

> Of all wit's uses the main one
> Is to live well with who have none.

dled and bridled for others booted and spurred,[1] etc.

BURNET.

DISPROPORTION

All vice is built on the apparent disproportion there is between the temptation to do wrong and the motive to do right. The contest that exists between these opposite influences is like no other strife in nature. It is no combat between beings of the same blood, of equal might, of the like nature, between sword and sword, or wit and wit.[2]

IMMORTALITY

That fate and metaphysical aid do deem that I shall be great or small, is of little moment, so that the great hope of spirits militant be sure. For who can doubt but that, in the ages of intercourse that impend with spirits of every degree of grandeur, be it of thought or of virtue, he can fail to find his own level, or fear to be robbed of his just fame? But shake down this blessed doctrine of the Resurrection, towards which the wise and good, the countless genera-

1 Quoted in essay on *Aristocracy*, Works, vol. x, p. 45 and note. The name is usually spelled Rumbold.

2 Mrs. Julia Ward Howe relates Mr. Emerson's instruction to her, when a young girl, that the Angel must always be stronger than the evil spirit.

tions of men as they scanned in their little day the impending future, have darted their desiring eyes — to which every conclusion of the intellectual power and every effort of the moral power have pointed, from the first glimmering of human history, and you have done more for ruin than if you had shaken down the stars from their courses. And after this downfall, all things here below, or there above, are so insignificant to us, who are to be connected with them but a moment, that fame which we nickname immortality is but the shadow of a shade.

HISTORY

'T is not always easy to separate what principles are robust and stable, what in humanity is immoveably moored, from what is tossed upon the waves of time. Few things need more philosophy than the study of history. For it is not easy or safe to look long on these turning wheels, lest we grow giddy. The best good that is reaped, is the glorious congregation of final causes, that is marshalled as this Muse descends from age to age; the indisputable tribute they bring of obedience and honour to Deity. The examination of a single idea with the eye of exact philosophy leads to atheism and to universal doubt; is susceptible of all the criticism with which Mr. Hume assailed the sources of knowledge. But many ideas confederated compel men to believe. I need observe that 't is no result of accumulated inquiry that has brought into doubt the faithfulness of the senses; for, in Plato's *Phædon*, Socrates mentions that the poets sing that "we neither see nor hear truly"; but what was moonshine then is philosophy now.

I have heard Shakspeare's "Blow winds and crack your cheeks," and the rest, accused of false taste and bombast. I do not find this fault. And though I might not allow it in another, even in his mad king, yet I am not offended by this passage in *Lear*. For as the Romans were so idolatrous of Cato's virtue that when he had drunk wine they would rather believe that intemperance was virtue than that Cato was guilty of a vice, so I am afraid to circumscribe within rhetorical rules, the circuits of such a towering and majestic mind, and a taste the most exquisite that God ever informed among men.[1]

"We seem to recognize a truth the first time we hear it."   FONTENELLE.

1 The three last paragraphs are dated 1825.

I would write something worthily on the most affecting of topics, upon the personal character and influence and upon the death of Jesus Christ, a being whose nature has divided the opinions of men more than did ever any question; who was so great as to leave foundation for the idea that he was a portion of the Deity, and, in the opinions least reverent, that he was first of men; a being who would be called renowned, did not fame and what men call glory sink before his majesty into things offensive and ridiculous; a human being whose influence on the fortunes of human society — taking out of account all supernatural influence — has been far the most powerful foreign influence that ever acted thereon; a being whose character was so pure and whose death was so sublime as, if no consequences had followed, would for himself have attracted the greatest admiration.

[Here follow several quotations from Mme. de Staël's *Germany*.]

I find in Burke almost the same thought I had entertained as an original remark three years ago: that nothing but the moral quality

of actions can penetrate through vast intervals
of time.

.　　.　　.　　.　　.　　.　　.

"The Translator," says Butler, "is a small
Factor that imports Books of the growth of one
language into another; but it seldom turns to
account, for the commodity is perishable, and,
the finer it is, the worse it endures transporta-
tion, as the most delicate of Indian fruits are by
no art to be brought over."

(From "XVI")

The spirits of the wise sit on the clouds
And mock the ambition of man,
For his breath is vapour, his beauty the colour of a
　　　cloud,
And his body and soul are parted by a sun, a storm,
Or the feeble fork of a poor worm:
And who shall tell his household
Whither the soul of the dead man is gone?
Is it gone to live in torture,
Enduring a dread resurrection into pain,
And perceive mortal plagues in an immortal body,
Sighing to the heavy centuries, that bring
No light, no hope in their immeasurable train?
Is it gone to farther regions of unequal lot,
To a land where the colours of love and disgust
Are blended anew in the texture of the web,

And the web is stained with black and bloody clouds?
Is it gone to harmonies of joy,
To the ardour of virtue and the wealth of truth?
Is it gone to blank oblivion,
The mockery of hope and virtue, and the death of
     God?
Alas! Alas! Alas!
Wo is me! for the sad survivor!
Tho' Fortune threw good, not evil, in his way,
Showering the roses of pleasure and the laurel of
     Fame,
Whilst his brother breasted the driving snows—
Alas for the sad survivor!
He walks the long streets of his native city,
But the peopled street is like the desolate sea.
Men study his face and its lofty lines,
And love the graceful tones of pride and power
Rolled with rich thunder of eloquent words.
In the bosom of his own land
They love him and they honour him,
And they think his heart leaps at the voice of their
     praise.
But their thoughts are dark and their eyes are dim,
And they cannot see that a noble nature
Must pine, or be matched with noble things.
It is ill with the living, it is well with the dead.
It is better with the dead who live
Than it is with the living who die daily.
Oh Life, thou art a house wherein Fears inhabit;

And when Man, poor pilgrim, enters the doors,
They flock unto him with icy hands,
They lead him in their shivering company,
And if he come to a shining room,
They tell him it leads to a dungeon tower.

SONG

This cup of life is not so shallow
  That we have drained the best,
That all the wine at once we swallow,
  And lees make all the rest.

Maids of as soft a bloom shall marry
  As Hymen yet hath blessed,
And finer forms are in the quarry
  Than Phidias e'er released.

[The damps of Autumn brought increase to Emerson's symptoms. The invitations to preach which came to him were gratifying, but after each occasion his chest felt the strain. His condition was low; consumption distinctly threatened him. At this crisis his good (half-) uncle, Reverend Samuel Ripley, came to the rescue and insisted on his going South for the winter and there remaining until his health improved; and he advanced the necessary funds and gave letters of credit. There can be little doubt that

Emerson's life was saved by Mr. Ripley's kindly forethought and generosity. Waldo stayed at home until he could see his loved brother Edward, just returned from France, and then took ship for Charleston, South Carolina, on the 25th of November.]

(From "XVI," Cabot's S)

For versatility of Genius, see Livy, *de* Cato the Elder; Shakspeare, *de* Henry V,—"Hear him debate of Commonwealth affairs," etc., etc.; Aubrey, *de* Bacon; Byron, *de* Cæsar; Plutarch, *de* Themistocles; Milton, *de* Education; and Stewart, Fred. III's bottle in cellar; Jack of all trades, good at none — What's worth doing, worth doing well.

"No profit comes where is no pleasure taken :
In brief, sir, study what you most affect."

Nature notches the edge of the petal, and hurls the globes in orbits.

(From Cabot's R)

AT SEA; Sunday, *December* 3, 1826.

'T is a nine days' wonder to me, this voyage of mine. Here I have been rolling through the weary leagues of salt water, musing much on myself and on man, with some new but incoherent thinking. I revolved a thought I had somewhere found, that dangers were companions of illustrious minds; and applying it to society, which may, like individuals, by its education and fortune emerge from obscurity and grow illustrious, I perceived that in its progress it would overtake dangers not known to its infancy. It would embrace dangers and ennoble itself by its company. The men of this age work and play between steam-engines of tremendous force, amid the roaring wheels of manufactories, brave the incalculable forces of the storm, here in the seat of its sovereignty, and fulfil in these perilous crises all the minute offices of life, as calm and unawed as they would compose themselves to sleep in the shade of a forest. Such facts assert a sovereignty in the mind that is very dear to the philanthropist.

After a day or two, I found I could live as comfortably in this tent, tossed on the ocean, as if it were pitched on the mountains ashore. But it is the irresistible sentiment of the first day, whilst your philosophy is sea-sick, to fancy man is violating the order of nature in coming out here where he assuredly has no business; and that, in virtue of this trespass on his part, the wind has a right to his canvass and the shark to his body. Whilst his philosophy is distempered, so is his imagination. The whole music of the sea is desolate and monitory. The wave and the cloud and the wind suggest power more than beauty to the ear and eye. But the recovery is rapid, and the terrible soon subsides into the sublime.

(From " XVIII," 2d)

CHARLESTON, SOUTH CAROLINA,
December 13.

I have for a fortnight past writ nothing. My bosom's lord sits somewhat drowsily on his throne. It is because I think not at all that I write not at all. There is to me something alarming in these *periods* of mentality. One day I am a doctor, and the next I am a dunce, that is, so far as relates to my own resources. An educated man who thinks for himself can, of course, at any time, by contact with a powerful mind, whether by conversation or by a book, be easily wrought upon, and go into action. But put away these foreign impulses, and the mind will be treacherous to its alleged immortality, inasmuch as suspended action, independent of the waking and sleep of the body, assaults the notion of spiritual life. The true account of the scarecrow is this. At sea a fortnight elapses in which I always remember myself to have been, in times past, a channel through which flowed bright and lofty thought. But I find in me no disposition, no power to recreate for myself the same brilliant entertainment. I come to land, and the weary days succeed each other as on the desolate sea, but this coveted power does not return, and every attempt to force the soul is heavily baffled. Now suppose it should never return; the causes are concealed, the sun and the moon are hidden which affect the ebbs and flowings of the intellectual tides.[1] They are determined by something out of me and higher than me. If the virtue that is gone out of me be withheld, I have parted with what in life was best, and eternity will lose its dread attractions. Eternity is only desirable when regarded as the career of an inquisitive mind. It would be a disappointment, a prolonged sorrow to him who mourned the loss of the sense which only could unlock its treasures. Yet during the days of this eclipse the notice of the loss of light

---

[1] Unsure the ebb and flow of thought;
The moon comes back — the Spirit not.
See *Poems* (Appendix), "The Poet."

sometimes rises into apprehension lest it might not return. This is our boasted human dignity and majesty and so forth. We are such bubbles that when we mount, we see not how; and when we grow great, we cannot commend ourselves.

(From Cabot's R)

CHARLESTON, SOUTH CAROLINA,
December 16.

It is an old remark, that there are no discoveries in morals. It is the leading object of our existence, to form moral character, and the laws of morals are therefore written on the heart in luminous and ineffaceable characters. . . . But there are problems of moral science, questions of no easy solution, and it would be the grossest error to suppose that from the scanty lights of nature the young and ignorant were equally competent to decide them with the experienced moralist.

It cannot be. All men are equal on this point precisely in the sense in which we say in general all men are born free and equal. They all have the same kind of moral science in different degrees, and in each sufficient for his wants. The little child refuses to tell a lie with the same confidence in the rectitude of his refusal that the archangel feels when he persists in his allegiance to the most High, and defies the Tempter. But the child can give no reason for his perception, nor see one step beyond of its harmony with Nature.

But there are discoveries in morals: 1, in the case of every individual who loves to search the sources of action, the manner in which God has connected and fortified us by the graduated forces of the passions,— Tut, tell me he makes no discoveries, from the time he first blushed, to the hour when he analyzed Shame; and 2, there are discoveries made in morals from age to age. . . . The silent progress of human refinement does from time to time disclose more and more insight of the moral frame of man.

. . . .

Understand now, morals do not change, but the *science* of morals does advance; men discover truth and relations of which they were before ignorant; therefore, there are discoveries in morals.

It is under this persuasion that we think it a matter of importance to adapt the exercises of public worship to the changing exigences of society. If ethics were an immovable science, the primeval altar of the Jews might serve as the model of our holy place. . . .

We see that we are standing on a higher stage; that we are instructed by a better philosophy, whose greater principles explain to us the design, whilst they comprehend, themselves, the petty provisions of the less.—We leave the ritual, the offering, and the altar of Moses; we cast off the superstitions that were the swaddling clothes of Christianity, the altercations of novices, the ambition that created a hierarchy, the images and the confessional; and would accommodate the instructions of the Church to the wants of worshippers. We already descry the broader light blazing before us when we shall have emerged from the porches of the temple and stand in the temple itself. . . . Then the champion of the Cross will be able to turn from this ungrateful task, in which ages have so unprofitably elapsed, of stripping off the manifold coats under which prejudice and falsehood had concealed the truth —and come at last to the dear and lofty employment of pointing out the secret but affecting passages in the history of the soul. . . .

It has been ever a favourite topic of the pulpit to warn men against the great vice of every day,—assuming the shew of godliness when their hearts are strangers to its power,—no man in the world but pretends to a more perfect virtue than he possesses,—and to denounce against this most prevalent sin the future vengeance of heaven. I am inclined to consider this a very imperfect statement, as so falling very far short of the power and conviction it ought to carry. Instead of denouncing a future contingent vengeance, I see that vengeance to be contemporary with the crime. Instead of a cold delineation of the discord between hypocrisy and just moral feeling, I see the attempt at disguise, in every instance, to fall shamefully short of its own ends. I see that its plot is wise and its hands cunning, but in all its purposes, betwixt the work and the reward, comes in upon the evil doers a dark and strong hand which turns them back with shame upon the way they came. The true statement which I would introduce . . . is that the assumption of a shew of virtue does not and cannot impose on men, and that a successful hypocrisy does not exist, and quiet natures suffer most in the apprehension of pain.

[STRIFE OF THEOLOGIANS]

It has been remarked that notwithstanding the prodigious impression which theological controversies respecting the nature of Jesus Christ have made on human history, and the passions they daily excite in men's minds, the real difference between the sentiments of the disputants when rigidly analyzed is very subtle, and is inconsiderable. For the Trinitarian, whilst he names the name of God, is very careful to separate the idea of God from his account of the life of Jesus Christ, but considers him only in his human nature; considers him as a man. Hence it happens well that, to whatever party names education or inclination has attached us, we sympathize all on the same affecting views of the life and passion of our Lord.

MANNERS

Manners seem to be more closely under the influence of climate. They belong more to the body than the soul, and so come under the influence of the sun; they are accommodations of the motions of the body to moods of the mind. In Lapland, men are savage: in Norway, they are plain-spoken and use no ceremony, in England, some; in France, much; in Spain, more. In like manner, no man has travelled in the United States from the North to the South without observing the change and amelioration of manners. In this city, it is most observable, the use of the conventions of address among the lowest classes, which are coarsely neglected by the labouring classes at the North. Two negroes recognize each other in the street, though both in rags, and both, it may be, balancing a burden on their heads, with the same graduated advances of salutation that well-bred men who are strangers to each other would use in Boston. They do not part before they have shaken hands and bid good-bye with an inclination of the head. There is a grace and perfection too about these courtesies which could not be imitated by a Northern labourer where he designed to be extremely civil. Indeed I have never seen an awkward Carolinian.

AUTHORS OR BOOKS QUOTED OR REFERRED TO IN JOURNALS OF 1825 AND 1826

Bible;

Homer; Socrates; Plato; Demosthenes; Epicurus;

Plutarch; Seneca; Juvenal; Marcus Antoninus; Origen;

Machiavelli; Luther; Montaigne;

Bacon; Shakspeare; Ben Jonson, *Alchymist;*

Milton; Pascal, *Pensées;* Dryden, *Song for St. Cecilia's Day, Absolom and Achitophel;*

Newton; Burnet; Prideaux; Fontenelle; Leclerc;

Le Saurin; Pope; Butler, *Analogy;* Voltaire; Johnson, *Lives of the Poets;* Hume, *Essays;* Vattel; Rousseau, *Émile;* Buffon, *Natural History;* Warton, *Essay on Pope;* Burke, *Speeches;* Gibbon, *Roman Empire;* Eichhorn; Paley, *Natural Theology;*

Mitford, *History of Greece;* Herder; Playfair; Dugald Stewart; Jeffrey; Mackintosh; Thomas Brown, *Lectures on the Philosophy of the Human Mind;*

Napoleon; De Staël, *Germany;* Scott; Wordsworth, *Excursion, Intimations of Immortality, Dion;*

Byron, *Marino Faliero;* Campbell, *The Last Man;*

Dr. Channing; Edward Everett, *Phi Beta Kappa Oration;* Webster, *Funeral Oration on Adams and Jefferson;*

Sampson Reed, *Growth of the Mind.*

JOURNAL XVIII

1827

[From "XVIII," 2d, Cabot's Q and R, and a Pocket Note-book]

(From Cabot's R)

CHARLESTON, S. C.
January 4, 1827.

A NEW year has opened its bitter cold eye upon me, here where I sought warm weather. A new year has opened on me and found my best hopes set aside, my projects all suspended. A new year has found me perchance no more fit to live and no more fit to die than the last. But the eye of the mind has at least grown richer in its hoard of observations. It has detected some more of the darkling lines that connect past events to the present, and the present to the future; that run unheeded, uncommented, in a thousand mazes wherever society subsists, and are the moral cords of men by which the Deity is manifested to the vigilant, or, more truly, to the illuminated observer. It does not always

— this gifted observation — it does not always presuppose a regulated soul. A man may be a shrewd judge of the finest shades of character, whose own conscience is contaminated with habitual guilt. But such a man is not blind to the discrepancy betwixt his morals and his mind. He perceives the discord, and cannot perceive it without alarm. For he has an instinctive dread of the tendencies to harmony in the Universe which he has often observed, and which betoken some future violence to root out this disorder. If the string cannot be made to accord, it must be broken.

It is a just thought which was lately presented to me and which fell in entirely with my own notions of compensation, not yet fully unfolded, that it is beyond the compass of the most subtle policy, when once the consideration of principle has been set aside, to regulate affairs so as always to succeed; or, (as in the instance on which the remark was grounded) so as to keep for a man the popularity for which his duty was abandoned. For the order of Providence in the world fights against such a man; and somewhere on his way, maugre all his forecast and all his fetches, he will be unexpectedly circumvented and thrown out.

NOTE-BOOKS

If an ingenious man lived long enough, he might learn to talk by system, in a manner out of all comparison better than men now use. Suppose him to keep a book of commonplaces, and, as his knowledge grew, to put down on the page of each the theories that occurred. It is clear that in process of time it would embrace all the ordinary subjects of human discourse. He would n't talk so well as those who have the natural talent. Nature has fetches which art cannot reach; bewitching felicities, affecting pauses, that the mere practice of a moderate genius would n't attain. But something would doubtless be accomplished that would put to shame the cheap, extemporaneous draggle-tail dialogue that takes place in our evening companies, even among men of letters and ambition, from candle-light till the bell strikes nine and breaks up the company.[1]

1 Mr. Emerson's own practice, from youth to age, of keeping journals in which he, on the moment, faithfully recorded his thought or observation or sentence, and made his corollary, then or later, thereon, was the basis of all his writings, — the poems, the lectures, the books,— and gave a strange interest even to his occasional speech on public events.

Men lose their temper in defending their taste.

A man becomes sensible, now and then, of the existence of a kind of country gentlemen in the regions of genius, a sort of taciturn critics who have in them a solitary talent, it may be a love of eloquence, an image enshrined in their souls of eloquence so beautiful and so glorious that the successful orator, if he could open the doors of the mind and behold, would find his satisfaction changed to admiration and move all the springs of wonder, turn his summit of success into a starting-post. Such a man seems to belong elsewhere. He is a column in the desert. e. g. R. M. G.[1]

It is the rare fortune of those who are born in these times and this country to be born for the blessing of the world.

There's a free masonry among the dull by which they recognize and are sociable with the dull, as surely as a correspondent tact in men of genius.

[1] Perhaps Robert Marion Gourdin, an attractive Southerner, brother to John G. K. Gourdin, Emerson's chum. He studied medicine after leaving college.

THE FLAG

It is surprising what frivolous things excite our strongest emotions. An old rag of blue and red bunting — the national flag waving in the air of these outposts of society — makes all my patriotism glow again.[1]

IRON

It was formerly said that he " who has the most iron will be master of all this gold." In our times, War has surrendered his supremacy to Trade. But the experience of nations has shewn that the manufacture of iron is an unerring index of the degree of civilization. The consequence is that the position of Solon is still emphatically true, though in a sense very wide of that which was in his mind, that he who has most iron will have all the gold.

1 Probably the flag on the old fort at St. Augustine, Florida. The cold at Charleston had driven him farther South. He had written to his brother William, " I am not sick, but luke-sick. I have but a single complaint, a certain stricture on the right side of my chest which always makes itself felt when the air is cold or damp, and exertion of the lungs is followed by an aching. The worst part of it is the deferring of hopes; and who can help being heart-sick ? "

In your charity, the merit is always commensurate with the sacrifice.

ST. AUGUSTINE

For fifteen winter days
I sailed upon the deep, and turned my back
Upon the Northern lights, and burning Bear,[1]
And the cold orbs that hang by them in heaven,
Till, star by star, they sank into the sea.
Full swelled the sail before the driving wind,
Till the stout pilot turned his prow to land,
Where peered, 'mid orange-groves and citron blooms,
The little city of Saint Augustine.
Slow slid the vessel to the fragrant shore,
Loitering along Matanzas' sunny waves,
And under Anastasia's verdant isle.
I saw Saint Mark's grim bastions, piles of stone
Planting their deep foundations in the sea,
And speaking to the eye a thousand things
Of Spain, a thousand heavy histories.
Under these bleachèd walls of old renown
Our ship was moored.

                An hour of busy noise,
And I was made a quiet citizen
Pacing my chamber in a Spanish street.
An exile's bread is salt, his heart is sad, —

---

1 Another form of the third line was,
      On the twin Bears, fast tethered to the Pole.

Happy, he saith, the eye that never saw
The smoke ascending from a stranger's fire!
                                Yet much is here
That can beguile the months of banishment
To the pale travellers whom Disease hath sent
Hither for genial air from Northern homes.
Oh, many a tragic story may be read,—
Dim vestiges of a romantic past,
Within the small peninsula of sand.
Here is the old land of America
And in this sea-girt nook, the infant steps,
First foot-prints of that Genius giant-grown
That daunts the nations with his power to-day.
Inquisitive of such, I walk alone
Along the narrow streets unpaved and old,
Among few dwellers, and the jealous doors
And windows barred upon the public way.
                                I explored
The castle and the ruined monastery,
Unpeopled town, ruins of streets of stone,
Pillars upon the margin of the sea,
With worn inscriptions oft explored in vain.
Then with a keener scrutiny, I marked
The motley population. Hither come
The forest families, timid and tame;
Not now, as once with stainèd tomahawk
The restless red man left his council fire,
Or when, with Mexique art, he painted haughtily
On canvas woven in his boundless woods

His simple symbols for his foes to read.
Not such an one is yon poor vagabond,
Who in unclean and sloven apathy
Brings venison from the forest, — silly trade.
Alas! red men are few, red men are feeble,
They are few and feeble and must pass away.

And here,

The dark Minorcan, sad and separate,
Wrapt in his cloak, strolls with unsocial eye;
By day, basks idle in the sun, then seeks his food
All night upon the waters, stilly plying
His hook and line in all the moonlit bays.
Here steals the sick man with uncertain gait,
Looks with a feeble spirit at things around
As if he sighing said, " What is 't to me?
I dwell afar; — far from this cheerless fen
My wife, my children strain their eyes to me,
And Oh! in vain. Wo, wo is me! I feel
In spite of hope, these wishful eyes no more
Shall see New England's wood-crowned hills again."

. . . .

Heard the roaring on the beach long before
we saw land, and the sea was full of green twigs
and feathers.

(From Pocket Note-book)

St. Augustine, January 16, 1827.

The colonies observe the customs of the parent country, however ill they may be adapted to

the new territory. The Dutch cut canals in Batavia, because they cut canals in Holland, but the fierce sun of the E. Indies stagnated the water and slew the Dutch. In like manner the Spaniards and the Yankees dig cellars here because there are cellars in Madrid and Boston; but the water fills the cellars and makes them useless and the house unhealthy. Yet still they dig cellars. Why? Because there are cellars in Madrid and Boston.

Over the gate of the Fort is an inscription which, being in Spanish, and in an abbreviated character, I was unable to read. After many inquiries in town, I could not find an individual who had ever read it, or knew anything about it. Mr. Gay, the public interpreter, took the card on which I had written what letters were not defaced of the inscription, and succeeded in decyphering the following record : —

Regnando en España el Señor Don Fernando Gobernador y Capitan General de esta plaza de San Agostino de la Florida y su provincia el Mariscal de Campo Don Alonzo Fernandes d'Heredia se concluio este castillo el año de 1756 dirigiendo las obras el Capitan ynceniero Don Pedro de Brozas y Garay.

Which runs in English thus : —

" Don Ferdinand VI being king of Spain, and the Field Marshal Don Alonzo Fernandez d'Heredia being Governor and Captain General of this place of St. Augustine of Florida, and of its province, this fort was finished in the year 1756. The works were directed by the Captain Engineer Don Pedro de Brozas y Garay."

It is commonly said here that the fort is more than a century old. It seems there was an old one of much earlier date standing on the same site, which was the foundation of the present erection.

There are two graveyards in St. Augustine, one of the Catholics, another of the Protestants. Of the latter, the whole fence is gone, having been purloined by these idle people for firewood. Of the former, the fence has been blown down by some gale, but not a stick or board has been removed, — and they rot undisturbed ; such is the superstition of the thieves. I saw two Spaniards entering this enclosure, and observed that they took off their hats in reverence to what is holy ground. In the Protestant yard, among other specimens of the Sepulchral Muse, the following epitaph is written over the body of Mr. Happoldt, " a native of Germany":—

Rest in this tomb, raised at thy children's cost;
Here sadly summoned what they had and lost
For kind and true, a treasure each alone,
A father, brother, and a friend in one;
O happy soul, if thou canst see from high
Thy large and orphan family.

[St. Augustine is the] oldest town of Europeans in North America; 1564; full of ruins,—chimneyless houses, lazy people; horsekeeping intolerably dear, and bad milk from swamp grass, because all the hay comes from the north. 40(?) miles from here is nevertheless the richest crop of grass growing untouched. Why? because there is no scythe in St. Augustine, and if there were, no man who knows how to use one.

[DETERMINATION OF RIGHT]

(From Cabot's R)

It occurs to me in reading the history of the Revolution of 1688, that where, as in that case, the Providence of God and the progress of mankind imperiously demand the final success of a cause, the particular events on which it might be beforehand supposed the general result would hang are disastrous, and yet without affecting that general result. A determined bias is given to the mass, which is preserved amid all the lesser revolutions which it fulfils, by the foreign attractions to which it is subjected in its average orbit. James gains the victories, but William gains the crown. It is the same with the American Revolution.

[In the expression of doubts in the latter part of the following entry, and perhaps in some allusions later, there seem to appear reflections of the writer's conversation with a new and notable friend. At St. Augustine he met Napoleon Achille Murat, eldest son of Joachim Murat, Napoleon's brilliant cavalry leader, to whom he gave his sister Caroline as wife, and made him king of Naples. But for the overthrow of his uncle the Emperor, and the tragic death of his father, Prince Achille Murat might have succeeded to that troublesome kingdom. Happily he sought his fortunes in the New World and became an enthusiastic American. He had married a Virginian lady,[1] a grand-niece of Washington, and was a planter near Tallahassee.

Emerson by chance met Murat, who was two years the elder, and the young men were drawn to one another. Murat, brave, frank and friendly,

1 A Mrs. Gray, a widow of sixteen, née Catherine Willis. Her father, Colonel Byrd Willis, lived near Fredericksburg.

had a very active mind, but was skeptical as to religious dogmas. Emancipated from the Church of Rome, he was disgusted with the low forms of the Methodist and Baptist worship that he found in the new community. Emerson, of course, was much disturbed at the frank agnosticism of this admirable youth, and gave him his first ideas of the liberal and humane views of the Channing Unitarians. The result of their discussions appears in a letter from Murat, which will be given a little later, also in the references to Boston and the Unitarians in Murat's intelligent and enthusiastic letters on "America and the Americans" to a friend in Belgium, which were published in translation in a little book so entitled, after Murat's death in 1847.]

[DARK HOURS]

St. Augustine.

A child in a vessel thinks the shores remove when the ship leaves the shore. When the affections depart from God, God appears to depart from the soul. His image fades fast from his sanctuary and when he ceases to be seen he is thought to cease to be.

There is a tremendous sympathy to which

we were born by which we do easily enter into the feelings of evil agents, of deep offenders in the hour of their temptation and their fall. We catch with intelligent ear the parley between the tempter and the tempted ; we measure with sad alacrity the joys of guilt.

This is a part of our condition, a part of our free agency, and necessary to us as moral probationers. Let us, then, since it lies in our power, observe these gradations by which he that stands in his purity suffers himself to decline to his fall.

What hinders me from doing my will? I am perplexing myself with scruples that never entered the minds of thousands of persons, fellow-beings of mine who have lived and acted in similar circumstances. Why should I embarrass my existence? voluntarily give up this enjoyment of life, which is equivalent to so much life itself, because of certain ideas, certain imaginations which occur to nobody else, or, if they occur, are defied? Who calls on me to be the solitary servant, or the victim rather, of what is called Conscience, when all my neighbours are absolved from its authority. Conscience, Virtue—to be sure these are words of wonderful efficiency, but there have been men who have denied their foundation in the nature of man. Yet these are the alpha and omega of the argument, these two words are all the obstacles that stand between me and my advantage. They seem to me of some account, I am accustomed to revere them. I honour men that honour them. Yet there are many prejudices which I well remember to have influenced my conduct when a child, which I now despise and ridicule. These too may be but superstition, and a few years hence I shall wonder that I could ever be so pusillanimous as to regard them. Besides, what am I in the general system of being but an iota, an unregarded speck? Why then suppose that my puny arm is chained to one or another action by all this apparatus of invisible agency, that all my solitudes are swarming with commissioned witnesses, that every word I utter is overheard, that every thought I entertain is observed, that every insignificant passage of my life is brought into judgment? Alas! I fear me there is something fabulous in this prodigious array of solemn images with which divines and philosophers would bear me down and persuade me that the health of this wide universe of moral beings of an extent that affrights the imagination — and the Omnipotence of God over all — are nearly concerned in this pitiful contingency (of mine) whether I shall act, or whether I shall forbear. Why, this is the very folly of the dotard, who thinks when a passing hurricane darkens a few leagues around his hovel, that the consummation of the world is come, whilst half the globe beside is basking in sunshine. I am wiser than this. I better rate my just value in the world. I can fulfil my purposes without being affrighted by these disproportioned bugbears.

And what is the amount of all that is called religion in the world? Who is he that has seen God of whom so much is known, or where is one that has risen from the dead? Satisfy me beyond the possibility of doubt of the certainty of all that is told me concerning the other world, and I will fulfil the conditions on which my salvation is suspended. The believer tells me he has an evidence, historical and internal, which make the presumption so strong that it is almost a certainty, that it rests on the highest of probabilities. Yes; but change that imperfect to perfect evidence, and I too will be a Christian. But now it must be admitted I am not certain that any of these things are true. The nature of God may be different from what is represented. I never beheld him. I do not know that he exists. This good which invites me now is visible and specific. I will at least embrace it this time by way of experiment, and if it is wrong, certainly God can in some manner signify his will in future. Moreover I will guard against any evil consequences resulting to others by the vigilance with which I conceal it. . . .

January 30, 1827.

But now comes the analysis of this shallow philosophy. He that was sinless before declines from his integrity. He says, I have sinned ; But I live; I am in health; I shall not sin again; and how am I the worse? and no man shall know it. Vain, blind man! alas ! the laws which he spurned, the laws of the moral Universe have taken hold on him and assert their insulted supremacy. He thought himself too insignificant to provoke the animadversion of the Most High and that he might sin unnoticed in the immensity of God's government. But God has not so poorly framed the economy of his administration. He devised no fallible police, no contingent compensations. He secured the execution of his everlasting laws by committing to every moral being the supervision of its own character, by making every moral being the unrelenting, inexorable punisher of its own delinquency. In the hour when he sinned, that hour his own fate

avenged on him the majesty of the laws he had
broken.

(From Pocket Note-book)

TALLAHASSEE

Tallahassee, a grotesque place, selected three
years since as a suitable spot for the Capital of
the territory, and since that day rapidly settled
by public officers, land speculators and despera-
does. Much club law and little other. What are
called the ladies of the place are, in number, eight.
"Gov. Duval is the button on which all things
are hung." Prince Murat has married a Mrs.
Gray and has sat down in the new settlement.
Tallahassee is 200 miles west of St. Augustine,
and in the journey thither you sleep three nights
under the pine trees. The land in its neighbourhood is rich. Here is the township of Lafayette.

I saw here a marble copy of Canova's bust
of Queen Caroline of Naples, Murat's wife. It
did not strike me as at all wonderful, though
Canova's busts of the Buonapartes are said to
be his finest works.[1]

1 It would appear from this passage, although there is no
other mention of it, that Emerson accepted an invitation of
Murat to ride with him to the new settlements in West Florida.
I was told in Tallahassee that Murat's plantation was at some
distance to the eastward from that small capital with its beautiful surroundings.

[In a letter written to his brother Charles, January 27, Mr. Emerson said: "Whoso is in St. Augustine resembles what may be also seen at St. Augustine — the barnacles on a ledge of rocks which the tide has deserted : move they cannot; very uncomfortable they surely are; but they can hear from afar the roaring of the waters and imagine the joy of the barnacles that are bathed thereby. The entertainments of the place are two, billiards and the sea-beach, but those whose cloth abhors the billiards — why, theirs is the sea-beach. A small, gray-coated gnat is wagoner to the queen of fairies, and we who walk on the beach are seers of prodigious events and prophets of noble natures."

To William he wrote, a day or two later: "The air and sky of this ancient, fortified, dilapidated sand-bank of a town are really delicious. I am very decidedly relieved from my stricture, which seems to hold its tenure from Boreas. It is a queer place. There are eleven or twelve hundred people, and these are invalids, public officers, and Spaniards, or rather Minorcans. What is done here? Nothing. . . . I stroll on the sea-beach and drive a green orange over the sand with a stick. Sometimes I sail in a boat, sometimes I sit in a chair. I read and write a

little, moulding sermons for an hour which may
never arrive. For, though there may be preaching
in the world to come, yet . . . it will be hardly
after the written fashion of this pragmatic world."
(See letters, of greater length, in Cabot's Memoir, vol. i.)]

(From Pocket Note-book)

The Minorcans are very much afraid of the
Indians. All the old houses have very strong
walls and doors, with apertures through which a
musket can be discharged. They are delighted
to find that under the American flag the Indians
are afraid of the whites. Some of them, however,
do not like to venture far out of the town at this
day. "But what are you afraid of? Don't you
know General Jackson conquered all the Indians?" "Yes, but General Jackens no here now."
"But his son is, for, you know the Indians call
Colonel Gadden his son." "Ay, ay, but then
the Indians, for all that."

I saw by the city gates two iron frames, in the
shape of a mummy, with iron rings on the head.
They were cases in which the Spanish governor
had hung criminals upon a gibbet. There is a
little iron loop on one side, by the breast, in

which a loaf of bread and a vessel of water were contained. Thus provided, the wretch was hung up by suspending the ring over his head to a tree and left to starve to death. They were lately dug up full of bones.

(From Cabot's R)

PECULIARITIES OF THE PRESENT AGE

1. Instead of systematic pursuit of science, men cultivate the knowledge of anecdotes.

2. It is said to be the age of the first person singular.

3. The reform of the Reformation.

4. Transcendentalism. Metaphysics and Ethics look inwards — and France produces Mad. de Staël; England, Wordsworth; America, Sampson Reed; as well as Germany, Swedenborg. . . .

5. The immense extent of the English language and influence. The English tongue is spreading over all North America except Mexico, over Demerary, &c., Jamaica, &c., Indostan, New Holland and the Australian islands.

6. The paper currency. Joint stock companies.

7. The disposition among men of associating themselves to promote any purpose. (Millions of societies.)

" I have seen," said a preacher, in Northampton, "a drunkard who acknowledged his fault, a profane man who confessed profanity, a loose man who owned his licentiousness, &c., but I never saw an ungrateful man who owned his ingratitude. An ungrateful man! A monster in the universe."

The argument for Necessity can never be got the better of. It is like a goose which,—fight it down as much as you will,—always cackles of victory. It always turned on you as you retired. So of Berkeley's Idealism.

There is hope of one who has a vein of genius that he will be a friend to virtue. For there is between virtue and genius a natural, an eternal affinity, and where one is found, the other may be looked for, as in South America a gold mine is said to indicate the vicinity of diamonds.

The bodies of intemperate men are the tombs of immortal minds.

St. Augustine, *February* 2, 1827.

With a little thinking, passive almost amidst our sensations, and rounding our lives with a little sleep, we count off our days with a prodigal hand. The months depart, and soon I shall measure back my way to my own people. But I feel how scanty is the addition I have made to my knowledge or my virtue. Day by day I associate with men to whom my society yields no noticeable amount of advantage or pleasure. I have heard of heights of virtue and lives of philanthropy. I am cold and solitary, and lead a life comfortable to myself and useless to others. Yet I believe myself to be a moral agent of an indestructible nature, and designed to stand in sublime relations to God and to my fellow men; to contribute in my proper enjoyments to the general welfare. What then, young pilot, who by chart and compass pointest out to others the shoals they must shun and the haven they must seek—art not thyself a castaway? Will you say you have no call to more austere virtue than you daily exhibit? Have you computed the moral influences of this quiescence, this waking torpor of the soul and found them adequate to what may in equity be demanded of you? Young pilot! you dare not say Aye.

16 *February,* 1827.

My weight is 141 lbs.

It is not these speculations which are most abstruse that either deserve or receive the best reward from fame. The only dispensers of fame are the middle class of mankind, and they will not value the far-sought abstraction, no matter how inaccessible or sublime, more than the fowl on the dunghill regards the pearl. It came from distant climes, it was got with toil, it was hoarded with care, yet having no suitableness to the wants of the finder, is less valued than a kernel of corn. But those writings which indicate valuable genius treat of common things. Those minds which God has formed for any powerful influence over men, have never effeminately shrunk from intercourse with unnurtured minds. They scorned to be tender and squeamish. Human destiny is not nice. They have taken hold with manly hand on its vulgar wants; on poverty and riches; on pain of body and pain of mind, on the inconveniences of goodness, and the compensating hope. "Most poor matters point to rich ends." Besides the advantage of being understood, it is a groundless fear that the author loses a jot of true dignity by this humility in the choice of topics; for the high and low points of human life are so nearly allied that no man of powerful sense ever found himself on any subject far removed from the sources of what is deeper in human thought. It is a near neighbourhood, that of greatness of destiny and lowness of lot; that of mind and matter; that of man and God. It is like our natural existence. Though we be pigmies of a few feet, it is not a dungeon wall which confines us to the earth. There is nothing between us and the infinite Universe. So our life, which had its beginning a few summers ago from a sorry succession of some dull material causes, walks with God on the other side through time and chance, through the fall of suns and systems, through unbounded ages, unhurt and immortal. 'T is the rich treasure in earthen vessels. Such being the character of our life, such must also be the character of its descriptions.

If a man carefully examine his thoughts he will be surprised to find how much he lives in the future. His well being is always ahead. Such a creature is probably immortal.

(From Pocket Note-book)

The worthy father of the Catholic church here,

by whose conversation I was not a little scandalized, has lately been arrested for debt and imprisoned in St. Mark's. This exemplary divine on the evening of his arrest said to Mr. Crosby, "If you can change ten dollars for me, I will pay you the four which I owe you." Crosby gave him six, which the father put in his waistcoat pocket, and, being presently questioned, stoutly denied that he had anything from him. But Crosby was the biggest and compelled him to restore the money. I went yesterday to the Cathedral, full of great coarse toys, and heard this priest say mass, for his creditors have been indulgent and released him for the present.

I met some Indians in the street selling venison. I asked the man where he lived? "Yonder." "Where?" "In the big swamp." He sold his haunch for 5 bits. The purchaser offered him one bit, and a bill worth half a dollar and counted on his fingers this, *one*, and this, *four*. "You lie," said the Indian — which I found was his only word for *no*. I gave him a half bit for "piccaniny." Indian notions about the Creation, and three pairs, and three boxes.

Col. Humphreys [is] Indian Agent.

(From "XVIII" 2d)

TO HIS BROTHER EDWARD

February, 1827.

Much of what we learn, and to the highest purposes, of life is caught in moments, and rather by a sublime instinct than by modes which can be explained in detail. I acquire, when musing on my office and my hopes, notions which might savour of enthusism to an unprepared ear. If any unlucky Charles light on these sentences and call them obscure, tell him with Pindar, "It sounds to the intelligent."

TO HIS BROTHER CHARLES

23 *February,* 1827.

How is it with the ambitious youth? he of the sometime melancholy temperament, he that was called ardent, eloquent, irresistible scholar; he who loved greatness, and defied fair women; he who adored virtue on the great scale, but was squeamish at viewing it on a small one; he who had enthusiasm from nature, but it was almost all evaporated in the kneading; he whose taste would be correct, were it more manly, and whose form would be good, were it more stout—thyself? I am prone to mercy, and would draw

your character to the life, so that your own eye
should acknowledge the fidelity of the portrait-
ure. The memory is sharp, when home is distant and the dim congregation which my fancy
nightly and daily visits always appear in costume,
each in his virtues and vices. . . .

You are in the heyday of youth, when time
is measured not by numbering days, but by the
intervals of mentality, the flux and reflux of the
soul. One day has a solemn complexion, the
next is cheerful, the south wind makes a third
poetic, and another is "sicklied o'er with a pale
cast of thought,"— but all are redolent of knowledge and joy. The river of life with you is yet
in its mountain sources, bounding and spouting
on its way, and has not settled down into the
monotony of the deep and silent stream. Vouch-
safe, then, to give your poor brother some of
these sweet waters. Write, write. I have heard
men say (Heaven help their poor wits), they
would rather have ten words *viva voce* from a
man than volumes of letters to get at his opinion. I had rather converse with them by the
interpreter. Politeness ruins conversation. You
get nothing but the scum and surface of opinions,
when men are afraid of being unintelligible in
their metaphysical distinctions, or that the sub-

tlety and gravity of what they want to say will draw too largely on the extemporaneous attention of their company. Men's spoken notions are thus nothing but outlines, and for the most part, uninviting outlines of a subject, and so general as to have no traits appropriate and peculiar to the individual. But when a man writes, he uncovers his soul, he divests himself of his manners and all physical imperfections, and it is the pure intellect that speaks. There can be no deception here. You get the measure of his soul. Instead of the old verse, " Speak that I may know thee," I write, ' Speak that I may suspect thee ; write that I may know thee." Take your pen therefore and give me the secret history of the sanctuary you call yourself; what new lights illuminate, what fragrant affections perfume it; what litanies are sung; what works are daily done in its industrious recesses, and to what god is it consecrated? And if you have any inclination to retort, and play the La Bruyère on me, I defy you. It will give me extreme pleasure to see you miss the mark, and more if you hit it.

February, 1827.

Pascal wrote to expose the contradictions existing in human nature, to show that it was vile and sublime, and to furnish an account of the extremes. Young also stated and discussed the paradox. But a competent account has not, in my judgment, been given. Every man of reflexion has felt a contiguity between what was minute and what was magnificent, which was never stated in words. There is not a thing so poor and refuse in the world but that has some aspects and connexions which are grand. The chaff on the wind, the atom swimming in the sewer, fill a place in the system of matter as essential as the sun in heaven. And how, then, can man be low? If, on one side, his feet are in the dust, on the other there is nothing between his head and the infinite heavens.

Yea, yea, though I may fail to make it apparent in language, I feel that close by meanness is grandeur. In a beggar's weeds, in a servile office, the imagination starts out with a noble recoil, and in that moment whispers "Ye are gods." Never so lowly but we remember that we are tenants of infinite spaces and survivors of the sun and the stars.[1] "Power," said Pythagoras, "is never far from necessity," a stern saying which is both analogy and exemplification to my homily.

What set me forth on this odd declamation was the curious moral quality we call patriotism, which seems to flourish best, like flowers, in lowest grounds. Wise men perceive that the advantage of the whole is best consulted in consulting the real advantage of the particular, and do not therefore dissipate their affection or their force. But the dusty artisan who needs some consolation for the insignificant figure his sordid habits and feelings make in comparison with the great, and in comparison with his own conscience and conceptions, is fain to remember how large and honourable is the confederacy of which he is a member and, that, however low his lot, his resources are yet reckoned an integral part of that awful front which the nation presents to the world. Hence the unaffected, boisterous enthusiasm with which any spirited allusion to the idea

---

1 The above passage recalls Mr. Emerson's verses beginning "Let me go where'er I will" *Poems* (Appendix), and also the often quoted lines in the *Voluntaries* :—

> So nigh is grandeur to our dust,
> So near is God to man, etc.

of Country is always received by a mixed assembly. But it is not only plebeian clay that is thus touched. The sciolists also.

. . You say the sermon on prayer wanted unction and authority, and allusion to a venerable name. Let me suggest that the Son of God, if he listens from on high to the feeble efforts of his mortal ministers, may more approve the piety which finds the original foundation of his Father's law complete and competent, than that which adds awkward abutments to the work of Omniscience from the second dispensation. The true account, I take to be this. Men were so ignorant and besotted they could not see the perfection of morals. Jesus Christ was sent to remove the blindness from their minds. They are now able to see the majestic proportions and the sufficiency of the first Law. And it needs no corroboration.

(From Pocket Note-book)

St. Augustine, *February* 25.

I attended mass in the Catholic Church. The mass is in Latin and the sermon in English, and the audience, who are Spaniards, understand neither. The services have been recently interrupted by the imprisonment of the (clergyman) worthy father for debt in the Castle of St. Marks.

The people call the place Botany Bay, and say that whenever Presidents and Bishops or Presbyteries have danglers on their hands fit for no offices they send them to Florida.

When the woods are burned 'tis said they set the rivers in Florida on fire.

(From "XVIII," 2d)

BIBLE

The Bible is an engine of education of the first power. It does more than all other books. It is an index everywhere of light. All over the world where that book is found and honoured there is light; where it is not found there is darkness. The Sabbath doth more for education than all books and schools and institutions beside, united. It is one seventh of the week. It is one seventh of the year. It is one seventh of life. The child that hath lived in the light of no other opportunity, at seven years has had one year of education. The man at threescore years and ten has had ten years of religious education.

It is a sound doctrine that faith is virtue. If God sent revelations daily, none could plead the merit of faith.

(From Pocket Note-book)

St. Augustine, *February* 27.

A fortnight since I attended a meeting of the Bible Society. The Treasurer of this institution is Marshal of the district, and by a somewhat unfortunate arrangement had appointed a special meeting of the Society, and a slave-auction, at the same time and place, one being in the Government house, and the other in the adjoining yard. One ear therefore heard the glad tidings of great joy, whilst the other was regaled with "Going, gentlemen, going!" And almost without changing our position we might aid in sending the Scriptures into Africa, or bid for "four children without the mother" who had been kidnapped therefrom. It was singular enough that, at the annual meeting of this Society one week after, the business should have been interrupted by an unexpected quarrel of two gentlemen present, both, I believe, members of the Society, who with language not very appropriate to the occasion collared each other, and were, not without difficulty, separated by the interference of some members. There is something wonderfully piquant in the manners of the place, theological or civil. A Mr. Jerry, a Methodist minister, preached here two Sundays ago, who confined himself in the afternoon to some pretty intelligible strictures upon the character of a President of the Bible Society who swears. The gentleman alluded to was present. And it really exceeded all power of face to be grave during the divine's very plain analysis of the motives which probably actuated the individual in seeking the office which he holds. It fairly beat the "*Quousque, Catilina.*"

March 1.

I found here a gentleman from North Carolina who gave me some account of the monstrous absurdities of the Methodists at their Camp Meetings in that State. He related an instance of several of these fanatics jumping about on all fours, imitating the barking of dogs and surrounding a tree in which they pretended they had "treed Jesus."

(From Cabot's R)

St. Augustine, East Florida,
March 11, 1827.

To believe too much is dangerous, because it is the near neighbour of unbelief. Pantheism leads to Atheism.

I am an exile from my home ; heavily
And all alone I walk the long seashore,
And find no joy. The trees, the bushes talk to me,
And the small fly that whispers in my ear.
Ah me ! I do not love the look
          Of foreign men ;
      And woe is me that I forsook
      My little home, my lamp, my book,
      To find across the foaming seas
          This cheerless fen.

I care not that it should be said
By lords and grooms
That nature in my land is dead
And snows are scattered on her head,
Whilst here the fig and citron shed
          Their fragrant blooms.

      And dulcimer mosquitoes in the woods
      Hum their sly secrets in unwilling ears
      Which, like all gossip, leave a smart behind.

March 25th, weighed 152 lbs.

TO MISS EMERSON

(From " XVIII," 2d)

ST. AUGUSTINE, *March*, 1827.

I fancy myself better lately, through the blessing of God and the use of this fine air. And if

it please him that I shall wholly recover, I agree to the sentiment of your letter that I shall be a wiser and better man. He has seen but half the Universe who never has been shown the house of Pain. Pleasure and Peace are but indifferent teachers of what it is life to know. And though the mind touched with poetry must have a God, and the heart will reveal one, if history does not, yet the smooth man of taste and ease will be satisfied with a very indistinct and shadowy personification mixing on every side with the unintelligent forms of nature — some spirit too vague, if not too kind, to rebuke and punish his sin and pride. But the decay of his hopes; the manifested inefficacy of efforts into which he has pushed the pith and resources of all his nature; suffering and the grievous dependence on other men which suffering brings with it,— these things startle the luxurious dreamer, and alarm him with necessities never experienced before. These suggest the possibility of relations more intimate and more awful than friendship and love. They bring to light a system of feelings whose existence was not suspected before; they place him in a connexion with God that furnishes a solution of the mystery of his being.

Yet is the lesson of resignation hard to learn,

and I believe is seldom taught the young. . . .
It is easier for the venerable saint, whose warfare
is accomplished and whose brows are crowned, to
sing his hymn whilst the faggots are lighted, than
it is for a youth whose yet unmeasured powers
and yet immature virtues have already suggested
an unbounded confidence in himself; one for
whom the soothsayer Hope

> "Has turned the iron leaves of Fate's dark book
>   To read high dooms " —

.   .   .   .

These and such as these are, my dear Aunt,
the thoughts of every young man whose projects
of life are menaced by disease. I have made the
case extreme, you see, and instead of painting
myself, have given you one better and brighter.
But if you complain of long words and trite
thoughts, I confess I am fair game.

(From Cabot's U)

[FAREWELL TO ST. AUGUSTINE]

There liest thou, little city of the deep,
And always hearest the unceasing sound
By day and night, in summer and in frost,
The roar of waters on thy coral shore.
But, softening southward in thy gentle clime,
Even the rude sea relents to clemency,

Feels the kind ray of that benignant sun
And pours warm billows up the beach of shells.
Farewell; and fair befall thee, gentle town!
The prayer of those who thank thee for their life,
The benison of those thy fragrant airs,
And simple hospitality hath blest,
Be to thee ever as the rich perfume
Of a good name, and pleasant memory!

EXTRACT FROM A LETTER TO WILLIAM

CHARLESTON, *April* 23, 1827.

MY DEAR BROTHER, —

I arrived here yesterday, after a direful passage of nine days from St. Augustine. The ordinary one is one or two days. We were becalmed, tempest-tossed, and at last well nigh starved, but the beloved brother bore it not only with equanimity, but pleasure, for my kind genius had sent me for my ship-mate Achille Murat, the eldest son of the old King Joachim. He is now a planter at Tallahassee and at this time on his way to visit his uncle [Joseph Bonaparte] at Bordentown. He is a philosopher, a scholar, a man of the world; very skeptical but very candid, and an ardent lover of truth. I blessed my stars for my fine companion and we talked incessantly. Much more of him when I shall see you.

(From Cabot's R)

CHARLESTON, *April* 6, 1827.

A new event is added to the quiet history of my life. I have connected myself by friendship to a man who with as ardent a love of truth as that which animates me, with a mind surpassing mine in the variety of its research, and sharpened and strengthened to an energy for *action* to which I have no pretension, by advantages of birth and practical connexion with mankind beyond almost all men in the world, — is, yet, that which I had ever supposed only a creature of the imagination — a consistent Atheist, — and a disbeliever in the existence, and, of course, in the immortality of the soul. My faith in these points is strong and I trust, as I live, indestructible. Meantime I love and honour this intrepid doubter. His soul is noble, and his virtue, as the virtue of a Saddu-cee must always be, is sublime.

. . . .

(From "XVIII," 2d)

TO MISS EMERSON

CHARLESTON, *April* 10, 1827.

. . . I fancy myself wiser for my excursion. To be sure, one need not stir from the chimney corner for that. . . . But I rake the bright atoms faster together by quitting the fireside and sallying out after them, than by waiting for them in the slow and uncertain communication of books. Besides, to sluggish natures and manners impolite, travelling is the best lesson. When the man is at home, his standing in society is well known and quietly taken; but when he is abroad, it is problematical, and is dependent on the success of his manners. If he can assume the part of a gentleman, he is acknowledged as such. There is much entertainment also in the business of ascertaining the degree and character of a hundred casual acquaintances, and observing how far your preconceived notions tally with your experience of any companion as he gradually discloses himself. For me, who, like all men of a religious temper, love to consider myself as a favoured child of the Divinity, who is unrolling the Universe before me for my particular instruction; and, with an exact reference to my exigences and state of preparation, is bringing into my neighbourhood now one, and now another man, agent or combination of agents, until, by just degrees I am strengthened in each immortal fibre for the scenes of magnificent action which another world shall disclose for me, — it is very pleasant to retire with these views into my shell, and salute the comers as they pass in procession with a very majestic indifference — much as I would behold so many ingenious puppets which another hand is guiding. Nevertheless, I shall not deny that there are some who take such a strong hold of my attention that I am fain to quit my stoic fur, and fairly go out of my circle and shake hands and converse with them. Now I know, my kind Aunt with all her electrical imagination, will think I am talking of women. Alack-a-day! it surely is not so. Wo is me! with all the chivalry that is in my soul, backed by all the muse, I pass in cold selfishness from Maine to Florida and tremble lest I be destined for a monk. No, I was speaking of *men*, and another time I will give you an account of one whom it was my good fortune to meet in East Florida, a man of splendid birth and proud advantages, but a humble disciple in the school of truth.

[As the foregoing is the last place but one in the journal in which Murat is mentioned, and the friends never met again, it seems best to say a last word about him here in connection with the letter he wrote to his Northern friend in the autumn, here introduced. Although the young Murat is not mentioned by name in Mr. Emerson's works, their pleasant companionship is thus recalled in the essay " Society and Solitude " in the volume of that name. " If we recall the rare hours when we encountered the best persons, we there found ourselves, and then first society seemed to exist. That was society, though in the transom of a brig, or on the Florida Keys."

Achille Murat went abroad a few years later, and his military instincts led him to take a commission in a Belgian cavalry regiment, but the " Holy Alliance " did not approve of a brilliant nephew of the dreaded Emperor (who was said, too, to have borne a strong resemblance to his uncle) receiving a military training from a friendly power bordering on France, and for this reason the regiment is said to have been disbanded. Murat then lived for a time in England, he and his wife befriending Louis Napoleon, then an impoverished exile, who, when emperor, showed his gratitude to his " Cousin Kate " when she was a widow after the Civil War. The Murats returned to their plantation in West Florida, where they spent the rest of their lives.

Achille Murat, returning from the Old World, with all its attractions, enjoyed keenly plantation life with his brave wife in the frontier territory. He served in the Seminole War. An entertaining account of the Murats appeared in *Munsey's Magazine* a few years ago, entitled "An American Princess." They were childless. Prince Murat died in 1847. His remains and those of his wife lie in the graveyard of Tallahassee.

As to his agnosticism, the widow of Governor Long of Florida told me that her husband was Murat's second in a duel. As he took his pistol he said quietly, "You know I expect nothing hereafter," and stood up to give and receive fire, which happily was without fatal results to either combatant.]

LETTER FROM ACHILLE MURAT TO R. W. EMERSON

POINT BREEZE,[1] *September* 3, 1827.

MY DEAR SIR, — I have received nearly one month ago, your very polite letter, which I

1 Point Breeze, near Bordentown, New Jersey, was the home of Joseph Bonaparte who, forced by his brother, the Emperor, to be successively King of Naples and King of Spain, was thankful to spend his later days in quiet in America. In the letter the spelling of the original is preserved.

would have answered sooner but for my ill
health. I have not left my bed since the middle of July, and since three weeks I have been
afflicted with a Paralisis in my hands and arms
which prevents me using my pen. This, as you
may well think has entirely put a stop to my
plans, study and literary pursuits. I had here
lost sight of the discussions which we intended
to have together, but I intended as well as yourself to be able to continue it without interrup-
tion, before engageing in it. I must tell you,
however, candidly, that the state of my mind
has been altered since our meeting. Your system has acquired as much in proberbility as
mine has lost in certainty, both seem to me
now nearly equally proberable. I have accord-
ingly one only test left — that of expediency.
On this subject I still lean on my side, in a
refined state of society, although in barbarous
time of obscurity and ignorance your theory
may be more useful. A necessary prelimanary,
however, is to assertain how far we can have an
absolute notion of truth. This is paramount to
all subsequent indigations. As soon as I shall
be home (about the beginning of November)
and I shall be able to do anything, I shall em-
ploy myself in writing a monography of truth,

PRINCE NAPOLEON ACHILLE MURAT

for which I have been collecting materials, and of which, I believe I have spoken to you. As I shall not move from my house for a long time, I shall be fully at leasure to engage myself, at the same time, in any kind of polemical warfare which may lead to the mutual improvement of our minds.

The time I was here before being sick, was not entirely lost. I prepared for the *American Quarterly Review*, an article on Florida, but the constant misfortune which has followed me since several years did not leave me in this my first literary experiment in English. It was highly approved and spoken of by the Editor of the Review, who wanted only to make a few alterations in the style, which I, of course, readily granted. For that purpose he gave it to some underscribe, who, as little provided of commonsense and feeling of propriety as of knowledge of the matter, did take the unwarrantable liberty not only to add a review of the two works of Bertram, which I *purposedly* had discarded, but went further, and without making any alteration in my style in those parts which he conserved, changed compleately sence and meaning of others, so as to make me say exactly the contrary of what I conscientiously think. As the article now stands, it is evident to any other mind but of the able revisor, that it pulls in diferent directions and wants unity of objects. You will easyly see that the sentence which terminates the article on the Indians, is not from my hand, and is jaring with all the rest of the article. Where I had provided a regular portico for the entrance of the edifice, he has added a superstructure of historical scraps and stupid reflections which spoils the whole. If you hear anybody cite me as the author of this article, please to contradict it. I do not know I ever felt so mad about anything before.

I have been in Philadelphia to hear Mr. Furnace preach and heard him with great pleasure. Your church is increasing very rapidly in Geo. — why should it not extend to Tallahassee, and you come there to substitute, reason, learning and morality, to nonsense, ignorance, fanaticism ; even those who do not think as you do, would be glad of it for decency's sake, then we are far from that age of reason, where truth alone, resplendent, unbleamished, unmixed with errors, will be the proper food for man. I thank you very much for the interest you take in my welfare, and I assure you that feeling is perfectly reciprocal. We have met by chance, but I hope that the friendship you have inspired me, and you tell me I can claim from you, will be not the least lasting for it. Mrs. Murat appreciates your kind remembrances and has not forgotten to threaten me with your name whenever a harsh expression finds its way up my throat.

Your friend and Servant,
ACHILLE MURAT.

(From "XVIII," 2d)

FROM MISS EMERSON TO MRS. RIPLEY[1]

Yes, from my epicurean leisure, if it so please you, I scarcely peep out, but let the mutation go on which is one day to be lost in the fine elements. "Struggle for existence"—what a

---

1 Mr. Emerson's good uncle, Rev. Samuel Ripley, had married Miss Sarah Alden Bradford of Duxbury, a descendant of Governor Bradford of the Old Colony and of John Alden. She was a woman of great beauty of character and person, combining remarkable intellectual and domestic gifts, an accomplished scholar and the strength of her husband's school for boys at Waltham. With open mind, she eagerly read the new works on science and philosophy, whether in French, German or English. These naturally shook her faith in the dogmas of the day and she frankly told the change in her views in her letters to her valued friend, Miss Emerson. These, of course, drew out sharp criticism. She showed this letter to Mr. Emerson and allowed him to copy the passage.

phrase for one like you about the bubble life! How much better the ease of Mr. Horse and Mrs. Cow and Miss Sparrow. — And these might fill the earth with much more comfort to themselves if Mr. Man and Woman were not in company — and would prove to other spectators that there was a designing and good Creator, — one surely as good as the Deity of old and late skeptics, who refer not only all the powers of our mind, but God also, to the fortuitous concourse of atoms; that such a being *must* necessarily have resulted from these, operating from eternity. Well, such a being (which leaves us, it is said, all as before for natural and revealed religion) is better than none. Were atheism the order of the universe, would it be better to take part in active life? Would not death be indeed terrible then? To have loved and been loved would indeed be death to die! How much better to be a quiet dreamer; to lose by little the breath; to contract the sails of life; to despise honour and patriotism and friendship, — for indeed they would be but phantoms to embitter the grave. But then, where could be this thing — this wondrous substance which loves and hates and prophesies and reasons *a priori*, or was able to? But I know this is begging the question, and I had lain all to sleep, and it seemed so natural for my neighbours; but without any logic in me up started such a mind as S. A. R. and overset the theory. Anything, the whole of Calvinism, is nothing so absurd as that her spirit, her anything that acts, should slumber, and by the work of ages again chance in the form of a lily or a lobster.

"Can't believe." Commit a crime — form an intrigue, such as Queens and great outlaws do; blot the fair fabric of your fame, quench the torch which has been light for others, and you will have faith enough. Conscience will do an office which reason seems slow in doing. Early education would then react like a penal angel. And is it thus? is human nature in its best estate so ungracious a thing that fear will influence where love is useless? Oh no, the budding of the trees, the gentle breezes will dispel the demon. Alas! their buds wither and the morning soon clouds. But man has an invincible appetite for sorrow and apprehension of some kind which increases with his years, and it is only the old book which can quiet and sublime them.

Well, you'll say, What a canting old maid this has become. She has forgotten how many bright thoughts I gave her callous brain on the subject

of faith. Oh, these after-births — the bible-be-
liever don't like them, don't respect them, since
the glory of Socrates and such like have given
place to a higher Prophet Your would-be faith
is stumbled at a gibbet. A gibbet. He [i. e., the
criminal] never had any education. Has gone
where He who hung on a cross will procure
means to instruct him. Besides what's his crime?
Some sudden theft or rash murder — naught of
ambition which don't wash out; look not at him,
but at some long-faced hypocrite, some cruel
slave-holder, some lying office-seeker, or some
carnivorous man that feeds on human character
and grows fat on the entrails of human defects.

How little can we recapitulate without vomit-
ing at mortal condition, and resigning that the
knot should be cut, if it cannot be untied by the
revelation. Adieu. You speak of those who
dream about future influence and knowledge. It
is natural that the active should : they can hardly
imagine an existence where they are not efficient,
and why should not this part of the constitution
go forward? The Mystics, I believe, think a
higher order of virtue attainable, and I admire
the Mystics without knowing them.

(From Cabot's R)

CHARLESTON, S. C., *April* 17, 1827.

Let the glory of the world go where it will,
the mind has its own glory. What it doth, endures. No man can serve many masters. And
often the choice is not given you between greatness in the world and greatness of soul, which you
will choose, but both advantages are not compatible. The night is fine ; the stars shed down
their severe influences upon me, and I feel a joy
in my solitude that the merriment of vulgar society can never communicate. There is a pleasure in the thought that the particular tone of
my mind at this moment may be new in the
universe ; that the emotions of this hour may be
peculiar and unexampled in the whole eternity
of moral being. I lead a new life. I occupy new
ground in the world of spirits, untenanted before. I commence a career of thought and action
which is expanding before me into a distant and
dazzling infinity. Strange thoughts start up like
angels in my way and beckon me onward. I doubt
not I tread on the highway that leads to the
Divinity. And why shall I not be content with
these thoughts and this being which give a majesty to my nature, and forego the ambition to

shine in the frivolous assemblies of men, where the genuine objects of my ambition are not revered or known? Yet my friend is at home in both these jarring empires, and whilst he taxes my powers in his philosophic speculations, can excel the coxcombs, and that, *con amore*, in the fluency of nonsense. Nevertheless I cannot but remember that God is in the heavens, God is here, and the eye of my friend is dull and blind and cannot perceive Him. But what matter if this Being be acknowledged or denied, if the faith cannot impose any more effective restraint on vice and passion, than morals unsupported by this foundation?

CHARLESTON

In Charleston, I like well the decoration of the churches with monuments. It no doubt has a powerful tendency to attach.

The negroes in Charleston have a new theory of the seasons, viz., that the number of people from the North bring the cold with them.

When thy soul
Is filled with a just image, fear not thou
Lest halting rhymes or unharmonious verse
Cripple the fair conception. Leave the heart
Alone to find its language. In all tongues

It hath a sovereign instinct that doth teach
An eloquence which rules can never give.
In the high hour when Destiny ordains
That thou bear testimony to its dooms,
That hour a guiding spirit shall impart
The fervid utterance art could never find.

" LISTEN "

A poet represented as listening in pious silence,
"To hear the mighty stream of tendency." There
is much wisdom, — let me say there is much
duty in his employment.[1]

(From Cabot's R and U)

CHARLESTON, S. C., 1827.

He must have
Droll fancies sometimes cross his quiet thoughts,
Who in my vagrant verse shall look to find
A holiday from study or from toil,
And consolation to his mortal care.
Such idler will not be a man of name,

[1] Compare in *Poems*, " Wood Notes II ": —

> Hearken! Hearken!
> If thou wouldst know the mystic song,
> Chanted when the sphere was young.
>
> .   .   .   .   .
>
> To the open ear it sings
> Sweet the genesis of things
> Of tendency through endless ages,
> Of star-dust and star-pilgrimages, etc.

But must be, and therein resembles me,
A little liable to ridicule,
Because he cares a particle too much
For the opinion of the fickle world;
And notes how Merit does not swim to place
In th' tides of this world, — and feels the scandal
    oft
Of low salute to men of meaner mould;
And yet has felt, albeit with scorn the while,
A kind of justice in the Seneschal,
The uncivil fate, that made his fortunes vile.
I am frank, my friend, your eye has found
A gypsy muse that reads your lineaments
To tell the faithful fortunes of your life.

Go to, I'll feed my humour to the full,
And still expand the pleasant commentary.
Who loves my verse is one whose roving eye
Detects more beauty than his tongue will own
In art and nature. Nay his traitor tongue,
Sometimes consenting to the coxcomb's jest,
Derides the beauty, which delights his soul.
He is a man, who, though he told it not,
Mourned in the hour of manhood, while he saw
The rich imagination that had tinged
Each earthly thing with hues from paradise,
Forsake forever his instructed eye;
Bewailed its loss, and felt how dearly bought
Was wisdom, at the price of happiness.

Ah me! Sometimes in [heady wantonness[1]]
And sometimes when the dainty south-wind blew
Its soft luxurious airs, and called the clouds,
Mustering their hosts from all the sunny bays,—
Then, when the piping wind and sounding sea
And tossing boughs combined their cadences,
The sweet and solemn melody they made
Enticed him oft in heady wantonness
To scoff at knowledge, mock the forms of life,
Cast off his years, and be a boy again.
Then has he left his books, and vulgar cares,
And sallied forth across the freshened fields,
With all the heart of high-born cavalier
In quest of forest glades hid from the sun,
And dim enchantments that therein abide.

I had rather follow him than talk to him;
Fast, fast he leaves the villages behind,
As one who loathed them, yet he loathes them not,
And snuffs the scents which on the dallying gale
The woods send out as gentle harbingers
Bro't from their inmost glens to lure the step
Of the pleased pilgrim to their alleys green.
I know the pleasures of this humour well,
And, please you, reader, I'll remember them:
First, the glad sense of solitude, the sure,

[1] These words were struck out in the manuscript, because
he preferred to use them in the eighth line below, but neglected
to fill their places.

The absolute deliverance from the yoke
Of social forms, that are as tedious
Oft to a fretful and romantic man
As a mosquito's song at summer eve.
In the wood he is alone, and for the hollow chat
Of men that do not love, and will not think,
He has the unpretending company
Of birds and squirrels and the fine race of flowers.

[These verses were carried on at home in U,
and dated August 16.]

He forms his friendships with the flowers
Whose habits or whose hue may please him best;
Goes by the red and yellow populace
That with their vulgar beauty spot the plain,
To find the honoured orchis, seldom seen,
The low pyrola with a lilac's smell,
Or the small cinque-foil, the wild strawberry's friend.
He speculates with love on nature's forms,
Admires a calyx much as Winkelmann
The architecture of a Doric pile;
Not more he doted on the line
Of frieze or triglyph or on architrave,
Than doth this dreamer on the slender shaft,
With arms and stipules graced, that lifts in air
The lily or the loose-strife, tapestried with leaves;
And close below,
The faithful capsule to transmit its race,

Like from its like, to another year of flowers,
Once more to be the food of tuneful bird
Low stooping on swift wing, or busy bee,
Or the small nameless eaters that can find
A country in a leaf.

(From Cabot's R)

ALEXANDRIA, *May* 5, 1827.

My days run onward like the weaver's beam. They have no honour among men, they have no grandeur in the view of the invisible world. It is as if a net of meanness were drawn around aspiring men, through which their eyes are kept on mighty objects, but the subtile fence is forever interposed.

"They also serve who only stand and wait."

Aye, but they must wait in a certain temper and in a certain equipment. They must wait, as the knight on the van of the embattled line, standing in the stirrups, his spear in rest, his steed foaming, ready for the career with the speed of a whirlwind. Am I the accomplished cavalier?

COMPENSATIONS

In the view of Compensations nothing is given. There is always a price. Purity is the price at which impurity may be sold. If I sell my cruelty

I shall become merciful of necessity. No man ever had pride but he suffered from it; or parted with it for meekness, without feeling the advantage of the blessed change.

The angels — see Psalm 91. — The virtues are the angels.

TO HIS BROTHER EDWARD

May 8.

Glad of Dr. Channing, as some amends for the dullness, I fear I can't say degeneracy, of the pulpit in the whole country. If men abhorred nonsense as much as injury, a new race of Iconoclasts would outrun the fury of the Knoxes in demolishing our pews and spires. I suppose whenever the average intellect of the clergy declines in the balance with the average intellect of the people, it must happen that the churches will be shut up and a new order of things begin. The hazard of such a revolution who can tell? And yet I have hardly been to church this winter without feeling that the beam of the balance trembled already. I am consoled by the reflection that there is much in man that operates to postpone the convulsion, or to guide the ship in the event of a storm.

TO MISS EMERSON

Alexandria, D. C., *May* 15.

I am writing here in pleasant durance till the sun will let me go home. . . . I am not sure I am a jot better or worse than when I left home . . . only in this, that I preached Sunday morning in Washington without any pain or inconvenience. . . . I have not lost my courage or the possession of my thoughts. . . . It seems to me lately that we have many capacities which we lack time and occasion to improve. If I read the *Bride of Lammermoor*, a thousand imperfect suggestions arise in my mind, to which could I give heed, I should be a novelist.[1] When I chance to light on a verse of genuine poetry, it may be in a corner of a newspaper, a forcible sympathy awakens a legion of little goblins in the recesses of the soul, and if I had leisure to attend to the fine tiny rabble, I should straightway become a poet.

1 Mr. Emerson's strange fondness, retained from the time of first reading this novel, appeared at the Scott Centennial occasion in 1871. He said, " *The Bride of Lammermoor*, which almost goes back to Æschylus for a counterpart as a painting of Fate, leaving on every reader the impression of the highest and purest tragedy." See *Miscellanies*, Centenary Ed., p. 465; also *Essays*, First Series, p. 35.

In my day dreams, I so often hunger and thirst to be a painter, beside all the spasmodic attachments I indulge to each of the sciences and each province of letters.[1] They all in turn play the coquette with my imagination, and it may be I shall die at the last a forlorn bachelor jilted of them all.

But all which makes these reveries noticeable is the indirect testimony they seem to bear to the most desirable attributes of human nature. If it have so many *conatus*, they are not in vain, but point to a duration ample enough for the entire satisfaction of them all. They suggest a just idea of the world to come, which has always been made repulsive to men's eyes from the inadequate representations of systems of religion which looked at it only in one aspect, and that (I am forced to use a word in a limited sense it ought not to bear) a *religious* one. But I am satisfied the future world ought not so much to be regarded as the place of final moral reward, but as the after state of man, since it is probable that

1 The heads drawn in pen and ink on the margins and blank spaces of the earlier journals show much native skill and observation of feature and expression. He had no instruction, except the example of his friend and schoolmate, William H. Furness.

a moment of that infinity holds no more relation of reward to the past than doth a moment of the present life, for every moment of this life involves a relation of reward. And in this regard it is assuredly more consistent with our most elevated and therefore truest notions of God, that the education of man should there be carried on by furnishing space and excitement to the development of every faculty that can add accomplishment to the noble being. And though our poor tools of art, the colours, the pallet, the chisel, rhyme, and the pipes and strings of sound, must yield to finer and more efficient means, yet it would be to neglect those tokens of intended intellectual progress disclosed in our nature, to doubt that scope would be afforded to the compassing of the great ideal *results* of which these tools are now the poor, inadequate instruments.

THE PRESIDENT

ALEXANDRIA, *May* 19, 1827.

Mr. Adams went out a swimming the other day into the Potomac, and went near to a boat which was coming down the river. Some rude blackguards were in it, who, not knowing the character of the swimmer, amused themselves with laughing at his bald head as it poppled up and down in the water, and, as they drew nearer, threatened to crack open his round pate if he came nigh them. The President of the United States was, I believe, compelled to waive the point of honour and seek a more retired bathing-place.

NEW YORK, *June* 2.

I am sometimes fond, when I am uncomfortable, because to retreat on our own affections is the best way to put a rampart between us and fortune.

(From Pocket Note-book)

Lions seen in Philadelphia

1. Deaf and Dumb Asylum.
2. Academy of Arts.
3. Philosophical Society.
4. Sully's painting rooms.
5. West's Picture.
6. Waterworks of Schuylkill.
7. Mrs. Royall.
8. Hall of the Declaration of Independence.
9. Market.

Lions of New York

1. Broadway and Battery.
2. City Hall.
3. Van Buren and Emmett.

[Mr. Emerson worked his way slowly homeward, cautiously heeding any remonstrances from his chest at too rapid changing of latitude. He had opportunities to preach, and did so, in St. Augustine, Charleston, Washington, Philadelphia, and New York. He reached the ancestral home in the third week in June, and joined his mother at the Manse, his grandfather's house, where they were for the time the guests of Dr. Ripley. Invitations to supply the pulpit of his father's church in Boston came to him. The improvement due to the Southern journey shows in the return of courage and energy which appears in his writings.

Yet he still had uncomfortable warnings that he was, as he said, "all clay, no iron." In a letter written to his brother William in the end of June, he wonders whether, after all, he must give up the Ministry, for, he said, "my lungs in their spiteful lobes sing sexton and sorrow whenever I only ask them to shout a sermon for me." He took a better room in Divinity Hall for the rest of the year. He was asked to preach in Northampton for several weeks in the early Autumn.]

[From Cabot's U]

AT THE OLD MANSE

CONCORD, *June*, 1827.

Awed I behold once more
My old familiar haunts; here the blue river,
The same blue wonder that my infant eye
Admired, sage doubting whence the traveller came,—
Whence brought his sunny bubbles ere he washed
The fragrant flag-roots in my father's fields,
And where thereafter in the world he went.
Look, here he is unaltered, save that now
He hath broke his banks and flooded all the vales
With his redundant waves.
Here is the rock, where yet, a simple child,
I caught with bended pin my earliest fish,
Much triumphing,— and those the fields
Over whose flowers I chased the butterfly,
A blooming hunter of a fairy fine.
And hark! where overhead the ancient crows
Hold their sour conversation in the sky.

These are the same, but I am not the same,
But wiser than I was, and wise enough
Not to regret the changes, though they cost
Me many a sigh. Oh, call not nature dumb;
These trees and stones are audible to me,
These idle flowers, that tremble in the wind,
I understand their faery syllables,

And all their sad significance. This wind,
That rustles down the well-known forest road, —
It hath a sound more eloquent than speech.
The stream, the trees, the grass, the sighing wind,
All of them utter sounds of (ad)monishment
And grave parental love.
They are not of our race, they seem to say,
And yet have knowledge of our moral race,
And somewhat of majestic sympathy,
Something of pity for the puny clay,
That holds and boasts the immeasurable mind.

I feel as I were welcome to these trees
After long months of weary wandering,
Acknowledged by their hospitable boughs.
They know me as their son, for side by side,
They were coeval with my ancestors,
Adorned with them my country's primitive times,
And soon may give my dust their funeral shade.

(From Cabot's R)

THE STORM

Fast, fast across the savage sea
My little bark is blown;
Down in the ocean mournfully
The stars sank one by one.
Jesu Maria ! pray for me,
My hope is well nigh gone.

And now the heavens, which gleamed before,
Were sealed with windy clouds,
And I beheld the stars no more,
No more in shining crowds,
But loud above, the tempest tore
The canvas and the shrouds.

[The following lines, written at this time, were appended as a last verse to the little poem "Fame," written in 1824, given earlier in these extracts, and printed in the *Poems* (Centenary Ed., Appendix, p. 384).]

Go then, sad youth! and shine;
Go sacrifice to Fame.
Put Love, Joy, Health upon the shrine,
And Life to fan the flame.
Thyself, poor dupe! for praises barter
And die to Fame an honoured martyr.[1]

(From "XVIII," 2d)

TO MISS EMERSON

June, 1827.

Although I strive to keep my soul in a polite equilibrium, etc., I belong to the good sect of

---

[1] In copying them later still, he changed the last two lines to

"Being for seeming bravely barter,
And die to Fame a happy martyr."

the Seekers, and conceive that the dissolution of the body will have a wonderful effect on the opinion of all creed-mongers. How the flimsy sophistries that have covered nations, unclean cobwebs that have reached their long dangling threads over whole ages, issuing from the dark bowels of Athanasius and Calvin, will shrink to nothing at that sunburst of truth; and nobody will be more glad than Athanasius and Calvin. A glorious moment; and yet a young man does not wish it arrived. I do not think it will be dreadful to me, and yet wish to interpose thirty or forty years of strong life between me and it. In my frigidest moments, when I put behind me the subtler evidences, and set Christianity in the light of a piece of human history, much as Confucius or Solomon might regard it, I believe myself immortal. The beam of the balance trembles, to be sure, but settles always on the right side. For otherwise all things look so silly. The sun is silly, and the connexion of beings and worlds such mad nonsense. I *say* this, I *say* that in pure reason I believe my immortality, because I have read and heard often that the doctrine hangs wholly on Christianity. This, to be sure, brings safety, but I think that I get bare life without. I have no pleasure in the curiosity that hence arises to be falsified at that undeceiving hour. I covet no surprises *then*. I am content, if I can, to know what shall befall me. There's one consideration, however, one check without which I am persuaded the soul would leap in its dark womb, the body, at the approach of the future. I mean the fear of death itself, the instinctive melancholy which long trained philosophy does not strip off. If it be really true, and we plodders are to be so grand and infinite — mere beams of glory — spirits, — one would think the soul would be so enamoured of the strong suggestion that it would run before to meet its fate. But it is sedate instead, or, as you would say, wallows in the mire of life. I hope you won't scold a letter which adds nothing, even by guess, to the mass of truth, but to me 't is pleasant in idleness to hover on the verge of worlds we cannot enter, and explore the bearings of the piled mists I cannot penetrate.   R. W. E.

(From Cabot's R)

Concord, *June* 29, 1827.

The man who bates no jot of courage when oppressed by fate, who, missing of his design, lays hold with ready hand on the unexpected

event, and turns it to his own account, and in
the cruelest suffering has that generosity of perception that he is sensible of a secret joy in the
addition this event makes to his knowledge, —
that man is truly independent, — "he takes his
revenge on fortune" — is independent of time
and chance; fortune may rule his circumstances,
but he overrules fortune. The stars cannot
thwart with evil influences the progress of such
a soul to grandeur. — See Taylor's *Holy Living*,
p. 128, Philadelphia Edition.

I have seen a skilful experimenter lay a magnet among filings of steel, and the force of that
subtle fluid, entering into each fragment, arranged them all in mathematical lines, and each
metallic atom became in its turn a magnet communicating all the force it received of the load-
stone.

[A GOOD HOPE]

August 16.

There is a pleasure that has no alloy, in a hope
so confident and steadfast, that it pushes forward, through good report and evil, to the
accomplishment of its end, that it acts as what
is spiritual should act, with a scorn of material

obstacles, with a divine contempt for all that men think will hinder and bring it to nought ; and lo! instead [of] a heavy defeat, it springs elastic, and, as 't were, refreshed from apparent discomfiture, neither contracting its sail nor bating one tittle of its joyful pride. When bystanders say, Look, there is a lion in the way, it answers, But I am a man and mightier than lions. When they say, Men counterwork, it replies, Aye, but I go in the strength of God.

It is what is unseen in all actions that gives them their character. It is what is unseen that gives splendour in the view of wise men.

. . . .

TO MISS EMERSON

August 24, 1827.

When I attended church, and the man in the pulpit was all clay and not of tuneable metal, I thought that if men would avoid that general language and general manner in which they strive to hide all that is peculiar, and would say only what was uppermost in their own minds, after their own individual manner, every man would be interesting. Every man is a new creation : can do something best, has some intellectual modes or forms, or a character the general result of all such, as no other agent in the universe has; if he would exhibit that, it must needs be engaging, a curious study to every inquisitive mind. But whatever properties a man of limited intellect feels to be peculiar he studiously hides; he is ashamed or afraid of himself, and all his communications to men are unskilful plagiarisms from the common stock of thought and knowledge, and he is of course flat and tiresome.

'Tis an old and vulgar maxim, Take care of the minutes, and the hours will take care of themselves; but like many old and vulgar things 't is better than gold of Ophir, wisely used.

The Emperor Napoleon is as much a proof of heaven and eternity as the life of St. Paul. He proves how impossible it is to satisfy the human soul. But he neglected, and the world neglects, to draw the right inference from their failures.

FOR A SERMON ON SOLITUDE

There is a story of a man who on his deathbed called to him his profligate son and left him large possessions, only exacting of him the promise to spend an hour every day alone. The son kept his word and became a wise and good man.

Of Mr. Adams it was memorably said by President Kirkland, " For fifty years he rose before the sun."

" Whenever Agesilaus made an excursion, he lodged in the temples most renowned for sanctity; and whereas upon many occasions we do not choose that men should see what we are about, he was desirous to have the gods themselves inspectors and witnesses of his conduct."

Plutarch.

GENIUS AND DOMESTICITY

Aunt Mary used her thimble twice as a seal to once for her needle, and I have heard my mother remark that her own was too much worn ever to make the indented impression on wax that Aunt Mary's did.

The Alpine flower that grew in fearless beauty amid storm and cold under the awful shadow of the avalanche will wither and die in the sunny gardens of the plains.

THE UNIVERSAL MIND

NORTHAMPTON, *October*, 1827.

. . . There prevailed anciently the opinion that the human mind was a portion of the Divinity, separated for a time from the infinite mind, and when life was closed, reabsorbed into the Soul of the world; or, as it was represented by a lively image, Death was but the breaking of a vial of water in the ocean. But this portion of the Divine mind in childhood and youth they thought was yet pure as it came from God and yet untainted by the impurities of this world. There was much of truth in the beautiful theory.

SONNET

Written in Sickness

I bear in youth the sad infirmities
That use to undo the limb and eye of age.
It has pleased Heaven to break the dream of bliss
That lit my onward path with bright presage,
And my unserviceable limbs forego
The sweet delights I found in fields and farms,
On windy hills, whose tops with morning glow,
And lakes, lone mirrors of Aurora's charms.
Yet I think on them in the sleepless night —
Still breaks that morn, though dim, in Memory's eye,

And the clear soul doth the foul train defy
Of pale Disease that would her peace affright.
Please God, I'll wrap me in my innocence
And bid each awful muse drive the damned harpies
        hence.

Cambridge, No. 14 Divinity Hall,
        December 7, 1827.[1]

[In December he went on a visit (probably
an invitation to preach) to Concord, New Hampshire; hence the notification, in the following
entry, to the possible future reader of his journal, for there he met Ellen Louisa Tucker, and
fell in love. She was the daughter of Mr. Beza
Tucker, a Boston merchant who had lately died,
and her mother had married Mr. W. A. Kent
of Concord, N. H.]

(I ought to apprize the reader that I am a
bachelor and to the best of my belief have never
been in love.)

1 In this journal, the eighth line was written, —

        And lakes that mirrored all Aurora's charms ;
for which it seemed better to substitute the form given by Mr.
Emerson in a later copy (in Cabot's U). In the last line of that
copy, however, he substituted "dark" for "damned," probably because he deemed the latter unbecoming in one of his
profession, yet, as stronger, it is here retained.

Robinson Crusoe when he was in any perplexity was wont to retire to a part of his cave which he called his thinking corner. Devout men have found a stated spot so favourable to a habit of religious feeling that they have worn the solid rock of the oratory with their knees. I have found my ideas very refractory to the usual bye-laws of Association. In the graveyard my muscles were twitched by some ludicrous recollections, and I am apt to be solemn at a ball. But, whilst places are alike to me, I make great distinction between states of mind. My days are made up of the irregular succession of a very few different tones of feeling. These are my feasts and fasts. Each has his harbinger, some subtle sign by which I know when to prepare for its coming. Among these some are favourites, and some are to me as the Eumenides. But one of them is the sweet asylum where my greatest happiness is laid in, which I keep in sight whenever disasters befal me, and in which it is like the life of angels to live.

SONG

The cup of life is not so shallow
That we have drained the best,
That all the wine at once we swallow,
And lees make all the rest.

Maids of as soft a bloom shall marry
As Hymen yet hath blessed,
And fairer forms are in the quarry
Than Phidias released.[1]

TO MISS EMERSON

November 20, 1827.

It is difficult to speak with confidence of religious feeling. The mind recurs at once to history for authority. It finds the great multitude of the best men who have lived and left a name to be what the enthusiast calls " Cold and prudent Christians" — Bacons, Lockes, Butlers, Johnsons, Buckminsters. But the enthusiast admits or insists on the fact that the world is against him, and appeals confidently to the received language of religion in every age, which has always expected the suffrage only of a minority. At the same time he proudly cites a concurrent line of elect souls, coming down from the beginning, who saw the light that was not vouchsafed to the world, and were not disobedient to the heavenly vision. The apostles, the early martyrs, the Ebionites, the tenants of Thebais, the Bene-

1 These verses appear to have been written earlier in the year,— it is impossible to tell just when,— but this seems an appropriate place for their introduction.

dictines, the Waldenses, the Puritans, the Mo-
ravians, down to Pascal, Wesley, and Cowper,
beside what has been done and suffered from
kindred motives by unnumbered devotees in
"the mysterious East," out of the pale of
Christianity, and many indications of the same
spirit before its advent, as the Gymnosophists
of India, and Essenes of the Jews: all these bear
witness to a principle in human nature ineradicable in the shifting influences and forms of society, firm in the flux of ages, that suggests and
sanctions the crucifixion of the flesh before the
mighty image of God within the soul. Moreover, in our wariest, most philosophic hours
the heart compels us to respect even what we
deem the extravagant issues of devotion. The
proper emotion is wonder : the proper duty perhaps a diligent study of the phenomenon and of
ourselves ; but I think no good man will laugh
at Wesley, and no wise man be secure of his
own superiority. 'T is always grateful to find men,
the solidity of whose understanding is beyond
dispute, giving themselves heartily to devotion.
The piety of Newton is inestimable: and there
is something awful in the gravity and apprehensive contrition of Johnson's closet. It gives a
start to the secure spirit, like his who

". . . heard the bell of the convent toll
For a departing sinner's soul."

Nevertheless we are not to be bound by suggestions of sentiment, which our reason not only does not sanction, but also condemns. 'T were to throw our pilot into the sea in compliment to the winds. And when the mystics tell me, as the mystics will not hesitate to do, that there is sin in every good work until I have the assurance clear as the sun in heaven of a new connexion of God with my soul, of a new birth, or what not, I shall give them no regard; I shall be content, while the laws of my nature remain the same, with "the beggarly elements of justice and charity"—self-condemned, I own, at the lax discharge of my known duties, but not curious to add to my genuine grief horrors for imaginary and remediless delinquencies. Does this reasoning seem to you unsafe? Is it not to be applied to all that we judge false doctrine, coming under whatever authority of names and age? Were it not a crime of which account would be demanded, and involving possibly hereafter many more than myself, if I should surrender to the casual and morbid exercise of the sentiment of a midnight hour the steady light of all my days, my most vigorous and approved thoughts, barter the sun for the waning moon? 'T is all idle talking. In the extreme it is plain enough. But the difficulty I contemplated consists in finding the proper mean; in discerning how much (for certainly something) is laudable, and how much extravagant in their theory of duty; in learning how much we lack of the love of God, and in adjusting life betwixt reason and feeling; e. g., it may be plausibly denied that 't is worth while to get rich, or to make acquisitions in science. But shall a wise man refrain?

December 17, 1827.

. . . But now and then the lawless imagination flies out and asserts her habit. I revisit the verge of my intellectual domain. How the restless soul runs round the outmost orbit and builds her bold conclusion as a tower of observation from whence her eyes wander incessantly in the unfathomable abyss. I dimly scrutinize the vast constitution of being into which this present shall be absorbed, in which we shall look back, peradventure, to Christianity as to a rosary on which, in the morn of existence, we learned to count our prayers, and think it idle to pause in the train of mighty meditation, to remember in our ancient pupilage the rudiments of those stupendous moral energies we shall wield at that hour. But no; no thought, no perception of truth, how limited soever, can become insignificant. God communicates with the thoughts of men; and to whatever magnificence of nature and acquisition we may attain, the whole past will always be the instrument of future works.

. . . Connexion between God and the Soul,— What is religion but this connexion? Is not this the thought that always invests human nature, though in rags and filth, with sublimity, — that wheresoever a man goeth, there goes an animal containing in his soul an image of the Being by whom the Universe subsists? The Mind is his image and mirror. Is it not that, with whatever depravations blotted and disguised, God makes the main idea therein to which all others arrange themselves as threads of steel to a magnet, or as all the magnets of the world to the polar axis? Is not the mind in health just in proportion as that idea is clear? If that is obscured, is there not death in the mind? (I use mind in its largest sense, for I see that the intellect may be vigorous, as in Laplace, and refuse to honor its Maker.) But I am confounded by the anomaly. These views seem to me to hold. I cannot understand the feelings of the Atheist. I cannot believe Atheism and genius to consist. And yet what motive for the pretence? Doesn't the heart say Hallelujah amid its prayers for Bacon, Newton and Locke, for Socrates and Cicero? If there were no lobsidedness, no disease in the Soul, the idea of Deity would be its exact and constant measure of its progression. When that was great, the mind was great. Its own glory would keep even pace with the glory it gave. Is not this unutterably beautiful and grand, this life within life, this literal Emanuel, *God within us*? When this shall have been taught worthily to men, the wailing spirits of the prophets may bend from their spheres, for the Principle of Evil shall come to his end, and God shall be all in all.

AUTHORS OR BOOKS MENTIONED OR REFERRED TO IN JOURNALS OF 1827

Bible;
Pindar; Socrates;
Cicero; Seneca; Epictetus; Plutarch, *Lives*;
Athanasius;
Philippe de Comines; *Mémoires*;
Calvin.
Bacon; Shakspeare;

Jeremy Taylor, *Holy Living and Dying;*
James Harrington, *apud* Hume;
Pascal; Locke; Newton; La Brùyère;
Cowper; Young; Berkeley; Butler;
Madame de Staël; Scott, *Quentin Durward,
Bride of Lammermoor, Rokeby;*
Buckminster, Channing, *Sermons;*
Sampson Reed, *Growth of the Mind.*

JOURNAL XIX

(From "Sermons and Journals," 1828-29, and Cabot's
Q and R)

[SOME letters, written by Emerson to his brothers
and aunt during the winter and spring of this
year, which are quoted by Mr. Cabot in his
Memoirs, show the good sense with which at
this critical period he yielded to necessity instead
of fighting Fate, like his brother Edward. Thus
the elder brother saved and the valiant younger
brother lost his life. In one of these letters,
Waldo says : " I am living cautiously, yea, tread-
ing on eggs, to strengthen my constitution. It is
a long battle this of mine between life and death.
. . . So I never write when I can walk, and especially when I can laugh." This accounts for the
scanty journal-writing in this year, and he refused many flattering invitations to preach. Thus
his proper health gradually reasserted itself.]

(From Cabot's R)

January, 1828.

Montaigne says he is sorry Brutus's treatise
on Virtue is lost, because he would hear one,

who so well understood the practice, discuss the theory of virtue. 'T is well said. It is always dangerous when an appeal is made from the sermon to the preacher, when the bold reason of the hearer quotes his life against his doctrine.

Demades told the Athenians that he had observed that they never treated of peace except in black clothes; so, says Plutarch, men never reduce their diet except amidst cataplasms, clysters and medicines; so also men do not turn for enjoyment to another world till their hopes in this have failed them.

"Age gives good advice when it is no longer able to give a bad example."

We think ill of a man who has an ill gait, or a defective utterance, or bad countenance, and shun his acquaintance, but a man who wastes his time does not excite aversion.

It has been observed that particular sects have their own physiognomy. But we keep the same face and air from year to year; — it shows that we have wasted our time.

It is said public opinion will not bear it. Really? Public opinion, I am sorry to say, will bear a great deal of nonsense. There is scarce any absurdity so gross, whether in religion, politics, science, or manners, which it will not bear. It will bear the amazing conference of New Lebanon. It will bear Andrew Jackson for President. It will bear the convicted ignorance of Captain Symmes. It will bear the obscenities of the Boston Theatre. Lord Bacon never spoke truer word than when he said, There's more of the fool in the world than the wise.

I have once or twice been apprehensive that I was reading in vain, that the cultivation of my mind did not turn to any good account in my intercourse with men. I am now satisfied of the contrary. I have every inch of my merits. More is conceded to me than I have a just title to. I am oftener compelled to deplore my ignorance than to be pleased with my knowledge. I have no knowledge that I do not want.

January, 1828.

In Concord, N. H., I visited the prison and went into the cells. At this season they shut up the convicts in these little granite chambers at about 4 o'clock P. M. and let them out about 7 o'clock A. M. — 15 dreadful hours.

EXTRACTS FROM WORDSWORTH [1]

(From Cabot's Q)

" But in calm peace the appointed Victim slept
  As he had fallen, in magnanimity
  Of spirit too capacious to require
  That Destiny her course should change."

Dion.

" Tens of thousands rent from off the tree
  Of hopeful life, by Battle's whirlwind blown
  Into the deserts of eternity."   III, 218.

" Not in entire forgetfulness,
  And not in utter nakedness,
  But trailing clouds of glory do we come
  From God who is our home."

Intimations of Immortality.

" . . . From Cambrian wood and moss
  Druids descend, auxiliars of the Cross,
  Bards nursed on blue Plinlimmon's still abode."

Ecclesiastical Sonnet, X.

" There is a radiant but a short lived flame
  That burns for poetry in the dawning east."

  1 Because of the confused manner in which the journals were
kept during this unsettled period, it is hard to tell whether these
extracts and the Essay on Poetry which follows were written
in 1825 or the end of 1826.

" Know — that he who feels contempt
    For any living thing hath faculties
    Which he hath never used ; that thought with him
    Is in its infancy."

> *Lines left upon a Seat in a Yew Tree.*

" Intent to trace the ideal path of right
    More fair than heaven's broad causeway paved with
        stars
    Which Dion learned to measure with delight."

> *Dion.*

" A soul by force of sorrows high
    Uplifted to the purest sky
    Of undisturbed humanity."

" How touching when, at midnight, sweep
    Snow-muffled winds and all is dark."

> *Sonnet I, On the River Duddon.*

" From her unworthy seat, the cloudy stall
    Of Time, breaks forth triumphant Memory."

" But Shapes that come not at an earthly call
    Will not depart when mortal voices bid."

(From Cabot's Q)

1828?

NOTES ON POETRY.[1]

A fault that strikes the readers of Mr. Wordsworth is the direct pragmatical analysis of objects, in their nature *poetic*, but which all other
poets touch incidentally. He mauls the moon
and the waters and the bulrushes, as his main
business. Milton and Shakspeare touch them
gently, as illustration or ornament. Beds of
flowers send up a most grateful scent to the passenger who hastens by them, but let him pitch
his tent among them and he will find himself
grown insensible to their fragrance. And it
must have occurred frequently to our reader
that brilliant moonlight will not bear acquaintance. Nothing is more glorious than the full
moon to those who ride or walk under its beams.
But whoso goes out of doors expressly to see
it returns disappointed. Mr. Wordsworth is a
poet with the same error that wasted the genius

1 It may be of interest to compare with these early judgments what Mr. Emerson said of Wordsworth in 1840 and
in 1843; see in *Natural History of Intellect*, " Papers from the
Dial," "Modern Literature," and " Europe and European
Books "; also in *English Traits*, chapters i and xvii.

of the alchemists and astrologers of the Middle Age. These attempted to extort by direct means the principle of life, the secret substance of matter from material things; and those to extract intelligence from remoter nature, instead of observing that science is ever approximating to truth by dint of application to present wants, and not by search after general and recondite Truth. Mr. Wordsworth is trying to distil the essence of poetry from poetic things, instead of being satisfied to adorn common scenes with such lights from these sources of poetry as nature will always furnish to her true lovers. We feel the same sort of regret that is occasioned when Aristotle forsakes the Laws of the Intellect and the Principles of Ethics for researches into the nature of mind.

> " The man who shows his heart
> Is hooted for his nudities, and scorned."
>
> YOUNG.

There's a great difference between good poetry and everlasting poetry.

Shakspeare alludes to himself nowhere in his drama. The sonnets. Homer keeps out of sight except in two places. A grand trait. It is like Providence. *Vide* Herder. *Mem.* Pope's account of his own resemblance to Providence in my blotting book.—A different age. In antiquity, nature towered above all man had done: it sunk the personal importance of man. The bard taught as the minister preaches, and felt an impertinence in introducing self. Now man has grown bigger, a commercial, political, canalling, writing animal. Philosophy inverts itself, and poetry grows egotistical.

Shakspeare immortalizes his characters. They live to every age and, as we say of Christianity, have a prospective adaptation. Ben Jonson's are all dead. Read *Alchymist* and the rest. They are all in brocade. We feel that they are a past generation, our great grandfathers and mothers. And so their motives and manners are in brocade, not vital to us; as the Euphuism of one. But universal man appreciates Shakspeare,— boys, rabble, every man of strong sense though uncultivated as ——. Exceptions rare. Gibbon,—but he had no acumen for poetry; that ear was deaf; witness his poetical opinions in notes. So Dr. Priestley, I guess, had no ear; he calls Mrs. Barbauld one of the best poets England can boast of (see his *Life*, p. 69). Milton does not get this general suffrage.

I find to-day one of Shakspeare's quibbles.

Miranda tells Ferdinand who carries wood to the pile,

> " When this burns,
> 'T will weep for having wearied you."

February, 1828.

A very unaccountable poem, that *Pelican Island*. A mixture of greatness with defects that don't appear to be slovenliness, like the slovenly greatness of Dryden, so much as want of delicate poetic perception; but all along, at intervals, glitter lines that might decorate *Paradise Lost*. And there's a general grandeur of conception. But in the minor poems he is decidedly an ordinary genius again. It is the singular merit of the *Pelican Island* that 't is original both in the design, which perhaps makes all its greatness, and in the execution. It is a poem worth ten *Excursions*, being generally a complete contrast to Wordsworth's verses. These abounding in fact, and Wordsworth wanting. These seizing coarse and tangible features for description or allusion, and Wordsworth the metaphysical and evanescent. This teaching body, and Wordsworth soul. This using a very large encyclopediacal diction, and Wordsworth affecting that which may be proper to the passions in common life. It seems

to me that who could write this could write ten
times as well. Milton would write it off in un-
premeditated manuscript and lay it up as a block
to be hewn and carved and polished. But Milton
would as soon have hanged himself as published
it as it stands. Had it been found and printed
by Montgomery's executors, instead of Montgomery, it would not surprise. The puzzle is
that there's quite a large portion of the Poem
is mere extemporaneous blank verse, only fit for
the fount of a newspaper.

(From Cabot's R)

DIVINITY HALL, *February* 14, 1828.

Burnap was very witty to-night.[1] He said
there was one man who had the queerest reputation — Dr. Watts — such a mixture of hea-
thenism and scholastic learning and Calvinism
and love and despair and mully-grubs — he was
the funniest old cock in the theological walk;
that that old Betty should be one of the three
legs that support the Trinity, and that the
church should go chanting his hymns for centuries, mistaking the effusions of belly-ache for

1 Rev. George Washington Burnap, at that time a divinity
student. He received the degrees of A.B., 1824; A.M., 1827;
S.T.D., 1849; from Harvard University.

the inspirations of David — was the greatest
phenomenon. Then, that he should write a treatise on Logic, and then one on the Improvement of the Mind! Then, that his sun should
set clear after being foggy all day! And Dr.
Doddridge! who owed all his fame to his getting up at five o'clock every morning and writing
for two hours what everybody knew and said
before.

Religion aims to make a man at peace with
himself. A man who is angry is not at peace
with himself, or who is proud, or who steals.
And, as we cannot determine the place of the
ship on the heaving sea except by reference to
the immoveable sun, so we find it impossible
to determine the state of the soul without
something outside, some fixed idea, as that of
God.

I would ask, What is God? with that awe
which becomes a man in this inquiry. It is no
idle curiosity. It is what we were made for. The
answer we offer to the question is always an unerring index of the purity of our religious views.
A savage will make one reply, a sage another,
an angel another; and, as their views of God
are, their views of man and of duty will be. . . .

ANECDOTE OF MR. OTIS AND JUDGE SPENCER

DIVINITY HALL, *March* 10, 1828.

. . . If you are in habits of intimacy with men, you have sometimes known two of your friends come to you at different times, and each, giving the character of the other, lament that he had not judgment. The fact probably was that both were right, for both wanted it. Judge Spencer of New York (who was left out in the new modelling of the courts in that State) told Judge Lyman that Mr. Otis came to see him on his way from Washington, and "I said to him, ' Well, my old friend, we are both disappointed — I have fallen and you have failed to rise ' — and I was very much mortified to have said this, for I found it touched Mr. Otis to the quick." Shortly after Mr. Otis came to Northampton and dined with Judge Lyman and spoke of this visit to Spencer and the conversation, and remarked, " that it really made him ashamed to see how much Judge Spencer was offended by so trifling a thing as this political disappointment." And how was the truth? I inquired of Judge Lyman ; " O," said he, "both felt it very much."

[OFFICE OF RELIGION]

... Men entertain very gross prejudices touching the very nature of Religion. I speak ... of good plausible people that go to church for decency's sake, but do not obey the commandments, nor observe the ordinances. They think it is a train of solemn pageants that we wish them to entertain in the mind, to lengthen the visage, to make long prayers, to read long sermons,— and not to fulfil their duties to the Universe. They are living. All the true aim of Religion is to set them right, enlighten them. They are on a wrong scent; they are undoing themselves; they are living like *animals*. We would have them live like *men*. They are acting for thirty or forty years. We would have them act as century-plants. They are scheming and talking, as if they belonged, like a toad or a ground-worm, to the acre on which they were born: they never leave the shop, they are village statesmen, cob-house architects ; we have found out that, though in the disguise of these rags, they are come of an imperial family ; that they are heirs of heaven and earth ; tidings have come full of astonishment and transport that their life, that seemed running fast to the last sands, is to be prolonged by a decree of Omnipotence ;

that it is not to be wasted any more in low places, but they are to be removed to the company of majestic minds and an infinite spectacle; that they are now to owe duties to the Sovereign of the Universe and to all the vast circle of intelligent beings.

Observe: — A prejudice exists that we would call them to a life of *contemplation*, and the nature of man demands a life of action. They would have reason. But it is not so. *We* call them to a life of action. We understand their ignorance. We find unutterably dear and beautiful what they esteemed, and what we once esteemed, sad and tragic. Joy is grave.

. . . .

[*Religio non solum*] *ad delectationem, sed ad animi magnitudinem, et ad mores conferat.*

[BACON] *De Augmentatione Scientiae*, Lib. II; cap. 13.

(From " Sermons and Journals.")

[DO NOT OVER-RATE ACTION]

We are very apt to over-rate the importance of our actions. Men of a very religious turn of mind are apt to think (at least their language gives this impression) that the designs of God in the world are very much affected [by], if not dependent upon what shall be done or determined by themselves, or their society, or their country. We lose ourselves in the details of the prejudice, till we are blind to the absurdity that we are making the everlasting progress of the universe hang upon the bye-laws of a Missionary Society or a Sunday School.

The true way to consider things is this: Truth says, Give yourself no manner of anxiety about events, about the consequences of actions. They are really of no importance to us. They have another Director, controller, guide. The whole object of the universe to us is the formation of character. If you think you came into being for the purpose of taking an important part in the administration of events, to guard a province of the moral creation from ruin, and that its salvation hangs on the success of your single arm, you have wholly mistaken your business. Creep into your grave, the universe hath no need of you. How foolish! For what hast thou which thou didst not receive? and cannot He who gave you this power commit it to another, or use it himself?

It is proposed as a question, whether the business of the preacher is not simply to hunt out and to exhibit the analogies between moral and material nature in such manner as to have a bearing upon practice.

[INSPIRATION]

CONCORD, *May*, 1828.

. . . I find a kindling excitement in the thought that the feeling which prompts a child to an act of generosity is the same which guides an archangel to his awful duties; that in the humblest transaction in which we can engage we can introduce these stupendous laws which make the sovereignty of the creation, the character of God. It seems to me, in obeying them, in squaring my conduct by them, I part with the weakness of humanity. I exchange the rags of my nature for a portion of the majesty of my Maker. I am backed by the universe of beings. I lean on omnipotence.

FRIENDS

The character of our friends is a sacred property which is very important to us. . . . In moments when our own faith wavers, when we are disturbed with melancholy doubts, the unfailing refuge of the mind is in that little honoured number of good men and women among our friends, whose probity is our anchor, that, like a squad-

ron of angels, gather on the mount before us and
send out from their seraph faces courage and light
into our hearts.

There is something respectable in being master of the tongue. . . . Consider the force of
character ; the impressiveness of the silence of a
good man. I have known a pause in speech do
more than a harangue. Consider also the beneficent consequences of collecting and reporting the
good of all men.

[WRITING DOWN]

DIVINITY HALL, *July* 10, 1828.

I am always made uneasy when the conversation turns in my presence upon popular ignorance
and the duty of adapting our public harangues
and writings to the mind of the people. 'T is all
pedantry and ignorance. The people know as
much and reason as well as we do. None so quick
as they to discern brilliant genius or solid parts.
And I observe that all those who use this cant
most, are such as do not rise above mediocrity
of understanding.

[SAUNTERINGS]

I am not so enamoured of liberty as to love to be idle. But the only evil I find in idleness is unhappiness. I love to be my own master, when my spirits are prompt, when my brain is vegete and apt for thought. If I were richer, I should lead a better life than I do; that is, better divided and more able. I should ride on horseback a good deal; I should bowl, and create an appetite for my studies by intermixing some heat and labour in affairs. The chief advantage I should propose myself in wealth would be the independence of manner and conversation it would bestow and which I eagerly covet and seldom quite attain, and in some companies never.

It is a peculiarity (I find by observation upon others) of humour in me, my strong propensity for strolling. I deliberately shut up my books in a cloudy July noon, put on my old clothes and old hat and slink away to the whortleberry bushes and slip with the greatest satisfaction into a little cowpath where I am sure I can defy observation. This point gained, I solace myself for hours with picking blueberries and other trash of the woods, far from fame, behind the birch-trees. I seldom enjoy hours as I do these. I remember them in winter; I expect them in spring. I do not know a creature that I think has the same humour, or would think it respectable. Yet the friend, the *anteros*, whom I seek through the world, now in cities, now in wilderness, now at sea, will know the delight of sauntering with the melancholy Jaques.

When I consider the constitutional calamity of my family, which, in its falling upon Edward, has buried at once so many towering hopes — with whatever reason, I have little apprehension of my own liability to the same evil. I have so much mixture of *silliness* in my intellectual frame that I think Providence has tempered me against this. My brother lived and acted and spoke with preternatural energy. My own manner is sluggish; my speech sometimes flippant, sometimes embarrassed and ragged; my actions (if I may say so) are of a passive kind. Edward had always great power of face. I have none. I laugh; I blush; I look ill-tempered; against my will and against my interest. But all this imperfection, as it appears to me, is a *caput mortuum*, is a ballast — as things go, is a defence.

My practice conforms more to the Epicurean, than to the Stoic rule,

"I will be flesh and blood;
For there was never yet philosopher
That could endure the toothache patiently,
However they have writ the style of gods
And made a pish at chance and sufferance."

Wo is me, my brother, for you! Please God to rescue and restore him ! [1]

EDUCATION

I like to have a man's knowledge comprehend more than one class of topics, one row of shelves. I like a man who likes to see a fine barn as well as a good tragedy.

Sir Henry Wotton says of the institutions of Education, that they are more important than the laws, because, if young trees were at first well fastened at the root, they would little want any props and fence afterwards. He says also, by an analogy perhaps not so natural, that if such an unpliant and stubborn mineral as iron is will acquire by continuance a secret appetite, an habitual inclination to the site it held before,

---

[1] Edward's reason temporarily gave way because his conscience and his ambition spurred him to labours too great for his high-strung organization to stand. See in Emerson's *Poems*, "In Memoriam, E. B. E.," and the "Dirge"; also in Cabot's *Memoir*, vol. 1, pp. 140, 141.

how much more may we hope through [the] same means, — education being nothing but a constant plight and inurement, — to induce, by custom, good habits into a reasonable creature? — See *Survey of Education*.

He has two or three signs among children; *Tantum ingenii quantum irae*, Seneca; another, *tantum ingenii quantum memoriae*, Quintilian; a third, *tantum ingenii quantum imitationis*, Aristotle.

I do not love to be punctual because I love to be punctual.

SKETCH FOR A SERMON, BY E. B. E.

You are a son, and certain conduct you perceive to belong to you in this relation. You are a brother, and such and such duties, etc. You are a merchant. You belong to this city, and [it is] this or that in the deportment which makes up your virtue or your vice in your character as citizen. One step farther; you belong to this country as a confederacy of States, and hence come other new obligations. Farther still, you belong to mankind, and, as a man, owe something. But is this all? — You belong to one still more extensive family, brotherhood, community — the universe.

July 30, 1828.

A child is connected to the womb of its mother by a cord from the navel. So, it seems to me, is man connected to God by his conscience. God has given him a free agency, has permitted him to work his will in the world — doing wrong or right, but has kept open this door by which he may come in at all times and visit his sins with distress, or his virtues with pleasant thoughts. It is like the hydrostatic paradox, as naturalists call it; the ocean against a hair line of water; God against a human soul.

Est deus in nobis, etc., and, when outraged, this *deus* becomes *diabolus,* a spectre that no exorcism will bind.

DIVINITY HALL, *August* 18, 1828.

Keep a thing by you seven years, and you shall find use for it. You will never waste knowledge. I like the sentence of Locke; " that young men in their warm blood are often forward to think that they have in vain learned to fence, if they never show their skill in a duel."

One of the great defects of the world is this, that it is not enough that an objection has been fully answered. In my simplicity I should have thought Richardson's engaging novel of *Sir*

Charles Grandison a settlement of the subject of duelling: that all the common prejudices on that question were manifestly shown to be paltry. But no, it must be hammered into the head of society, as Latin nouns into the head of a blockhead at school.

October 31, 1828) }
February 11, 1828.[1]) }

[SELF RELIANCE]

It is better to depend on yourself and set at nought the judgment of society. . . . Is it not better to get out of the vapours that settle in this low air, its deceptive echoes, its false valuations, and sketch the map of the country from mountain ground? Is it not better to scorn and avoid the heaving fluctuations of its public opinion, refuse to be the victim of its changing estimation, and be all the universe to yourself?

DIVINITY HALL, *September* 11.

We are very powerful beings. Every mind may be brought to such a state as to have very little regard to inconvenience or physical obstructions. Let it [. . .] be felt by us that we exist

1 Here follow two passages written in cipher.

wholly in the mind; that all happiness is there, and all unhappiness; that the present condition and appearance is nothing. . . .

SITUATION

'T is a striking proof of the power of *situation* to drop a penknife or a glove upon the ground and see how they look there.

[COMPENSATION]

It is an important fact that a man carries about with him favour or disgrace. We impute our reception in society to the will of others and forget that we ourselves alone determine what that reception shall be, that a man may always, before he enters the door of a house, forestal his welcome by consulting his own mind. It will render him a true and faithful reply. . . .

Do you not see that every misfortune is misconduct, that every honour is desert, that every affront is an insolence of your own?

Don't you see you are the universe to yourself? You carry your fortunes in your own hand. Change of place won't mend the matter, you will weave the same web at Pernambuco as at Boston, if you have only learned how to make *one* texture. . . .

He that explores the principles of architecture and detects the beauty of the proportion of a column, what doth he but ascertain one of the laws of his own mind? The Kingdom of God is within you.

If you stammer in your talk or are cloudy, why then it is because your purpose is not pure. If the plan you explain is high-minded, generous on your part, why, then the reason you stammer is because you tell it to get credit for your magnanimity.

[READING]

I read things in Montaigne, Caius, that you cannot; much as he said himself. I will give you Scougal and you shall not find anything in it valuable to you. "It sounds to the intelligent." [1] The lapidary will let you choose a stone from a handful of chrystals, knowing that your eye is not skilful enough to detect the unpolished diamond.

I believe the law of Justice is very hard to keep. As to Charity, you can't help being charitable. It is easier to give than it is to withhold on twenty occasions. But Justice lasts all the time, and never mitigates her claim, and, after all, is a pitiful performance, for it never deserves praise. You can only sing, We are unprofitable servants.

1 Pindar.

In a tavern everybody puts on airs except the landlord: he is the poor devil, and the commonest sot of a teamster thinks he has the advantage of him.

[BEAUTY]

It is hard to yoke love and wisdom. It is hard to criticize the behaviour of Beauty. In her magic presence, reason becomes ashamed of himself and wears the aspect of Pedantry or Calculation. Sentiment triumphs, . . . quotes triumphantly the ancient theory (a sweet falsehood) that Beauty is the flower of Virtue. Experience looks grave, and though when the radiant eye peeps out upon him, he stands half convinced, yet still he musters his saws, his conspiring traditions and rules of the wise, his observations on the living, his analogies, and, what he chiefly relies on, the impressions formerly made on the same heart by other and loftier qualities which reason and stoicism justified. A pretty plea, no doubt, but if the Dæmon of the man should throw him into circumstances favourable to the sentiment, reason would stand on a perilous, unsteady footing.

The terms of intercourse in society are singularly unpropitious to the virtuous curiosity of young men with regard to the inner qualities of a beautiful woman. They may only see the outside of the house they want to buy. The chance is very greatly against her possessing those virtues and general principles which they most value. For they know of what delicacy and rarity is the nature of those fruits, and with what difficult and long separated steps they themselves reached them. Yet a mighty testimony is afforded to the moral harmony of human nature, in the fact that the deportment of a beautiful woman in the presence of her admirer never offends point blank against the great laws whose violation would surely shock him.

[THE SPLENDOUR OF ENGLISH POETRY]

Is it not true, what we so reluctantly hear, that men are but the mouthpiece of a great progressive Destiny, in as much as regards literature? I had rather asked, is not the age gone by of the great splendour of English poetry, and will it not be impossible for any age soon to vie with the pervading etherial poesy of Herbert, Shakspeare, Marvell, Herrick, Milton, Ben Jonson; at least to represent anything like their peculiar form of ravishing verse? It is the head of human poetry. Homer and Virgil and Dante and Tasso and Byron and Wordsworth have powerful genius whose amplest claims I cheerfully acknowledge. But 't is a pale ineffectual fire when theirs shines. They would lie on my shelf in undisturbed honour for years, if these Saxon lays stole on my ear. I have for them an affectionate admiration I have for nothing else. They set me on speculations. They move my wonder at myself. They suggest the great endowment of the spiritual man. They open glimpses of the heaven that is in the intellect. When I am caught by a magic word and drop the book to explore the infinite charm — to run along the line of that ray — I feel the longevity of the mind; I admit the evidence of the immortality of the soul. Well, as I said, I am afraid the season of this rare fruit is irrecoverably past; that the earth has made such a nutation of its nodes, that the heat will never reach again that Hesperian garden in which alone these apricots and pomegranates grew.

[FORGIVENESS]

DIVINITY HALL, *December* 20, 1828.

"Forgive our sins." Were it not desirable that we should have a guardian angel that should go on our errands between heaven and earth, that should tell us how God receives our actions; when he smiles and when he frowns; what petitions he hears with favour, and what he rejects? Well, we have such a report rendered back to us. Consider this prayer, Forgive our sins. I believe every man may answer to himself when he utters this ejaculation, the precise degree of consideration it has received from the Almighty mind. That consideration depends wholly upon the sentiment which accompanied the prayer. If when I say Forgive my sins, I am in a frame of mind that sorrowfully repents of all my perversity, if I am struck with a deep and contrite sense of the enormity of sin; if I feel the evil of guilt and the virtue to sin no more, then God hears me.

CONCORD, NEW HAMPSHIRE,

December 21, 1828.

I have now been four days engaged to Ellen Louisa Tucker. Will my Father in Heaven regard us with kindness, and as he hath, as we trust, made us for each other, will he be pleased to strengthen and purify and prosper and eternize our affection!

[On Edward's happy recovery of his mental balance, though his general health was permanently broken, Waldo took him, for a change, with him to Concord, New Hampshire, where he had engagements to preach for three Sundays in December.

In a letter to his brother William, announcing his engagement, he said : " It is now just a year since I became acquainted with Ellen . . . ; but I thought I had got over my blushes and my wishes when now I determined to go into that dangerous neighbourhood on Edward's account. But the presumptuous man was overthrown by the eye and ear, and surrendered at discretion. He is now as happy as it is safe in life to be. She is seventeen years old, and very beautiful, by universal consent."

A little before this time, Mr. Emerson had been asked by the Committee of the Second Church in Boston to become associate pastor, on account of the delicate health and need of travel of the Rev. Henry Ware, Jr., the pastor, and was considering whether he ought to accept the call.]

Ellen Tucker

JOURNAL

MINISTER OF THE SECOND
CHURCH OF BOSTON

JOURNAL XX

1829

(From " XVIII," 2d, " Sermons and Journal," Cabot's
S, U and Y)

(From Cabot's S)

TO ELLEN

ALL that thy virgin soul can ask be thine,
Beautiful Ellen, — let this prayer be mine.
The first devotion that my soul has paid
To mortal grace it pays to thee, fair maid.
I am enamoured of thy loveliness,
Lovesick with thy sweet beauty, which shall bless
With its glad light my path of life around,
Which now is joyless where thou art not found.
Now am I stricken with the sympathy
That binds the whole world in electric tie;
I hail love's birth within my hermit breast,
And welcome the bright ordinance to be blest.
I was a hermit whom the lone Muse cheers,
I sped apart my solitary years,
I found no joy in woman's meaning eye
When Fashion's merry mob were dancing by;
Yet had I read the law all laws above,
Great Nature hath ordained the heart to love;

Yet had I heard that in this mortal state
To every mind exists its natural mate;
That God at first did marry soul to soul,
Though lands divide and seas between them roll.
Then eagerly I searched each circle round,
I panted for my mate, but no mate found.
I saw bright eyes, fair forms, complexions fine,
But not a single soul that spoke to mine.
At last the star broke through the hiding cloud,
At last I found thee in the silken crowd;
I found thee, Ellen, born to love and shine,
And I who found am blessed to call thee mine.

TO MISS EMERSON

(From "XVIII," 2d)

January 6, 1829.

MY DEAR AUNT, — You know — none can know better — on what straitened lines we have all walked up to manhood. In poverty and many troubles the seeds of our prosperity were sown. . . .

Now all these troubles appeared a fair counterbalance to the flatteries of fortune. I lean always to that ancient superstition (if it is such, though drawn from a wise survey of human affairs) which taught men to beware of unmixed prosperity, for Nemesis keeps watch to over-throw the high. Well, now look at the altered aspect. William has begun to live by the law. Edward has recovered his reason and his health. Bulkeley was never more comfortable in his life.[1] Charles is prospering in all ways. Waldo is com-paratively well and comparatively successful — far more so than his friends, out of his family, anticipated. Now I add to all this felicity a par-ticular felicity which makes my own glass very much larger and fuller. And I straightway say, Can this hold? Will God make me a brilliant exception to the common order of his dealings which equalizes destinies? There's an appre-hension of reverse always arising from success. But is it my fault that I am happy, and cannot I trust the Goodness that has uplifted to up-hold me? In all these considerations I believe the sentiment of the old hymn is just:

" In every joy that crowns my days,
    In every pain I bear,
My heart shall find delight in praise,
    Or seek relief in prayer."

1 Robert Bulkeley Emerson, a brother between Edward and Charles in age, though amiable and well behaved, re-mained childish all his life, supported by his brothers, usually at the house of some worthy farmer.

The way to be safe is to be thankful. I cannot find in the world without, or within, any antidote, any bulwark, against this fear like this, — the frank acknowledgment of unbounded dependence. Let into the heart that is filled with prosperity the idea of God, and it smooths the giddy precipices of human pride to a substantial level, it harmonizes the condition of the individual with the economy of the universe. I should be glad, dear Aunt, that you, who are my oldest friend, would give me some of your meditations upon these new leaves of my fortune. You have always promised me success, and now, when it seems to be coming, I chuse to direct to you this letter which I enter as a sort of protest against my Ahriman, that, if I am called, after the way of my race, to pay a fatal tax for my good, I may appeal to the sentiment of collected anticipation with which I saw the tide turn and the winds blow softly from the favouring west. As Bacon said, "You may know it was my fate, and not my folly, that brought me to it.". . .

(From " Sermons and Journals ")

CAMBRIDGE, *Sunday morning,*
January 17, 1829.

My history has had its important days within a brief period. Whilst I enjoy the luxury of an unmeasured affection for an object so deserving of it all, and who requites it all,— I am called by an ancient and respectable church to become its pastor. I recognize in these events, accompanied as they are by so many additional occasions of joy in the condition of my family, — I recognize with acute sensibility, the hand of my heavenly Father. This happiness awakens in me a certain awe: I know my imperfections: I know my ill-deserts; and the beauty of God makes me feel my own sinfulness the more. I throw myself with humble gratitude upon his goodness, I feel my total dependence. O God direct and guard and bless me, and those and especially *her*, in whom I am blessed.

She has the purity and confiding religion of an angel. Are the words common? the words are true. Will God forgive me my sins, and aid me to deserve this gift of his mercy?

What is the office of a Christian minister? 'Tis his to show the beauty of the moral laws of the universe; to explain the theory of a perfect life; to watch the Divinity in his world; to detect his footstep; to discern him in the history of the race of his children, by catching the tune from a patient listening to miscellaneous sounds; by threading out the unapparent plan in events crowding on events. The soldier in the army does not know the plan of the fight. . . .

The world, to the skeptical eye, is without form and void. The gospel gives a firm clue to the plan of it. It shows God. Find God, and order, and glory, and hope, and happiness begin. It is the office of the priest. . . .

[Mr. Emerson was still considering the acceptance of the call to the Second Church when another serious element was added to the problems. Signs of consumption appeared in Miss Tucker, sufficient to cause grave uneasiness. Dr. James Jackson, the leading physician in Boston, however, held out hope of her improvement, and so, after a frank talk with the committee, Mr. Emerson decided to accept the associate pastorship. Ellen seemed to improve much as Spring approached.

Naturally there are few entries in the Journal for some time to come. The new life brought other uses for the hours which for years had been devoted to writing.]

July 3.

My weight is 144 lbs.

NOVELS

[Boston] Chardon St., *July* 21.

The passion for novels is natural. Every child asks his Grandpapa to tell him a story. Cinderella and Red Ridinghood are the novels of the Two-shoeses, and Walter Scott is the grandpa of the grown up children.

There appeared in the world, as Civilization advanced, a marked character which was its creature — a fashionist. He never laughs, he never weeps, is never surprised, never moved. He is completely selfish. By his self-command he aspires to an influence over society which owes nothing to rank, wealth, office, talents or learning — the command of fashion. He derides and is cool, and so reigns. This person has been shown to the public under several names : Vivian Grey, Lord Etherington, Mr. Brummel, Lord Dalgarno, Pelham. But 't is all one rascal with all his *aliases*. Now the question arises whether these novels of fashionable life, whether these representations of this scoundrel, have a good or bad effect. It is an impertinent question. As long as the original exists, the copies will be multiplied. If the moral is bad, as it is, get rid of the character and the pictures will no more be made. Therefore let every man cultivate benevolence in himself.

[FRAGMENT]

I am not, I thank the gods,
Born a slave to priests or kings;
Both were bad, but what's the odds
To be the thrall of thoughts, or things?
There's blood alike on crown and mitre —
Pronounce, who can, which cap is whiter.

My humour, poor and proud, disdains
The monarch's crown and friar's frock;
My blood shall warm my proper veins
Nor stain the altar or the block.

[To confirm Miss Tucker's apparently improving health, a driving journey was made in August; Mr. Emerson and she in one chaise, her mother (Mrs. Kent), and her sister, Miss Margaret Tucker, in a carriage. They followed the route chosen by the patient, day by day, resting as they pleased, from Concord, New Hampshire, through Canterbury and Meredith to Centre Harbor; thence northward to Tamworth under Chocorùa, and on to Crawford's at the Notch. From there they went to Conway, and, *via* Squam Lake, to Plymouth; thence through Rumney and Wentworth to Hanover, and, descending the Connecticut Valley to Springfield, eastward through Worcester to Boston.

These verses to Ellen, and those which follow them, were written in September, at Pepperell, where, no doubt, Mr. Emerson was occupying the pulpit for a Sunday.]

(From Cabot's U)

Dear Ellen, many a golden year
May ripe, then dim, thy beauty's bloom,
But never shall the hour appear
In sunny joy, in sorrow's gloom,
When aught shall hinder me from telling
My ardent love, all loves excelling.

The spot is not in the rounded earth,
In cities vast, in islands lone,
Where I will not proclaim thy worth,
And glory that thou art mine own;
Will you, nill you, I'll say I love thee,
Be the moon of June or of March above thee.

And when this porcelain clay of thine
Is laid beneath the cold earth's flowers,
And close beside reposes mine,
Prey to the sun and air and showers,
I'll find thy soul in the upper sphere,
And say I love thee in Paradise here.

———————

I call her beautiful; — she says
Go to; your words are idle;
My lips began to speak her praise,
My lips she tried to bridle.
But, Ellen, I must tell you this,
Your prohibition wasted is,
Unless among your things you find
A little jail to hold the mind;
If you should dazzle out mine eyes,
As dimmer suns sometimes have done,
My sleepless ears, those judges wise,
Would say, 'T is the voice of the Peerless One.
And if your witchery decree
That my five senses closed should be,
The little image in my soul
Is Ellen out of Ellen's controul,
And whilst I live in the universe
I will say 't is my beauty, for better, for worse.

[On the last day of September, 1829, Ralph
Waldo Emerson was married to Ellen Louisa
Tucker, at the house of Colonel W. A. Kent,

her step-father; the bridegroom being then twenty-six years of age, and the bride eighteen. They immediately began housekeeping in Chardon Place, in Boston, Madame Emerson living with them.]

(From "Blotting Book 1829." Cabot's Y)

Quantum scimus sumus.

Quid sumus, et quidnam victuri gignimur.
                                    PERSIUS.

NEW JERUSALEM CHURCH

CHARDON ST., *October 9*, 1829.

I am glad to see that interpretations of Scripture like those of the New Jerusalem Church can be accepted in our community. The most spiritual and sublime sense is put upon various historical passages of the New Testament. The interpretation of the passages is doubtless wholly false. The apostle John in Patmos and our Saviour in his talking, meant no such things as the commentator says he meant. But the sentiment which the commentator puts into their mouths is nevertheless true and eternal. The wider that sentiment can be spread and the more effect it can have on men's lives, the better. And if the fool-part of man must have the lie, if truth is a pill that can't go down till 't is sugared with superstition, why then I will forgive the last in the belief that the truth will enter into the soul natively and so assimilantly that it will become part of the soul and so remain, when the falsehood grows dry and lifeless and peels off.

BOOK MEMORANDA

Vide John Smith, contemporary of Jeremy Taylor;

Huber on *Bees and Ants*;

Kirby and Spence, Introduction to *Entomology*;

Works of Derham, Niewentiet and Lyonet;

Coleridge's *Aids to Reflection*, p. 147;

Bayle, article "Simonides";

Pomponatius, Treatise *De Fato*, *Aids to Reflection*, p. 148;

H. More's *Antidote to Atheism*;

Dr. Donne's Sermons.

October 13.

There are people who exist to ask each other conundrums, and there are others who avail themselves of each other's knowledge to find out the plan of the solar system; to such different uses do we put this social principle.

October 15.

The way for us to be wise is to foresee the great tendencies and currents of the universe in the leanings and motions of the little straws which our eyes can see. We live among eggs, embryos and seminal principles, and the wisest is the most prophetic eye. Thus perhaps we might find out God's being from the strong instinct of the human soul to worship, from the magnifying idolatrous propensity we have. A great man we call a very great man : our friend, we call the best man ; and that not to others, for vanity's sake, but we try to convince ourselves that there is something that reaches a little beyond our apprehension in the knowledge, genius, delicacy, or magnanimity of the *protégée* reputation we take up cudgels for. "It is in honour of theism," says Aunt Mary, "that the effect of strong and exclusive attachment to natural science, that becomes disinterested and free of interest and fame, has a noble moral effect, as in case of some German philosophers. Alas that the religious affections should be developed in idolatry even of knowledge!" It would seem as if the soul had been made to go out of itself to apply itself in all its length and breadth to something else, that is, to God. Therefore we

approve when it goes out of itself and does thus
devote itself to friendship or to science; we approve, for we compare this action with selfishness; but when the idea of God is suggested,
then we feel these are but half; that the act is
true, but the object is untrue.

PRAYER

October 20.

The government of God is not on a plan, —
that would be Destiny; it is extempore. The
history of the universe is a game of which the
object to be gained is the greatest good of the
whole, and is attained by a long series of independent *moves*. The omniscient Eye makes each
new move from a survey of all the present state
of the game. Hence the efficiency of *Prayer*.
God determines from all the facts, and my earnest desires make one of the facts.

[SERENITY]

How ridiculous that the follies of the world
should vex you. Thus they become part and
parcel of you, — an excess of the social principle, — too eager and sick a sympathy. Presidents should not take sides in a battle of mos-
quitoes. Say with Plato, "Do not I think things

unsound because I am unsound?" as the blind man complained the streets were dark.

[HUMAN METAMORPHOSIS]

October 31.

I am made unhappy by talking with Mr. ——, with all his reputed fine feelings and his profession and his genius. For he scoffs; slightly and elegantly, but still 'tis the poison of scoffing, and hardly can a man believe his immortality and deride any hallowed thing. "He that contemns, &c., has faculties which he has never used." We must beware of the nature of the spiritual world. It has this [so] terrible power of self-change, self-accommodation to whatsoever we do, that Ovid's Metamorphoses take place continually. The nymph who wept became a fountain; the nymph who pined became an echo. They who do good become angels; they who do deformities become deformed. We are not immoveably moored, as we are apt to think, to any bottom. And if we do wrong, and don't succeed, we think we can come back to where we were. That where is gone. I cannot live over my childhood. No more can I do right when I have vitiated all the springs of feeling and action. I have no ποῦ στῶ. I have then no eye to see the right, no fingers to feel it. I have only vicious members loving and doing wrong. That part of us which we don't use dries up and perishes.

November 7.

Every man by God's arrangements whilst he ministers and receives influence from all others is absolutely, imperially free. When I look at the rainbow I find myself the centre of its arch. But so are you; and so is the man that sees it, a mile from both of us. So also the globe is round, and every man therefore stands on the top. King George and the chimney-sweep no less.

TO MISS EMERSON

(From "XVIII," 2d)

November 15 [1829?]

They say that the progress of the human mind is not by individuals, but by society at large; that the Newtons and Bacons are mountain summits that catch the sunlight a little earlier, which is presently visible to all; so we gazers are spying to see if the giants of the generation are not now bathing in a purer element than we below. It is surely with no affectation and no good will that I suspend my judgment of things so vast, but a

state of mind wholly involuntary. All that I see
is full of intelligence and all that I know is *my*
approximation to the idea of God. When I see
a green lane open, I suppose that however beautiful in itself, with what bluebell and rosemaries
soever it may be adorned, it leads somewhere, and
in my simple manhood I am still guided by these
old truepenny reasons, all Hume and Germany
to the contrary notwithstanding. Then is not
one amazed, if amazement it be, which is rather
calm delight — to find, as he goes on, how perfectly the moral laws hold, how they pervade with
their delicate and subtle divinity all human life
— how truly too the material creation seems to
be their shadow and type, by its faithful analogies (the mind does not manufacture, but finds
them). Then every man's life is to him the idea
of a Providence. And moments are marked in his
memory of intercourse with God. Well now, if
he have sense, he must see that where all is so
wondrous, a miracle is no more, and a revelation
of immortality no more strange than his perception of its probability.

I think thus and so, receive the dispensation
gladly, but with my own interpretations, not
thinking it becoming or possible to give up the
certainty of natural reason for the highest un-

certainties, when at the same time 'tis so easy to account for the imperfect transmission of the revelation. But when you ask, What is God — I must answer with Simonides : The finite cannot comprize the infinite; we have faculties to perceive his laws, but himself how obscurely. He can be nothing less than our highest conception, and our conceptions continually soar higher — both the man's and the age's. So that the best man of our time is a nobler moral exhibition than the *God* of a much ruder time. We need not fear what Time may teach us, for that which is true must be that which is most desirable ; — because that which is true must be fittest for our nature, since all that exists is mutually conformed. At least we may gather so much prophecy from our inward informations.

PERSEVERANCE

(From Cabot's Y)

December 7.

Habit is the succour God sends in aid of Perseverance, that is, he decrees that what you have done laboriously you shall do easily. The great majority of men are bundles of beginnings. . . . Some very unseasonable circumstances occurred and the good purpose was postponed. Who is there here who does not remember his defeats; who that does not own himself the cause? The world is full of slippery, imbecile, undetermined persons, who carry a cowardice in their bosoms that invites attack. Here and there is a Hercules who persists in his purposes. . . . He cannot fail. If all the universe oppose he cannot fail. For the stake is nothing; the skill of his game is all. The soul he has made unconquerable, and so, at death, it bursts into eternity, like a God to win worlds. One of the reasons why perseverance hath such potency is because it gains by littles, and life is made up of littles, and happiness.

Everything has its price. Little goods are lightly gained, but the rich sweets of things are in the ribs of the mountain, and months and years must dig for them. For example, a jest or a glass of wine a man can procure without much pains to relieve his trouble for a moment; but a *habit of patience*, which is the perfect medicine, he cannot procure in a moment or a week or a month. It will cost thought and strife and mortification and prayer.

In some of the foreign manufacturing towns steam power is generated and vended in amounts to suit very different purposes. I conceive every man to be such a shop. His conversation and works in the world do generate a certain amount of power, which he applies here to certain objects, but these objects are arbitrary and they are temporary, will soon be removed, and he will be called on to apply the same habits, i. e., steam power, to new uses, and very different ones in heaven.

Give your good project a fair trial, a year, two years. It is of small matter if it should prove on the whole inexpedient. It has done *you* good, if it has not mankind; and so has given the state a better citizen for its next occasions.

TO MISS EMERSON

Boston, *December* 10, 1829.

My dear Aunt, — I hear nothing from you, though I sent an almost immediate answer to your catechism. You asked about the knee. I said nothing, for it was no better. Now 't is well, or all but well. I have walked far and wide to-day. A quack doctor, the pupil of Sweet, has cured me, and that in two or three hours. His name is Hewitt. He still attends me every evening, and will come presently, so my pen must scamper.

I am reading Coleridge's *Friend* with great interest. You don't speak of it with respect. He has a tone a little lower than greatness — but what a living soul, what a universal knowledge! I like to encounter these citizens of the universe, that believe the mind was made to be spectator of all, inquisitor of all, and whose philosophy compares with others much as astronomy with the other sciences, taking post at the centre and, as from a specular mount, sending sovereign glances to the circumference of things. There is an affectation of emphasis and typography, — a nobleman don't care how he looks ; but there are a good many of these Rousseaus in the world whose two eyes are one a microscope and t'other a telescope. But there are few or no books of pure literature so self-imprinting, that is so often remembered as Coleridge's.

Sunday night, 13.

I have got your letter and perhaps will try to answer it. But what a fight all our lives long between prudence and sentiment; though you contradicted once when I tried to make a sentence, that life was embarrassed by prudentials. The case in point is this : — My soul is chained down even in its thoughts, where it should be freest, lordliest. The Christmas comes, a hallowed anniversary to me as to others, yet am I not ready to explore and explain the way of the star-led wizards—am looking at the same Truth which they sought, on quite another side and in novel relations. I could think and speak to some purpose, I say, if you would take what I have got, but if I must do what seems so proper and reasonable, — conform to the occasion, — I can only say what is trite, and will, 't is likely, be ineffectual. This is a very disadvantageous example of that warfare that is in all professional life between the heroical and the proper.

People wag their heads and say, I can't understand Coleridge. Yet it is only one more instance of what is always interesting, the restless human soul bursting the narrow boundaries of antique speculation and mad to know the secrets of that unknown world, on whose brink it is sure it is standing — yea, can now and then overhear passing words of the talk of the inhabitants. I say a man so learned and a man so bold, has a right to be heard, and I will take off my hat the while and not make an impertinent noise. At least I become acquainted with one new mind I never saw before,— an acquisition in my knowledge of man not unimportant, when it is remembered that so gregarious are even intellectual men that Aristotle thinks for thousands, and Bacon for his ten thousands, and so, in enumerating the apparently manifold philosophies and forms of thought, we should not be able to count more than seven or eight minds. 'T is the privilege of his independence and of his labour to be counted for one school. His theological speculations are, at least, *God viewed from one position ;* and no wise man would neglect that one element in concentrating the rays of human thought to a true and comprehensive conclusion. Then I love him that he is no utilitarian, nor necessarian, nor scoffer, nor *hoc genus omne*, tucked away in the corner of a sentence of Plato.

USES OF BIOGRAPHY AND HISTORY

December 12.

Pericles is made noble and Luther indomitable to show Canis and Aspen their capabilities. Instead of generating complaint, it should beget all hope.

AUTHORS OR BOOKS MENTIONED OR QUOTED IN JOURNALS OF 1828 AND 1829

Homer ; Anaximander, *apud* De Gerando ; Simonides ; Democritus ; Socrates ; Plato ;

Virgil; Persius; Juvenal; Plutarch, *Lives* and *Morals;* Saint Augustine, *Confessions;*

Dante; Montaigne, *Essays;* Tasso;

Shakspeare; Ben Jonson; Bacon, *De Augmentatione Scientiae;* Sir Henry Wotton, *Survey of Education;* Herrick; Herbert; Milton; Marvell; Saint-Évremond, *Sense of an Honest and Experienced Courtier;*

Locke; Newton; Scougal, *Life of God in the Soul;*

Young; Pope, *Essay on Man;* Samuel Richardson, *Sir Charles Grandison;*

Spence, *Anecdotes, Observations and Characters;* Butler; Cotton Mather, *Essays to do Good;*

Hume, *Essays;* Priestley; Gibbon; Paley; James Montgomery, *The Pelican Island;*

Sir James Mackintosh; Degerando, *Derivation de la Science du Droit;*

Wolf, *Prolegomena ad Homerum;* De Staël, *Germany;*

Wordsworth, *Excursion, Sonnets, Dion, Intimations of Immortality,* etc; Byron;

Coleridge, *Friend, Literary Biographies, Aids to Reflection;*

Rev. Henry Ware, *Sermon;* Rev. Nathaniel L. Frothingham, *Sermon;*

Disraeli, *Vivian Grey;* Bulwer, *Pelham.*

JOURNAL XXI

1830

From Y, Ψ, and Blotting Book IV

[INTERACTION OF MINDS]

(From Y)

January, 1830.

"THE grandest visions external could not become intellectual, but by the chemistry of those acquired from the minds of others, — how far original inspiration influenced is uncertain, — as how far a constant agency in harmony with the laws of mind and matter influence at all times the seeker of moral excellence."

AUNT MARY.

I read in Plutarch's Political Precepts, that when Leo Byzantinus went to Athens to appease the dissensions in that city, when he arose to speak, he perceived that they laughed on account of the littleness of his stature. "What would you do," he exclaimed, "if you saw my wife who scarce reaches to my knees?" And they laughing the more he said, "Yet as little as we are, when we fall out, the city of Byzantium is not big enough to hold us."

It is strange that the greatest men of the time only *say* what is just trembling on the lips of all thinking men.

January 4, 1830.

Knowledge, even, God's own attribute and delight and mean, I fear it is but the cock's pearl when it is in a spirit which is not united to the great spirit. *Quantum sumus scimus.* It will not do for us to dogmatize. Nothing is more untrue to nature. The meanest scholar in Christian practice may often instruct the greatest doctor both in faith and practice. I have no shame in saying, I lean to this opinion, but am not sure. I do not affect or pretend to instruct. O no, it is God working in you that instructs both you and me. I only tell how I have striven and climbed, and what I have seen, that you may compare it with your own observations of the same object. It is important to have some *formal* observer, whether a keen-sighted one or not, in order to furnish some ποῦ στῶ, some *other point* to measure thought by.

That man will always speak with authority who speaks his own convictions, not the knowledge of his ear or eye, i. e., superstitions got in conversation, or errors or truths remembered from his reading, but that which, true or false, he hath perceived with his inward eye, which therefore is true to him, true even as he tells it, and absolutely true in some element, though distorted and discolored by some disease in the soul.

Omnia exeunt in mysterium.

BOSTON, *January* 7, 1830.

"*Quelle profonde philosophie,*" says De Gérando,[1] "*ne supposent pas les législations de Lycurgue et de Solon!*" A specimen, it seems to me, had I found it elsewhere, of that superficial admiration which is so common. Neither Lycurgus nor Solon need have been profound thinkers to have made their respective codes, but only practical, severe and persevering men. Wonderful capabilities both moral and intellectual, the formation of a code does indeed suppose, but in the general mind of man, and not in the individual. Lycurgus and Solon were alike in the dark

1 *Histoire Comparée des Systèmes de Philosophie, par M. De Gérando.*

with their contemporaries as to the extent, or the order, or the history of those capabilities which yet their codes recognized, and the common people they ruled recognized, and Degerando recognizes, and I recognize, — inevitably one and all.

Anaximander revives in De Staël. Anaximander said, "The infinite is the principle (*principe*) of all things." Anaxagoras, in Degerando, is the model of the true philosopher.

It is the praise of most critics that they have never failed because they have attempted nothing. It is generous in a youthful hero who bears an unspotted shield to adventure his fame in that difficult field of Metaphysics, where, from the intrinsic inaccessibilities of the positions, the strongest and the weakest assailants are brought nearly to a level, and where much may be gained by the losses of the individual. He will console himself, when he comes out smeared and baffled, with the saying of Wotton that "Critics are brushers of noblemen's clothes."

"The Eternal hath fixed his canon 'gainst self-slaughter," shall be my answer to the pyrrhonist.

The system of Aristotle, the labour of a thousand years, which had become the religion of the intellect of Europe, comes to be called an *experiment*; some happy genius epitomizes it in a word, and that becomes its history, the algebraic *x* by which it is to be designated, now that its value has been evolved and that it cannot be spared more room in the opulence of human knowledge, — repositories where it is huddled away.

January 18.

" I am more a Frenchman," said the Archbishop of Cambray, "than a Fénelon, and more a man than a Frenchman." This is quoted in Spence's *Anecdotes* to Chevalier Ramsay, who was secretary to Fénelon.

The greatness of human desires is surely one element of the greatness of man. The love of the marvellous, all the fantastic theories of mystics, the deification of the faculties, &c, &c, are in that view good.

Man's natural goodness is to do good to others. Remarkable what natural aids there are to this object. Love of praise strongest in strongest minds. If the tree did not bear its drupe, it would perish; if the animal did not give out its young, it would perish; if the soul do not bear its good deed, it will wither and die, it is made stronger, like the animal muscles, by use. If you cut off the tree's leaves and it cannot give out its juices to the atmosphere, it dies. If you feed the horse and not work him, he dies. A great deal of good we can't help doing. Example is inevitable. A miser and a sensualist do good by their hateful example. That's a shabby good.

January 22.

The question was debated before the Association this evening, whether we were not required to abstain from amusements, innocent to us, if we think them not innocent to others. The subject announced was self-denial, and the instance perpetually quoted was the Theatre. I think that self-denial is only one form of expression for perfection of the moral character. It means the denial of self-indulgences. It means the subordination of all the lower parts of man's nature to the higher, so that the individual doth nothing contrary to reason. Well, such a person cannot do wrong. He is that pure man to whom all things are pure. If such a person finds it any time his duty to go to the theatre, he will go there unchecked by fear of what harm his example may do. It is not very likely he will ever want to go there, for any good now, or in past time, apparent on the stage; but if he do, he must go. Nor will he do any harm. His example will never be quoted *bona fide* by any who goes with evil intentions. His going there cannot be mistaken. A self-denier creates a moral atmosphere about him, which sanctifies and separates his actions. One part of his example interprets another part of his example. He may safely trust his virtue to bear itself out in the world. Our Saviour sat with sinners, yet none ever thought of quoting him as sanctioning sin. What, then, may we be so free? And is nothing due to the judgments of others? No, not anything to the judgments of others, except as a commentary, an expositor frequently useful in bringing out the true sense of our own. Not anything to the judgments of others, but much, very much more, to our own than we are accustomed to give them. The true pinch of the question is that there is almost no such thing as this self-denial. It is not that men are careless of their influence on other men, but that they are careless of their own action.

Chemistry began by saying it would change the baser metals into gold. By not doing that it has done much greater things. Solon said, He that has better iron shall have all this gold. In modern times the best iron-manufacturing nations are the most civilized and run away with all the gold.

Objection to the subject of Providence that 't is too vast for human optics; pick up here and there a pebble contrivance, and say See! a God! as Newton thought. Every one of these instances valuable. Five or six facts, independently of almost no value, made the discovery of America in Columbus's mind, and it took as many centuries to accumulate them. One man sees a fact and secures it, which is to him altogether frivolous, but inestimable to the race, when seen in connexion with another fact not known for one hundred years after. Facts seek their inventions, happy marriage of fact to fact.

Sir Isaac Newton, a little before he died, said: " I don't know what I may seem to the world, but as to myself I seem to have been only like a boy playing on the sea shore, and diverting myself now and then finding a smoother pebble or a prettier shell than ordinary, whilst the great ocean of truth lay all undiscovered before me."

February 3.

"The greater God is, the greater we are. Homer was not grand in making his gods so mean." AUNT MARY.

February 10.

Is there not the sublime always in religion? I go down to the vestry and I find a few plain men and women there, come together not to eat or drink, or get money, or mirth, but drawn by a great thought. Come thither to conceive and form a connexion with an infinite Person. I thought it was sublime, and not mean as others suppose.

"The miraculous," says Sampson Reed,[1] "is the measure of our departure from God." And Brown says to the selfsame purpose, that the miraculous is no violation of the laws of nature, but a new agent interposes, *dignus vindice nodus*.

1 Mr. Emerson's Swedenborgian friend.

[Creeds grow from the structure of the creature]

February 11.

Every man makes his own religion, his own God, his own charity; takes none of these from the Bible or his neighbour entire. All feel that there is something demanded by the mind stronger and wiser than itself; that it is a thing essentially imperfect, that in its very structure demands more, as one half a pair of scissors, one sex, or a babe, and so every human creature makes its Jove, its Josh, its fairy, or amulet. Having got this thought well shaped and accommodated to their other knowledge they are easy, they are stronger than before, they will do wonders. If this idea is disturbed they are made uncomfortable, sometimes furious, sometimes depraved, sometimes dejected. Well then, it would seem that this idea is pointed at in all the structure of the animal, man. As nothing, it is discovered, is made without a meaning,—no hands, no intestines, no antennæ, no hair, without a distinct purpose disclosed as we study it, well then, is this *leaning* without a purpose, this inevitable, essential, natural *prayer* of all intelligent nature, without purpose? Is it not a finger pointing straight upwards at the Great Spirit? Then it is found that this superstition is cleansed into religion as the mind is informed.

The belief in God being thus gotten, Providence is the application of that belief to the government of the world. Just as great, or as little, as is the idea of God, just such is their opinion of Providence. The pagan believes in a little, jealous, snarling patronage that reaches him and his family and hates everybody else. It knows a little more and does a little better than a man. One god thwarts another, as man contends with man. The superstition of the fairies is the idea of a petty Providence. As his knowledge enlarges, that is, as his mind applies itself to a larger piece of the universe, he sees the unbroken prevalence of laws ; the grass grows in Bengal by the same order as in Massachusetts, the man of one district fears death like the man of the other, and knows what it is to love and to have and to want. . . .

Dr. Donne saith, " Encourage the catechizer as well as the curious preacher. Look so far towards your way to Heaven, as to the Firmament, and consider there that the star by which we sail and make great voyages is none of the stars of greatest magnitude, but yet it is none of the least neither, but a middle star. Those preachers which must save your souls are not ignorant, unlearned, extemporal men, but they are not over curious men neither. Your children are you, and your servants are you; and you do not provide for your salvation if you provide not for them who are so much yours as that they are you. No man is saved as a good man, if he be not saved as a good father, and as a good master, if God have given him a family." *Five Sermons*, p. 66.

February 24.

We are, by dint of self-command on one hand and omniscience on the other, as if a dead wall were built on one side of our plot of ground, and on the other it was not fenced by so much as a stake or a pin from the boundless expanse. A cunning dissimulator may shut out man's eye from so much as a glance at his thoughts, but God and all angels behold him on the spiritual side.

February 26.

Whether, saith Ellen, the spirits in heaven look onward to their immortality as we on earth, or are absorbed in the present moment?

[Because, in spite of all hope and tender care, the health of his young wife was failing, Mr. Emerson took her southward in early March, accompanied by her sister. Mr. Ware meanwhile had gone abroad and all the duties of pastor and preacher devolved upon Mr. Emerson. It is probable that he had to leave Mrs. Emerson with her sister and return to his post for a time. The poem " To Ellen at the South" was written a year earlier, April, 1829, and probably also " Thine Eyes Still Shined." Two of her poems, " The Violet" and one entitled " Lines written by Ellen Louisa Tucker," were printed by Mr. Emerson in the *Dial* ten years or more after her death. They are included in the Centenary Edition of the *Poems*. The following lines were probably written in 1830.]

And, Ellen, when the greybeard years
Have brought us to life's evening hour,
And all the crowded Past appears
A tiny scene of sun and shower,

Then, if I read the page aright
Where Hope, the soothsayer, reads our lot,
Thyself shalt own the page was bright, —
Well that we loved, wo had we not;

When Mirth is dumb and Flattery's fled,
And mute thy music's dearest tone,
When all but Love itself is dead,
And all but deathless Reason gone.

PREACHING

February 28.

Hudibras says,

" Rhymes the rudder are of verses,
　With which, like ships, they steer their courses."

It is not very much otherwise in preaching. Topics are the masters of the preacher. He cannot often write in the way he deems best and most level with life. He is obliged to humour his mind in the choice and the development of his subject. When the sermon is done he is aware that much of it is from the purpose, . . . and altogether it is unworthy of his conception of a good sermon. But to-morrow is Sunday. He must take this, or write worse, or have nothing. He hopes beside that parts of this discourse will reach all, and all of it touch or instruct individuals.

PRAYER

What is prayer? It is the expression of human wishes addressed to God. What is God? The most elevated conception of character that can be formed in the mind. It is the individual's own soul carried out to perfection. For no other Deity can he conceive. He is infinite as I am finite; he is sinless as I am sinful; he is all wise as I am all ignorant. He is strong as I am weak. Well, now prayer is the effort of the soul to apply itself in all its length and breadth to this sovereign idea, is the attempt to bring home to the thoughts so grand a mind and converse with it, as we converse with men. . . .

Burke said, "If I borrow the aid of an equal understanding, I double my own; if of a higher, I raise my own to the stature of that I contemplate." Well now, what must be the effect, judging from this plain analogy, of conversing with one who is wholly pure and benevolent, and whom we know we cannot deceive? It seems to me plain that we must grow godlike.

WEBSTER

March 3.

Read with admiration and delight Mr. Webster's noble speech in answer to Hayne. What consciousness of political rectitude, and what confidence in his intellectual treasures must he have to enable him to take this master's tone! Mr. Channing said he had great "self-subsistence."

The beauty and dignity of the spectacle he exhibits should teach men the beauty and dignity of *principles*. This is one that is not blown about by every wind of opinion, but has mind great enough to see the majesty of moral nature and to apply himself in all his length and breadth to it and magnanimously trust thereto.

Wednesday night.

The power that we originate outlives us, takes imposing and stable forms, and Cæsar becomes a dynasty; and Luther and Calvin each a Church; and Mahomet represents himself in a third of the human race.

April 24.

Noah Ripley, the good deacon, is himself an affecting argument for the immortality of the soul.

May 12.

It was said of Jesus that "he taught as one having authority," a distinction most palpable. There are a few men in every age, I suppose, who teach thus. Stubler the Quaker, whom I saw on board the boat in Delaware Bay, was one. If Sampson Reed were a talker, he were another. There is nevertheless a foolish belief among teachers that the multitude are not wise enough to discern between good manner and good matter, and that voice and rhetorick will stand, instead of truth. They can tell well enough whether they have been convinced or no. The multitude suppose often that great talents are necessary to produce the elaborate harangues which they hear without emotion of consequence, and so they say, What a fine speaker, What a good discourse; but they will not leave any agreeable employment to go again, and never will do a single thing in consequence of having heard the discourse. But let them hear one of these God-taught teachers and they surrender to him. They leave their work to come again; they go home and think and talk and act as he said. Men know truth as quick as they see it.

It is remarkable how this mastery shows itself in the tone that is taken, as much as in the facts that are presented. A tone of authority cannot be taken without truths of authority. It is impossible to mimick it. There is no favouritism in the public. Buckminster had it; Greenwood has it in some measure. F——m has not a particle. It proceeds directly from the perception of principles. Dr. Johnson was one.

BROOKLINE, *June* 7.

Conversion from a moral to a religious character is like day after twilight. The orb of the earth is lighted brighter and brighter as it turns, until at last there is a particular moment when the eye sees the sun, and so when the soul perceives God.

Every man contemplates an angel in his future self.

BROOKLINE, *June* 2, 1830.

. . . what value would belong to every man, if everyone literally told his own impressions from all he saw, and by the use of his conscience kept himself in the state of an observer. . . .

[DUAL CONSCIOUSNESS]

Dr. Channing spoke to me of a Frenchman who had written that there were two souls in the human body, one which never suspended its action, and had the care of what we call the involuntary motions, and was, in short, a gentleman who knew a good deal of natural magic, antipathies, instincts, divination and the like; and the other, the vulgar, waking, practical soul. Well, this theory, like all others, is founded on one glimpse of truth by a cross light. And such an intelligence is there in all men, that knows when men speak in simplicity, and when they speak conventionally. But observe, simplicity of character is not enough, of itself. All country people have it in great measures. It needs also a tender conscience, which shall lead men to improve themselves, to keep the ear and soul open to receive truth, and then this straightforwardness shall make them act and utter the truth. . . .

THE YEAR

The year is long enough for all that is to be done in it. The flowers blow; the fruit ripens; and every species of animals is satisfied and attains its perfection, but man does not; man has seen more than he has had time to do.

What it means to be one with God?

SOLITUDE

Go sit alone,—for the nations are a handful compared with that amount of being for whom the soul consults when she reasons of virtue,—and see what you can hope to be that is highest and best. See how goodness is the way to wisdom, and wisdom is the way to goodness. See how the soul, in the infinite vista of the future, foresees the hour when it shall desire nothing wrong, and therefore nothing false; when, desiring everything right, and everything right being done, it shall find that insensibly it beats pulse for pulse with the Heart of nature, that all its volitions are followed by instant effects, that it is united to God.

Is there any hiding of the character of an apple-tree or of a geranium, or of an ore, or of a horse, or of a man? A man is known by the books he reads, by the company he keeps, by the praise he gives, by his dress, by his tastes, by his distastes, by the stories he tells, by his gait, by the motion of his eye, by the look of his house, of his chamber; for nothing on earth is solitary, but everything hath affinities infinite. . . .

HUMILITY

BROOKLINE, *July* 15.[1]

Humility is properly the exaltation of the Spirit. . . . We are to be so humble as to be of the greatest possible service to all men. We are to be always accessible to truth as the proud are

1 After Mr. and Mrs. Emerson's return home in the early summer they lived in Brookline for better air (probably boarding). Madame Emerson and Mr. Emerson's brother Charles were with them.

not. Yet every sin are we to scorn with an imperial superiority. Then to keep an independence of all men, dazzling men and bad ones, how hard! It needs this great equilibrium, the relation to God, which sets all right. For if we depend on him for all things, [we] are his children. . . .

SELF RELIANCE

BROOKLINE, *July* 20, 1830.

. . . Milton, Bacon, Bunyan, Scougal, Herbert, Montesquieu: these are names of good men, but what dissimilar images do they suggest to the soul. Now this is not the thought of men, that to each belongs a separate nature which must be by him cultivated as an inalienable estate. As they say the vines failed because in America they wanted to grow madeira wine, instead of bringing out the native wines, probably equally good, of this region, so men fail as far as they leave their native moral instincts in the admiration of other characters. Let them on the contrary have greater confidence in the plan, yet to them unknown, which the moral Architect has traced for them. . . .

The elm is a bad oak, but a beautiful elm; and the beauty of the walnut or the sycamore is not felt by comparing them with different species, but with other individuals of their own.

The question arises doubtless, Have we not the power to make ourselves what we will by steadfast exertions? we do not snuff a scent that is laid already. We do not grow up like a plant according to a conformation of a seed. On the contrary, it is the privilege of our nature over that of flowers and brutes that we are our own law.

BROOKLINE, *July* 24.

Don't say that qualities are so radical in us that the fickle man can never persevere, let him try as he will, nor the selfish man ever distribute; for on the contrary, any quality of a man may be taken advantage of to lead him to any other that is desirable. I hate steady labour from morn till night, and therefore am not a learned man, but I have an omnivorous curiosity and facility of new undertaking. In voluntary exertions to gratify it, may I not become learned and acquire the habits of steady toil?

[WHO IS RELIGIOUS?]

It seems to me there are degrees in religion, and much is religion that is not called by that

name in minds that do oppose themselves to
what they call religion. A man of honour and
generosity, who would rather die than speak
falsely, has an aversion to religion, treats it with
a degree of contempt. Now I think this man is
religious, in the lowest degree. What he does
well, he does from his religious nature;

> " Pious beyond the intention of his thought,
>   Devout beyond the meaning of his will."

He is in the right way, and far more near,
therefore, to God, than the sensual religionist, as
a cripple in the right way will beat a racer in the
wrong. He is in the right way, and if he contribute all these generous sentiments in a high
degree, he will continually make advancements
unconsciously in religious excellence. He
thinks, perchance, that religion is Calvinism,
and so he hates it. By and by, in consequence
of his efforts at self-knowledge, his mind will
revolve so far that the increasing twilight will
give place to the Sun, and God will appear as
he is to his soul. I believe it is not a fact that
is very early known to children, that the sun is
the cause of the day. I am sure I was not myself acquainted with it, and while living and
growing and playing in his beams, and learning,

as all children do, the laws of light, I did not
imagine to what I was indebted; and when first
I was told, it seemed to me a thing absurd. Is
not this an emblem of the irreligious hero?

BROOKLINE, *August* 3, 1830.

My weight is 157 lbs.

August 18.

The sun shines and warms and lights us and
we have no curiosity to know why this is so;
but we ask the reason of all evil, of pain, and
hunger, and musquitoes and silly people.

August 28.

Alii disputent, *ego mirabor*, said Augustine. It
shall be my speech to the Calvinist and the
Unitarian.

BUCKMINSTER

September 1, 1830.

. . . Buckminster went into the pulpit on days
of deepest affliction in his parish for the loss of
excellent persons, with an alacrity and cheerfulness in his countenance that would have been
revolting levity in another man, and read psalms
and scriptures of praise. Yet no one was offended, but all felt that the intensity of his emotion was such, and the principle on which it was

founded was such, as to overmaster their private thoughts, and the mourner was carried away by the infection of his sublime joy, from the consideration of his petty griefs.[1]

So does a man ask himself if his subject be unseasonable or extravagant? Let him feel that none is so unseasonable but the force of his thinking upon it will make its excuse. Such is the intimate connexion existing between all truth, that no topic can be so unusual but a genuine teacher can show such a practical value in it as shall command your total attention, and make a mountain before your eyes out of a grain of sand.

September 3.

There are two kinds of pertinence. One to the circumstances, and one to the thing itself. What has been wholly pertinent to one case, (in the second and superior sense) will, I apprehend, always be found to have a degree of pertinence to every case. If the orator, as is common, attends only to the circumstantial pertinence, if he say, This man had yellow hair, large lips,

1 This is one of the earliest passages in the journal that appears in his published writings. It is found in an improved form, but without giving the name of the preacher, in "Eloquence," vol. vii, p. 83, of Collected Works, Centenary Ed.

long life, or he spent on this occasion a dollar and a quarter, or he lived in such a street and died on such a day, the discourse will not only be of necessity wholly impertinent to any other occasion, but, in my judgment, will be really impertinent to the occasion for which it was made. This is a mere carcass of circumstances destitute of all life and of all use to me.

But if he describe with minutest fidelity the moral portrait of the man, line for line, if he describe states of mind, the effect of temptation, and the modes of escape, the more minute his copying from the finest shades of thought in his original, the more deep and universal and permanent will the interest of the picture become. And let him change the names, and read it in Chinese in a bazar at Pekin, and he will find it is pertinent still to the human mind. So much for the doctrine so much prosed over of pertinent preaching.

September 6.

Mon amie à Concord.[1]

[HAPPINESS OR SERENITY?]

If a man be asked if he is happy, on his conscience, he will not affirm it; he will feel a scru-

1 Probably Mrs. Emerson had gone to visit her mother and sister at Concord, New Hampshire. She was now very delicate.

ple, I apprehend, precisely like that he would feel if he were about to say that he was sinless. And is there not any condition of the human heart when it is esteemed to have reached this climax? There is one remarkable exception; the state of religious progress, when a mind that has doubted of its spiritual safety emerges from the gloom into a state of peace, and says, I am happy. This is not strict language. If such a person be strictly dealt with, it will be found [he has] wants and imperfections yet. It is a joy and serenity but not happiness, though I think a nearer approach to it than any other circumstances that can be named. . . .

What happiness does a man feel uneasiness about? That which comes to him almost without his exertions, or anyhow which he feels he has not earned. And as all supereminent prosperity has a degree of this want of desert, it is always dashed with this feeling.

[TOWN AND FIELD]

. . . If a man loves the city, so will his writings love the city, and if a man loves sweet fern and roams much in the pastures, his writings will smell of it.

The argument which has not power to reach my own practice, I may well fear has not power to reach yours.

September 8.

Maxima debetur pueris reverentia.

September 9.

[BALANCING]

There are some kingdoms of Europe whose whole population for ages does not possess an equal interest in history with some single minds. The history of John Locke or of Isaac Newton is a far more important part of the stock of knowledge than the whole history of Poland or Hungary.

Well, what of this? You accuse yourself perhaps. Before God, Poland is a greater affair than Locke.

Mr. Stewart's works are like Dr. Clarke's description of the entrance of Moscow, all splendour and promise till you enter the gate, and then you look before and behind — but only cottages and shops.

Judge Howe advised his pupils to make study their business, and business their amusement.

September 10.

It is my purpose to methodize my days. I wish to study the scriptures in a part of every day, that I may be able to explain them to others and that their light may flow into my life. I wish not to be strait-laced in my own rules, but to wear them easily and to make wisdom master of them.

It is a resolving world, but God grant me persistency enough, so soon as I leave Brookline, and come to my books, to do as I intend.

SELF RELIANCE

BROOKLINE, *September* 27.

I would have a man trust himself, believe that he has all the endowments necessary to balance each other in a perfect character, if only he will allow them all fair play. I have sometimes wished I had not some acuteness or minuteness of observation that seemed inconsistent with dignity of character; but thus to wish seems to me now to be false to one's-self, to give up a tower in my castle to the enemy which was given me as a bulwark of defence. It is a wondrous structure, this soul in me, infinitely beyond my art to puzzle out its principle. I admire a flower and see that each lily and aster is perfect in its kind, though different in its proportions and arrangement of petals from every other aster in the field, and shall I not believe as much of every mind? — that it has its own beauty and character, and was never meant to resemble any other one? Every man has his own voice, manner, eloquence, and, just as much, his own sort of love and grief and imagination and action. Let him scorn to imitate any being, let him scorn to be a secondary man, let him fully trust his own share of God's goodness, that, correctly used, it will lead him on to perfection which has no type yet in the universe, save only in the Divine Mind.

It seems to be true that the more exclusively idiosyncratic a man is, the more general and infinite he is, which, though it may not be a very intelligible expression, means, I hope, something intelligible. In listening more intently to our own reason, we are not becoming in the ordinary sense more selfish, but are departing more from what is small, and falling back on truth itself, and God. For it is when a man does not listen to himself, but to others, that he is depraved and misled. The great men of the world, the teachers of the race, moralists, Socrates, Bacon, Newton, Butler, and the like, were those who did not take their opinions on trust, but explored themselves, and that is the way ethics and religion were got out.

September 29.

A man is invincible, be his cause great or small, an abstract principle, or a petty fact, whenever he expresses the simple truth. This makes the cogency of the talk of common people in common affairs. . . .

It ought to be considered that the meanest human soul contains a model of action greater than is realized by the greatest man. Nobody can read the life of Newton or Franklin or Washington without detecting imperfections in those astonishing instances of the conduct of life.

[VIRTUE MUST BE ACTIVE]

BOSTON, *October* 18.

There is very little enterprize in virtue. When men take to themselves the reproofs and exhortations of Scripture, they say, The rule is above my whole life. The mind performs a penitential act of perceiving its deficiency, but there it stops.

It declares war against the enemy, but it does not levy a troop nor make an excursion into his country. It languishes in inaction, and, at the end of a year, or of seven years, it is found no better, and therefore far worse than at the beginning — far worse, because the demand runs on increasing and the performance does not.

It were better to keep the blood warm with virtue by some brilliant act. It is as easy and natural to move, as to rest. Do a deed of charity; persevere to the end of a harassing work.

Better to give every sentiment the body of an outward action; as Johnson said, deal soberly by keeping early hours, righteously by giving alms, and godly by going early to church: Domestic virtues: Spartan, early rising, &c: temperance, fasting. Newton's mode of succeeding in his study was *by always thinking unto it*. A general attention to a man's personal habits, the habit of being sometimes alone, the habit of reading, the habit of abstraction, in order to find out what his own opinion is, the habit of controlling his conversation, the habit of praying, of referring himself always to God. Order has a good name in the world for getting the most sweetness out of time.

THE NIGHTINGALE'S SONG

The nightingale on her lonely thorn
In great gardens loud complaineth,
And all the woods where the sounds are borne
Are the sphere in which she reigneth
   By the empery of sound,
Wide through the dew above and around
   The birds lie mute
   To his breathing flute,
   And lordly man must linger
   And thank the wondrous singer.
Yet is it inarticulate sound
Nor mortal wit can give it sense,
And only heard a mile around
Thro' dusky lawns and hawthorn fence.

But thou, my bird of Paradise — [1]

FROM BLOTTING BOOK Ψ

1830

[The following note is written on the cover.]

Population of U. S. A. 12,821,181 souls.
   slaves   2,000,000.

CHARDON STREET, *October* 29, 1830.

It has been noticed that all a man's views are
of a piece. He is a friend of liberal religion ; he

[1] This unfinished poem appears to have been original.

will probably be found a friend of free trade, and of free press, and of free discussion of truth. On the contrary, is he a bigot? he will contract his views of education and of politics. This will happen where interest does not incline him to either side. But the manufacturer may wish a higher protecting duty *in the present circumstances*, though, on general questions, he adheres to the liberal party of the world. The improvement that a man makes in one part of his knowledge affects every other part, as the light that shines on one object illuminates all parts of the room.

All a man's conversation must be tinged by his occupations. His trade commonly furnishes his mind, and therefore his talk, with the analogies that furnish him with the most conviction; and the more natural wisdom *that* will give him, through increased skill or invention, or extension of its processes, the more will the spiritual wisdom also be augmented that he draws therefrom.

Can it be then that there should not be a retribution to our actions, if thus our nature is single, and feels throughout the condition of every part?

November 3, 1830.

Is it possible for religious principle to overcome the fear of death? It is commonly overcome, as Bacon observes, by every passion and humour in turn, love, honour, revenge, fun, &c. The instances are familiar of men habitually encountering the greatest risks, — sailor and soldier marching up to a battery for sixpence a day. And multitudes of the lower classes of mankind die continually with almost no exhibition of fear. In all these instances I apprehend it is not a conquest of the fear, but a setting it aside. It is want of thought. It is a dogged attention to the facts next them, and not a consideration of the event of death.

On the contrary, spiritual men exhibit not unfrequently strong apprehension, great gloom, as Dr. Johnson, at the thought of dissolution. The more delicate the structure of the mind, the stronger this emotion, I suppose ; and this for two reasons, first, because such persons have more to lose in losing life, and secondly, because they are not yet spiritual enough to overcome fear.

I suppose that he who . . . lives in the daily exercise of the purest and most expanded affections, especially has attained religious principles and loves to meditate on God and heaven, — I suppose that life is worth to him infinitely more than it is to a sensual wretch; life to him is a world of sweet and holy thought, and the idea of losing it is tremendous. I think therefore that Christianity has done much to increase the fear of death in the world by the general advance it has brought about in the cultivation of the moral powers, whilst it has yet failed to effect any large portion of society to that degree as to overcome this terror.

Secondly, I firmly believe that a fuller effect of Christian principles upon our hearts will be the disappearance of the fear of death. Men doubt their immortality because they doubt the real independent being of their moral nature. They fancy the thoughts of God, of goodness, of love, of ethics generally, may be visions of the mind, creations of the mind, and it and they may perish together.

I suppose that the reality, the independence of this part of our nature, can only appear to us by its use, that, in proportion as it is brought into exercise, its eternity will be felt. I have always noticed that when I had been occupied with diligence in any ethical speculation, with the law of compensations, for example, with the great conclusions that come from the analysis of the affections or any kindred question, — if from the midst of such thoughts I glance at the question of immortality, I have at that time a clearer conviction of it.

I have heard moreover a great many anecdotes of people in the last and the former generation, quiet simple people of Malden and Concord who had no books but Bible and psalter, and a less rational therefore, but far more fervid piety than is common now, who died without fear and with exaltation even, in the love of Christ. I suppose though they had neglected their minds, they had cultivated their moral power till it stood out to their minds a living soul, unaffected by any change of the body. This is true too of the apostles, who never speak of death as dreadful, to whom to die was gain. . . .

No man addicted to chemistry ever discovered a salt, or an acid, which he thought divine, never discovered a law which he thought God. No man devoted to literary criticism ever imagined that any of the thoughts that formed his study was God. But the man who cultivated the moral powers, ascended to a thought, and said *This is God*. The faith is the evidence.

A great deal may be learned from studying the history of Enthusiasts. They are they who have attained in different ways to this cultivation of their moral powers, and so to the perception of God. The reason why they are *enthusiasts* is that they have cultivated these powers alone; if they had, with them, trained all their intellectual powers, they would have been wise, devout men, Newtons, Fénelons, Channings. The Enthusiast, enraptured with the splendour of his discovery, imagines that whosoever would make the same must think as he has thought. In his wanderings he has come out upon the shore of the Ocean and, astonished, he believes you must walk through the same woods, climb the same mountains and be led by the same guide. Meantime the wise Christian sees and rejoices in the evidence brought by so many and independent witnesses that the Ocean has been discovered. The Swedenborgian thinks himself wholly different and infinitely more favoured than the Quaker or the Methodist. Yet is nothing more like than the mode in which they severally describe this common experience. Their likeness is greater than their difference.

November 5, 1830.

When a man has got to a certain point in his career of truth he becomes conscious forevermore that he must take himself for better, for worse, as his portion; that what he can get out of his plot of ground by the sweat of his brow is his meat, and though the wide universe is full of good, not a particle can he add to himself but through his toil bestowed on this spot. It looks to him indeed a little spot, a poor barren possession, filled with thorns, and a lurking place for adders and apes and wolves. But cultivation will work wonders. It will enlarge to his eye as it is explored. That little nook will swell to a world of light and power and love.

November 10, 1830.

I thought to-day, in reading Wayland's excellent sermon on Sunday Schools, that no better illustration could be to my doctrine of Perseverance preached some time ago than this, that whenever a man first perceives the supposed necessity of the use of ardent spirits throughout the community to vanish in his own mind — when first he sees in his thought the custom of drinking separate itself from the idea of society, and feels for the first time satisfied that it is a thing wholly accidental and not necessary, then the empire of Intemperance receives a fatal blow. As an illustration of persistency it should be the condition of the thought, that it comes in the prosecution of the project of reform; then, when he has got to that point, he is safe and victorious. And is not this the history of all advancement? We look at good and ill which grows together as indissolubly connected: if an improvement takes place in our own mind, we get a glimpse of an almost imperceptible line that separates the nature of the thing from the evil admixture. By a more diligent inspection that division will farther appear, till it peels off like dead bark. This is the sense of Coleridge's urged distinction between the similar and the same.

This is the merit of every reformer. One man talks of the abolition of slavery with perfect coolness, whilst all around him sneer or roar at his ludicrous benevolence. They with their sinful eyes cannot see society without slaves. He sees distinctly the difference, and knows that the crime is unnecessary. And this is the progress of every soul. What it joined before, it now severs, and sin and error are perpetually falling away from the eternal soul.

All our knowledge comes in this way. It is when a man perceives the essential distinctness of his mind and his body that he is a metaphysician. It is when the sword of the spirit doth divide his flesh and his spirit, that he perceives the immortality of his soul. There is a time when a man distinguishes the idea of felicity from the idea of wealth; it is the beginning of wisdom. There is a time when a man separates God from his works by a process of his own mind, and sees clearly that matter is one thing and the order and forms of matter another.

To the matter of patriotism, remember the saying of Anaxagoras when blamed for neglecting his country, "Wrong me not; my greatest care is my country," pointing to heaven.

The law is a sort of god or divine man to men, being the sense of equity or conscience applied, as close as men can, to the action of men. Yet is it plainly impossible, without prophecy, to fit it to all exigencies. It is for its spirit, for this human heart that is in it, that it has our reverence.

Means and ends. Goodness consists in seeking goodness for its own sake. Heaven is not something else than virtue. Truth must be sought, not for farther ends, but must be the ultimate end. Prayer too finds the end in the means. The world is driving ever at ulterior ends; the wise man is content to study the present event, and to disclose a world of valuable conclusions in the facts which the vulgar are shoving aside as the mere obstacles, scaffolding, steps, over which they must arrive at bread and wine.

I suppose most young men had rather run in debt or tell a lie than be known by the most elegant young man of their acquaintance to have made their dinner on onions from economy. Yet this last had been the act of Epaminondas, of Scipio, of Regulus, of Socrates, of Alfred, of Sidney, of Washington, of every great gentleman, Persian, Greek or Saxon, that ever lived; and the first would have been the action of Commodus, of Chiffinch, of Rochester, of Bonaparte, of Byron, of Brummel. Virtue is the only gentility. As soon as a young man is found to be incapable of virtue he should be bound out, as Montaigne says, prentice to make mince pies in some good town, though he were son of a duke.

Plotinus said as follows: " The animal life is aeriform and must be supplied with air. The eye is soliform and must be supplied with the sun. The soul is truth-like and must be fed with truth."

November 29.

Smother no dictate of your soul, but indulge it. There are passages in the history of Jesus which to some minds seem defects in his character. Probably a more full apprehension of his history will show you these passages in a more agreeable light. Meantime count them defects, and do not stifle your moral faculty, and force it to call what it thinks evil, good. For there is no being in the universe whose integrity is so precious to you as that of your soul.

November 30, 1830.

One mind may hold Europe in counterpoise. Locke and Poland.

December 10, 1830.

God is the substratum of all souls. Is not that the solution of the riddle of sympathy? It is worms and flesh in us that fear or sympathize with worms and flesh, and God only within that worships God of the Universe.

Is it not remarked by us that always we endeavour to find ourselves in other men? All our honest conversation aims at this point, to find the conviction in him that has appeared in me. Eloquence is the universal speech. Bad stammering, vulgar talk, is the issue of self in the individual. As fast as his nature rises, and truth appears, and good is sought, so fast he loses *mal*-loquence in eloquence. For 't is noticed that all eloquence is uniform, one. Everything bad is individual, idiosyncratic. Everything good is universal nature. Wrong is particular. Right is universal.

It has often occurred to me that a man was a reflection of my own self. I understand his smile and his scowl. So far we go along together and have one nature. The moment I do not understand him, the moment he departs from me, I am pained, for I feel that either he is wrong or I am. As long as that difference subsists, so long will our uneasiness on that point. It is an unshaken conviction of both, that both cannot be right.

An injury aimed at his body is individual, or at any of his opinions of institutions. But an assault upon his *truth* strikes me and every man as hard as it does him. A false sentiment has no country. It makes no difference whether it was uttered in France or Germany, in Cambridge or in Newgate. Every soul to whom it comes, feels the wound, and resists the enemy as if it were personal to itself alone. . . .

December 11.

Internal evidence outweighs all other to the inner man. If the whole history of the New Testament had perished, and its teachings remained, the spirituality of Paul, the grave, considerate, unerring advice of James would take the same rank with me that now they do. I should say, as now I say, this certainly is the greatest height to which the religious principle of human nature has ever been carried, and it has the total suffrage of my soul to its truth, whether the miracle was wrought, as is pretended, or not. If it had not, I should yield to Hume or any one that this, like all other miracle accounts, was probably false. As it is true, the miracle falls in with and confirms it. . . .

December 21, 1830.

When a truth is presented, it always brings its own authority, Doth it not? If anyone, denying Jesus, should bring me more truth, I cannot help receiving it also. I do not wish to make disagreeable or impossible suppositions, but say it for the extreme case. The value of Christianity must be shown, must it not, by showing the amount of truth it has brought? I am raised by the reception of a great principle to its height. And he who communicates, and applies, and embodies, a great principle for me, is my redeemer from the evil to which the want of it would have led me. Bacon showed the inanity of science not founded on observation. So he is the Restorer of science. He has not saved my life; he has not saved my estate; but he has saved me from one error, and to that degree is he honourable in my mind. Newton showed the law of gravity, and has directed all men to what will be true and will be false touching bodies, and so has saved a thousand errors.

December 22, 1830.

Forefathers' Day; 3 days more, Christmas. A man will make a better celebration of a holy day by clearing one principle than all the spruce and games and solemnities of Catholic or Episcopal Europe united.

The pain that a commandment gives us should be more welcome than all the pleasures of sin, for 'tis a pledge and a measure of the good we are capable of, of the excellency of the nature. But men forget this and take it wrong.

December 23.

The simplest facts are the most awful. Is it not the noblest fact with which we are acquainted that we are capable of being addressed on moral grounds? This fact is so close to the first fact of our *being*, that, like the circulation of the blood, or the gravity of bodies, it passes long unnoticed from the circumstance of its omnipresence.

December 29, 1830.

Hydriotaphia of Sir Thomas Browne smells in every word of the sepulchre. "That great antiquity, America, lay buried for thousands of years, and a large part of the earth is still in the urn unto us." "A gem of the old rock, *adamas de rupe veteri praestantissimus*." "We, being necessitated to eye the remaining particle of futurity, are naturally constituted unto thoughts of the next world, and cannot excusably decline the consideration of that duration which maketh pyramids pillars of snow, and all that is past a moment,"—p. 95. " To be studied by antiquaries who we were, and have new names given us like many of the mummies, are cold consolations

unto the students of perpetuity, even by everlasting languages," — p. 96.

"There is no antidote against the opium of
time."

Authors or Books quoted or referred to in Journals of 1830

Thales, Anaximander, Pythagoras, Xenophanes, Anaximenes, Heraclitus, Anaxagoras,
Democritus, Empedocles, Zeno, *apud* De Gérando, *Histoire Comparée des Systèmes de Philosophie ;*

Tertullian, *apud Life of William Penn* by
Clarkson ; Plotinus ;

Shakspeare ; Bacon ; Donne ;

George Herbert ; Samuel Daniel ;

Sir Thomas Browne, *Hydriotaphia ;* Milton ;
Bunyan ;

Locke ; Newton ; Scougal, *Life of God in the
Soul of Man ;* Fénelon ;

Swift ; Montesquieu ; Spence, *Anecdotes, Observations,* etc. ;

Dr. Johnson ; Hume, *Essays ;*

Huber, *Nouvelles observations sur les abeilles ;*

Goethe, *Wilhelm Meister* (Carlyle's translation);

Clarkson, *Life of William Penn ;*

Alison, *On the Nature and Principles of Taste;*
Paley; Dugald Stewart;

De Gérando, *Systèmes de Philosophie*, etc.;
Sermons of Greenwood, Buckminster, Wayland;

Landor, *Imaginary Conversations;*

Edinburgh Review, on Godwin;

Sampson Reed, *Growth of the Mind;* Dr.
Jacob Bigelow, *Botany;* Webster, *Reply to
Hayne.*

BLOTTING-BOOK IV

[This manuscript is hard to deal with. Begun
in the autumn of 1830, and continued next year,
it contains some jottings of later date. These, as
far as recognized, are omitted here. The book
also is a "double-ender." There is little original
matter, except the Hymn, but it seems to the
editors well to give some notes and quotations,
apparently made in 1830 and 1831, when Mr.
Emerson was introduced by the work of De
Gérando to the philosophers of the various
schools of ancient Hellas, and also, through him
and Anquetil-Duperron, learned something of
the teachings of Confucius and Zoroaster. Thus
he entered on the path that, years later, led to
the springs of Religion and Philosophy in the
remote past of the Orient.

At the same period he was forming acquaintance through articles by Carlyle and others in *Frazer's Magazine*, the *Foreign Review*, and other sources, with the German writers, and copied passages from translations of Goethe's *Wilhelm Meister*, *Elective Affinities* and his *Memoirs* by Falk; also extracts from Lessing, Schiller, Fichte, and Novalis. Always curious about advancing science, he read with interest Lee's *Life of Cuvier* and Sir Charles Bell *On the Hand*. Lastly, Walter Savage Landor's *Imaginary Conversations* gave him great pleasure and he copied long extracts from them.]

October 27, 1830.

I begin the *Histoire Comparée des Systèmes de Philosophie par M. De Gérando*. This leads me in the outset back to Bacon. (*De Augmentis Scientiae*.)

Bacon thought that philosophy in the highest sense of the word (*prima philosophia*) was deficient, by which he meant the great principles that are true in all sciences, in morals and in mechanics. He said (vol. 1, p. 96), "I see sometimes the profounder sort of wits, in handling some particular argument, will now and then draw a bucket of water out of this well for their present use; but the springhead thereof seemeth to me not to have been visited." By this I understand that generalization which gives the elevation to all the writings of Burke, of De Staël, and now of Sampson Reed. His definition of this philosophy is "That it be a receptacle for all such profitable observations and axioms as fall not within the compass of any of the special parts of philosophy or sciences, but are more common and of a higher stage" (vol. 1, p. 95).

(Metaphysics, in the *Advancement of Learning*, is removed from this philosophy and confined within narrower limits, namely, first, to the discovery of the " form," that is, the *essential nature* of physical things, as the nature of whiteness, of heat, of weight; and secondly, the discovery of "final Causes," as why we have eyebrows, why the skins of animals are covered with hair, fur, etc.)

M. De Gérando has understood Lord Bacon's project of a *literary history* as intended to develop this *highest philosophy* rather by furnishing the premises than drawing the conclusion.

Bacon (lib. III, cap. 4), in speaking of Natural History, proposes to have the fundamental points of the several sects and philosophies collected, so that men may see the several opinions touching the foundations of nature, not for any exact truth that can be expected in those theories, but because it will be useful to run over so many differing philosophies as so many different glosses or opinions of nature (*quarum una fortasse uno loco, alia alio, est emendatior*), "whereof it may be every one in some one point hath seen clearer than his fellows." But he expressly warns that it should " be done distinctly and severally, the philosophies of every one throughout by themselves, and not by titles packed and fagotted up together as hath been done by Plutarch." " For it is the harmony of a philosophy in itself which giveth it light and credence ; whereas if it be singled and broken, it will seem more foreign and dissonant."

It is this idea which De Gérando (Eng. vol. VII, p. 113) applies to the other of the *Prima Philosophia*, and proposes himself to pursue. Considering " Philosophy as the centre in which all the rays of light unite which direct the human mind in its different pursuits," he says further, " In like manner, the ideas which compose each philosophical doctrine in particular form a body and a whole by the connexion which they have in the mind of him who has conceived them. Every doctrine has then in itself its fundamental conditions which determine both the development of its details and the distinctive character of its face, so to speak, and the influence which it exerts around it."

" If then," continues the Baron, " there are in philosophy a small number of questions which, lying at the foundation of all the rest, should exercise over them a natural influence, and which should furnish the last data necessary to their solution; if the opinions which philosophers have formed respecting this small number of primary questions ought to determine by a secret or manifest consequence the whole after-course of their opinions by fixing the direction of their ideas, — if these fundamental questions, I say, could be known (*reconnues*), enumerated, strictly defined, we should have found a simple and sure means of marking in a general manner the primary conditions, the essential characteristics of each doctrine, we might find the terms which compose one of the most important laws of the intellectual world."

The first distinction that is made is that of Material and Work : changes, not creation.

First come the *Cosmogonies*. Indians, Chinese,

Chaldeans, Egyptians, Phœnicians, Persians, have a striking sameness in them, but all these are an intellectual offspring; no utility, mere curiosity.

Next come *Theogonies*, fruit of these, or rather, their expression. For to all the great powers and changes they give a genius, or God, and presently recite the history of world by a genealogy of gods. Then, system of emanations.

Idealism a primeval theory. The *Mahabarat*, one of the sacred books of India, puts in the mouth of Jschak Palak these express words; "The senses are nothing but the soul's instrument of action; no knowledge can come to the soul by their channel (*v. L'Oupnek-hat*, par Anquetil-Duperron, vol. 1, p. 467).

The rule "Do as you would be done by" is found in the "Invariable Medium" of the Chinese, but thrown into the 3d paragraph of the 3d chap. So the *Invariable Milieu* begins with these promising definitions. "The order established by heaven is called *Nature*. What is conformed to nature is called *Law*, the establishment of law (in the mind?) is called *Instruction*." (This "*Invariable Milieu*" M. Abel Remusat has translated into French in *Tome II. des Notices des Manuscrits*, 1818.) "What is pure thought?

That which has for object the beginning of things." *La Isechné*, ch. VIII, *dans le Zend-avesta*, par Anquetil-Duperron, vol. 1, 2d part, p. 141.

Peter Hunt's[1] uncle, sitting by his fire in Chelmsford, asked his nephew how he knew the tongs and shovel which he handled were actually there.

The Gnostics removed the sufferings of Christ from him, the Æon, to the body. And there is some confused idealism in the conversation of a soldier with Geo. Fox [Sewell's *History of the Quakers*, vol. 1, p. 85]. "Christ did not suffer outwardly," said Fox. [The Soldier asked him] "whether there were not Jews, Chief Priests and Pilate *outwardly?* "

Idealism seems a preparation for a strictly

1 Benjamin Peter Hunt was a boy who attended the country school in Chelmsford taught by Emerson in 1825, of whom the latter said, "He was a philosopher whose conversation made all the social comfort I had."

In 1860, Hunt, living in Philadelphia, wrote to his old schoolmaster, "It is now thirty-five years since you began your teachings to me, and, with the exception of those of the great, rough, honest, impartial world, I think they have been the best which I ever received from any man whom I have personally known."

moral life, and so skepticism seems necessary for a universal holiness.

First Class; the Ionian School.

Thales begins the Catalogue of acknowledged philosophers. He taught that "*Water was the beginning of all things.*" "In the liquid or fluid state," saith De Gérando, "all chemical changes take place, and it is in that same state that substances unite to, and identify themselves with organized bodies — " Thales was the first physician opposed to metaphysicians; the Newton who called attention from speculation to experience.

Next great principle of Thales ; *The essence of the soul is motion*, κινήτικόν τι, ἀεικινήτικον, αὐτοκινήτικον, i. e., thinks De Gérando, that he "taught the essence of the soul consisted in *free activity.*" Thus we can make mouse mean mountain everywhere. De Gérando thinks that he did not make *first principle* (ἀρχη) mean both *element* and *cause*, but only *element*, for he was physic, not metaphysic, studying laws of nature and not theology, and excluding divinity by supplying second causes for all particular phenomena. He incurred the reproach common to most physical philosophers, of Atheism. Yet doth it appear that, over all this matter, he set a universal cause, and Diogenes Laertius and Plutarch give these three maxims to him; *God is the oldest, for he was not made. The world is the most perfect, for it is the work of God. No action, no thought even is hid from God.*

Anaximander made this maxim, *Nothing can come of nothing*, and De Gérando says that this was the pivot on which long Greek Philosophy turned. . . . The next wondrous eruption of Anaximander was *The infinite is the beginning of all things ; an infinite altogether immutable and immense.* And surely such transcendentalism shows how close is the first and that last step of philosophy.

Anaximenes.

Hermotimus of Clazomene.

Anaxagoras.

Plutarch remarks "that the Contemporaries of Anaxagoras gave him the surname of νοῦς (mind) because he first had disengaged it from all mixture, presented it in all its simplicity, and its purity, and placed it at the summits of all being." I think this a very remarkable passage of the history of philosophy, as it casts light upon the disengagement also of the idea of God; for the greatest problem of the history of opinions is whether this idea is reasoned out or revealed.

Anaxagoras taught at Athens, but is reckoned in the Ionian School because, like them, he cultivated the Physical Sciences. But the great merit of Anaxagoras is thus told. Whilst the system of emanations, the systems of Pantheism, the opinions of the first Ionians themselves, had associated the elementary matter of all things to the first cause of all production, and thus conceive the Divinity as the *universal soul, the soul of the world*, the world itself as an animated whole identical in some sort with its author, Anaxagoras first detached, separated with precision and neatness these two notions until then confounded. The Universe is in his eyes an effect wholly distinct from its Cause.

This Cause has nothing common with the rest of beings. It hath its peculiar nature, one, eternal, acts on the world as workman on materials. So the idea of the first Cause, which until then was essentially defined by the attribute of *Power*, was determined by Anaxagoras to receive chiefly the attribute of intelligence.

De Gérando's authorities are Aristotle, *De Anima*, 1, 3. (Metaphys, 1, 3.) Plutarch, *Pericles*, and Cicero, *De Natura Deorum*.

Until him, a plurality of Gods. He first announced that the phenomena of the universe are strictly connected, that they form one whole, that *one order* reigns, that its Unity supposes One mind which ordains it. *Vide* Aristotle, *De Anima*, 1, 1. Metaph. 1, 3. By banishing God from each detail, magic, genii, etc., Anaxagoras was able to make this demonstration of God over all. Superstition opposes truth.

Anaxagoras said, one single soul ran through all being, ordering matter, but intimately present to man. He said moreover that the senses were little to be trusted. Anaxagoras was a nobleman, but forsook his estate for philosophy, was friend of Phidias and Pericles, and said that his country (pointing upward) was very dear to him.

Diogenes of Apollonia in Crete, another Ionian philosopher, rather went backward from Anaxagoras, confounding *cause* with matter. This materialism of theirs seemed to be incapacity of conceiving cause or principle, except as inherent in real substance; it was a substance of great subtilty expanded.

Archelaus of Miletus also retrograded. In morals, he taught Hobbism: " That men are born of the earth, have built cities, formed arts, made laws; the difference between just and unjust is not founded in nature, but in positive laws."

Second Class; the Italian School.

Pythagoras taught that *Numbers were the principles of things;* the *monad* one, eternal, simple, perfect; the *dyad* imperfect, matter, chaos.

"Beings are bound together by a chain of relations parallel or like to those which unite numbers.[1] All these relations converge to one centre. World forms one whole. Symmetry presides over the systems of their dependence and their connexion."

The Pythagoreans first gave the name κόσμος to the world — Beauty. Their notions of God were more material than the Ionians — soul of the world again — placed him at the centre. Mystics and spiritualizers were they; hierarchies of genii; much importance to dreams and predictions, and Pythagoras himself pretended to be an augur. But they bought this tribute paid to vulgar superstitions by fine notions of Providence. Philolaus says, "We are slaves, property of the Gods; they govern us, watch us, supply our wants." They first gave Virtue this definition, *Virtue is a harmony.*

Moderation, thought Pythagoras, the essential character of Virtue; the Empire over self to be

---

1 "A subtle chain of countless rings
The next unto the farthest brings," etc.
See *Poems*, "Mayday."

the means of obtaining it; inward peace as the fruit. He gave chiefly practical precepts, dietetic, etc., but Iamblichus attributed this to him, "*The love of truth and the zeal of good are the most precious present which God has been able to grant to man.*"

Pythagorean opinions.

"The soul is an emanation of the Divinity, a part of the soul of the world, a ray from the source of light. It comes from without into the human body, as into a momentary abode, it goes out of it anew; it wanders in ethereal regions, it returns to visit it; it passes into other habitations, for the soul is immortal." ("Man has some affinity not only with gods, but with animals; one mind runs through the universe.") "The soul breathes the representations of the images of things as a sort of air." "Reason contemplates all nature, it has a certain affinity with it. As light is perceived by the eye, sound by the ear, because of affinity between object and organ; so the universality of nature by reason, because of a consanguinity betwixt them."

Archytas of Tarentum has left this great maxim that "virtue ought to be sought for itself," also that "God is the source and means and end of all that is conformed to justice and reason." And a profound view of the double operation of the understanding. "What can decompound all particulars contained in a general principle, can arrive at truth and wisdom; can, in these notions, in a sort of mirror, behold God and the series of dependent beings."

Eudoxus said "Pleasure is the supreme good," but was a good man.

Third School; Eleatic.

The Eleatics asked *Why things are?* and sought the answer in the soul only, and wished to find the essence of things. Other philosophers demanded, "What is the generation of things?"

Xenophanes demanded, "Is there really any generation?" *Ex nihilo nil fit*, said Thales, and Xenophanes said therefore, "One thing can never come from another thing." Like must produce like. Then all is eternal. "Thought," said Xenophanes, "is the only real substance." He gave to the universe only a *phenomenal value*.

"God is one; there cannot be but one God. He is always like himself. He cannot be conceived under the human form; He is perfect. We can't apply to him either motion or limit. But he is not immoveable nor infinite," i. e.,

motion and limit as they belong to matter have
no relation to God's attributes.

Said Zenny, then, not wisely distributed things
into four elements, etc., and entitled himself to
the name of a Neptunian Geologist. " Xenophanes [said], " None perceives by the senses
things as they are. We must not then begin
from these opinions, got we know not how, but
from what is stable, from what reason discovers."
In the last part of his life he said, " he could not
be so happy as to know anything certainly.
Whichever side he looked all ran to Unity —
there was but one substance."

And Sextus Empiricus has preserved these
words from his poem on nature which are as
skeptical as one could desire. " No man knows
anything certain touching the Gods, nor upon
what I say upon the universal whole. None
can. For if one should chance upon the truth
he could not know that he had obtained it ; but
opinion spreads her veil over all things." But
it was of the external world, and never of metaphysical truths, that he was skeptical, saith De
Gérando. It was Idealism which he maintained.

Parmenides, poem on nature.
" Thought and the object of thought are but

one." These philosophers had confounded the abstract notion of being with its objective reality and thought they could conclude from one to the other. This great mistake has misled a number of metaphysicians down to Descartes himself, says De Gérando. He was the Idealist of antiquity.

There began from this Eleatic School the first philosophical dispute, this concerning the senses and the existence of matter. *Zeno* was charged with the defence of the Eleatics against the dogmatists, who relied of course on common sense and conscience.

Heraclitus said this good thing: that "a great variety of knowledge did not make wisdom, but it consisted in discovering the law which governs all things."

"All nature is governed by constant laws. The phenomena themselves, which appear discordant, concur in the harmony of the whole. It is an accord which results from discords. Meantime all change. Attraction, Repulsion." "The same cannot be conceived except by the same." "Conception cannot be except by a similitude between the object and the subject"; therefore reject the testimony of the senses, and hear reason.

Still, he said that the senses were open canals through which we inhale the divine reason.

Hence also from this admission *to the divine* he founded the authority of *Common sense*. " The judgments in which all men agree are a certain testimony of truth. That common light which enlightens all at once is only the divine reason spread through all thinking beings by an immediate effusion." " The understanding represents the march of the universe, such, as it has been preserved by memory; we arrive then, at truth, when we borrow from memory the faithful tablet of which the deposit is trusted to it. Wisdom is then accessible to all men." Virtue consists in governing the passions; wisdom in fidelity to what is true. The end of man is his own satisfaction. The body is to be used as an instrument only. Human laws receive their force from this divine law which rules all at its touch, which triumphs over all.

Hippocrates, the physician, [was] his disciple, an exact experimental philosopher. Hippocrates is called the result, the pride of the Eleatic School, Pythagoras of the Italian, Thales of the Ionian.

Always utility gives the medal, even though philosophers are the school-committee.

[HYMN] [1]

There is in all the sons of men
A love that in the spirit dwells,
That panteth after things unseen,
And tidings of the Future tells.

And God hath built his altar here
To keep this fire of faith alive
And set his priests in holy fear
To speak the truth — for truth to strive.

And hither come the pensive train,
Of rich and poor, of young and old,
Of ardent youths untouched by pain,
Of thoughtful maids and manhood bold.

They seek a friend to speak the word
Already trembling on their tongue,

1 This hymn was probably the first trial for that beginning
    " We love the venerable house
        Our fathers built to God,"
which was sung at the ordination of the Rev. Chandler Rob-
bins, Mr. Emerson's successor in the Second Church. Both
hymns are printed in the Centenary Edition of the *Poems*. In
this hymn, in the 5th stanza the original wording " humble
Sorrow's door" is given, as better than that found in a later
verse-book, — "meek Contrition's door," the form in the
volume referred to.   E. W. E.

To touch with prophet's hand the chord
Which God in human hearts hath strung.

To speak the plain reproof of sin
That sounded in the soul before,
And bid them let the angels in
That knock at humble Sorrow's door.

Sole source of light and hope assured,
O touch thy servant's lips with power,
So shall he speak to us the word
Thyself dost give forevermore.

"Man is a microcosm."
ARISTOTLE.

" Knowing the Heart of man is set to be
The centre of this world, about the which
These revolutions of disturbances
Still roll; where all the aspects of misery
Predominate; whose strong effects are such
As he must bear, being helpless to redress:
And that unless above himself he can
Erect himself, how poor a thing is man! "
SAMUEL DANIEL.

" The recluse hermit oft-times more doth know
Of the world's inmost wheels than worldlings can;

As man is of the world, the Heart of man
Is an Epitome of God's great book
Of creatures, and men need no further look."

                                        DONNE.

       He is in little all the sphere.

     .   .   .   .   .

Oh mighty love ! man is one world, and hath
Another to attend him.

                                        HERBERT.

" All things are yours."   ST. PAUL.

" There is a secret attraction towards all
points, from within us, diverging from an infinitely deep centre."   NOVALIS.

" What good were it for me to manufacture
perfect iron, while my own breast is full of
dross? What would it stead me to put properties of land in order, while I am at variance
with myself?"   GOETHE, *Letter to Werner*.

" If I wished to find some real inspiration,
some profound sentiment, some just and striking reflexions for my poetical compositions, I
saw that I must draw them from my own bosom."   GOETHE'S *Memoirs*.

" I, for my share, cannot understand how men have made themselves believe that God speaks to us through books and histories. The man to whom the universe does not reveal directly what relation it has to him, — whose heart does not tell him what he owes himself and others, — that man will scarcely learn it out of books, which generally do little more than give our errors names."

Wilhelm Meister.

"Every one of my writings has been furnished to me by a thousand different persons, a thousand different things, — the learned and the ignorant, the wise and the foolish, infancy and age have come in turn, generally without having the least suspicion of it, to bring me the offering of their thoughts, their faculties, their experience; often they have sowed the harvest I have reaped; my work is that of an aggregation of beings taken from the whole of nature; it bears the name of Goethe."

" The smallest production of nature has the circle of its completeness within itself, and I have only need of eyes to see with, in order to discover the relative proportions. I am perfectly sure that within this circle, however narrow, an entirely genuine existence is enclosed. A work of art, on the other hand, has its completeness *out of itself*; the Best lies in the Idea of the artist which he seldom or never reaches; all the rest lies in certain conventional rules which are indeed derived from the nature of art and of mechanical processes, but still are not so easy to decipher as the laws of living nature. In works of art, there is much that is traditional; the works of nature are ever *a freshly uttered word of God.*" Goethe.

"The great man is he who hath nothing to fear and nothing to hope from another. It is he who, while he demonstrates the iniquity of the laws and is able to correct them, obeys them peaceably. It is he who looks on the ambitious both as weak and fraudulent. It is he who hath no disposition or occasion for any kind of deceit, no reason for being or for appearing different from what he is. It is he who can call together the most select company when it pleases him."

" . . . My thoughts are my company. . . ." Landor.

" Character is a perfectly educated will."
NOVALIS.

" The gift of bearing to be contradicted, is, generally speaking, possessed only by the dead. . . ."   LESSING.

[A very long extract from Goethe's *Wilhelm Meister*, the *Wanderjahre*, on the three true religions is given.

Then follows (from Lee's *Life of Cuvier*) this statement of his fourfold division of the animal kingdom.]

" There exist in nature four principal forms or general plans according to which all animals seem to have been modelled, and the ulterior divisions of which, whatever name the naturalist may apply to them, are comparatively but slight modifications founded on the development or addition of certain parts which do not change the essence of the plan."

1. Man, and animals like him ;
2. Molluscous animals ;
3. Insects and worms ;
4. Radiated animals.

"Cuvier rejects the idea of a scale of beings as not founded in nature, but urges the 'necessity of considering each being, each group of beings, by itself, and not to make abstraction of any of its affinities or any of the links which attach it either to the beings nearest to it or the most distant from it.' The True method is to view each being in the midst of all others: it shows all the radiations by which it is more or less closely linked with that immense net-work which constitutes organized nature."

LEE's *Life of Cuvier*.

JOURNAL XXII

FROM Ψ

1831

January 10, 1831.

. . . I am not to help my neighbour because he is importunate, nor because *he wants*; (that does not express his claim on me) but because he is God's creature, as I am: and I have received all, and only hold all I have as *occasion* of exercising affections. His claim on me is through God, but this claim is nearest of any, for the Bible teaches us that God is in us, and in all, and there is therefore something in him which is another and the same as myself. I find myself in my neighbour, and the object of a charity is not to relieve want as an end, but by means of relieving that want, to justify myself to himself, or to fill both of us with God's approbation. He only is a perfect man through whom God's spirit blows unobstructed, who seeks with all his powers God's ends, seeks usefulness with every muscle, seeks truth in every thought.

Herein may be seen all the evil of the great controversy about faith and works. Works done as unto the Lord, and not unto men, contain faith; and he would be beside himself who should lift a finger against such.

Great men are great unto men, and not unto the Lord, and that is the reason why they are so much suspected. The greatest man is he that is not man at all, but merges his human will in the divine and is merely an image of God.

There is a greatness, however, that has been sometimes seen among the gladiators on our political arena, here and in England. I mean that elevation of reason that sees clearly great principles, and trusts magnanimously to them in the face of present odium, because it has some insight into their wholesome nature, and is sure they will work good in the end, and so justify themselves to the times and to posterity. This we call noble, and do not grudge our applause. It takes advantage of that moral advancement which the world has made, and is a tribute to that. This has been done by the Pitts and Burkes and Websters, and is second only to the praise of Godliness. They do not act as unto *men as they are*, but *to men as they ought to be*, and as some are. If there were no good men, they would not thus act, and they will not now act thus, steadily, invariably. If they acted to the Lord, they would thus act always, and they would find this course of action full of sweetness, and not full of chagrin, as Burke confesses it is.

January 24, 1831.

I believe it is true that the devout theist and the devout Christian will agree fully as to their duty. The preceptive part of Christianity enjoins no rules of action which are not binding on the theist. It enjoins love of relations, friends, country, mankind, and the strictest virtues, according to the ancient idea of virtue ; but with this first and last injunction, that they should be done as unto God.

If this is so, then to be an enemy to Christianity is to be an enemy to one's own self.

Let nobody suppose that what are by some sects called the peculiar, essential doctrines of Christianity — Regeneration, Justification by Faith — make an exception to this remark, or are not enjoined by the conscience. These doctrines, like everything in dispute, have been strained a great way, yea, out of all shape, but they are originally solemn verities, and in that shape, if presented by an ancient philosopher, would have to a sound mind absolute authority.

Ellen Tucker Emerson died, 8th February, Tuesday morning, 9 o'clock. . . .

CHARDON ST., *February* 13, 1831.

Five days are wasted since Ellen went to heaven to see, to know, to worship, to love, to intercede. . . . Reunite us, O thou Father of our spirits.

There is that which passes away and never returns. This miserable apathy, I know, may wear off. I almost fear when it will. Old duties will present themselves with no more repulsive face. I shall go again among my friends with a tranquil countenance. Again I shall be amused, I shall stoop again to little hopes and little fears and forget the graveyard. But will the dead be restored to me? Will the eye that was closed on Tuesday ever beam again in the fulness of love on me? Shall I ever again be able to connect the face of outward nature, the mists of the morn, the star of eve, the flowers, and all poetry, with the heart and life of an enchanting friend? No. There is one birth, and one baptism, and one first love, and the affections cannot keep their youth any more than men.

Her end was blessed and a fit termination to such a career. She prayed that God would speedily release her from her body, and that she might not make this prayer to be rid of her pains, " but because thy favour is better than life." "Take me, O God, to thyself," was frequently on her lips. Never anyone spake with greater simplicity or cheerfulness of dying. She said, " I pray for sincerity, and that I may not talk, but may realize what I say." She did not think she had a wish to get well. . . .

Heu! quantominus est cum reliquis versari, quam tui meminisse!

February 23, 1831.

The questions that come to me this evening are few and simple.

It is worth recording that Plotinus said, " Of the Unity of God, nothing can be predicated, neither being, nor essence, nor life, for it is above all these." Grand it is to recognize the truth of this and of every one of that first class of truths which are *necessary*. Thus, " Design proves a designer," " Like must know like," or " the same can only be known by the same," out of which come the propositions in ethics, "*Si vis amari, ama*," and "God without can only be known by God within," and "the scriptures can be explained only by that spirit which dictated them," and a thousand sayings more which have a *quasi* truth instantly to the ear, the real truth of which is this elementary fact in all, "like must know like." It would be well for every mind to collect with care every truth of this kind he may meet, and make a catalogue of "necessary truths." They are scanned and approved by the Reason far above the understanding. They are the last facts by which we approximate metaphysically to God.

March 13.

Paul says that his preaching was made effectual to the Gentiles by the same spirit as Peter's preaching to the Circumcision. He saith rightly. There is one light through a thousand stars. There is one spirit through myriad mouths. It will not do to divide or bound what is in itself infinite. Every word of truth that is spoken by man's lips is from God. Every thought that is true is from God. Every right act is from God. All these are as much done by his Spirit as the miracle of the Pentecost, they are of the same sort as that influence. The apostle who prophesied or who wrought a miracle, felt that his word or his act was as true to the occasion as he did when he lifted bread to his mouth that he might eat. The prophet understood his prediction; the apostle willed the cure of the cripple. If you ask how he wrought the miracle, I ask how you lift your arm. By God. I suppose that miraculous power is only more power. I suppose it is strictly of the same kind, for I suppose there is but one kind. There is but one source of power, that is God.

The reason why I insist on this uniformity and universality of spiritual influence is because any other view that can be taken of the Holy Ghost is idolatrous. If it be received into the mind as a person and separated from God and God's common operation, that moment the idea of God receives a wound in you. All that is added to the new power is taken from Him. A man tells me that the Spirit has been poured out in a great Reformation. Does he mean anything more or anything different from saying that God, in the infinite variety of his accustomed ways, has made some men better? If he does mean differently, he means wrong. Does he speak so fervently of the spirit as to imply more? I say he is doing injury to his own mind, and breaking up the thought of God into fragments; literally he is changing the glory of the incorruptible God into idols, made like unto good yet corruptible men. But, it will be said, The Comforter, the Advocate whom the Saviour speaks of, — did he mean nothing? Truly he meant what he said, The Comforter whom the Father will send you, that is the Spirit of Truth.

. . . I know well . . . many will not fail to say ; — To what purpose is this attempt to explain away so safe and holy a doctrine as that of the Holy Spirit? Why unsettle or disturb a faith which presents to many minds a helpful medium by which they approach the idea of God?

And this question I will meet. It is because I think the popular views of this principle are pernicious, because it does put a medium, because it removes the idea of God from the mind. It leaves some events, some things, some thoughts, out of the power of Him who causes every event, every flower, every thought. The tremendous idea, as I may well call it, of God, is screened from the soul.

Men are made to feel as if they ate their dinner and committed their common sins somewhere in the purlieus of the creation, behind a screen, for the Spirit of God works in a church, or in Judea, and not in the vulgar affairs of every day. The Spirit of God teaches us, on the contrary, that not a star rolls in space, that not a pulse beats in a single heart, not a bird drops from the bough, not an atom moves throughout the wide universe, but is bound in the chains of his omnipotent thought, — not a lawless particle.

And least of all can we believe — Reason will not let us — that the presiding Creator commands all matter and never descends into the secret chambers of the soul. There he is most present. The soul rules over matter. Matter may pass away like a mote in the sunbeam, may be absorbed into the immensity of God, as a mist is absorbed into the heat of the Sun; but the soul is the kingdom of God : the abode of love, of truth, of virtue. The bringing all minds into union with him is the work which God worketh from age to age.

CONCORD, *March* 4.

Our goodness is so low that it scarce seems to approximate to truth, and our knowledge so scanty that it does not approximate to virtue. But in God they are one. He is perfectly wise because he is perfectly good; and perfectly good because he is perfectly wise. . . . We say of a bad man that he will not believe because he cannot understand the great action of a moral hero. Did we ever see an exhibition of intellectual power by a good man that was not aided, enforced,—and that in the intellectual truth too, —by his goodness? Milton, Burke, and Webster get most of their wisdom from the heart. . . .

The Religion that is afraid of science dishonours God and commits suicide. It acknowledges that it is not equal to the whole of truth, that it legislates, tyrannizes over a village of God's empire, but is not the immutable universal law. Every influx of atheism, of scepticism, is thus made useful, as a mercury pill, assaulting and removing a diseased religion and making way for truth, and itself is presently purged into the draught. . . . Keep the soul always turned to God. Nothing so vast but feel that he contains it. If your idea of him is dim or perplexed, pray and think and act more. It is the education of the soul. It is the sure way of individual increase. Sincerity is always holy and always strong. Come good or ill, the pure in heart are in the right way. And presently and often, you shall be rewarded with clearer perception, the sense of more intimate communion. Dear friendship or solitary piety is often conscious that God's approbation rests upon it. . . .

Voltaire forsook good, aiming at truth, and grew up half, or less than half, a man, — a colourless plant grown in the dark. And many a religionist hurts the cause of religion by the opposite error.

It is all reception. More genius does not increase the *individuality*, but the *community* of each mind. In the wisdom or fancy (which is oft wisdom) of Bacon and Shakspeare we do not admire an arbitrary, alien creation, but we have surprize at finding ourselves, at recognizing our own truth in that wild unacquainted field. Who knows that he has got all the truth he might have? Who dares to think he has got all the good he might have? We dip our finger-tips in the sea that would make us invulnerable if we would plunge and swim. Out upon the cold, hard-eyed zealot whose whole religion and whole sect and all his missions and all his prodigality of means go to stifle the flame of holy love which young and heroic minds are nourishing, go to traduce the spirit of man.

. . . .

All wisdom, all genius, is reception. The more perfect the character and the more rich the gifts, the more would the individual seem sunk, and the more unmixed would the truth he possessed appear. He would exist merely to impart and to hang on the first cause, — a Socrates, a Jesus.

The moment you describe Milton's verse you use words implying, not creation, but increased perception, second-sight knowledge of what *is*, beyond the ken of others. Yet these are prophecy. . . .

Various psychological facts to be remembered: — Socrates's abstraction; Anaxagoras; Hermotimus burned in a trance; Plotinus; Marivaux' description of inequality of mental states; Newton's saying, that *attention* to what was true is all; Shakspeare and Bacon as *attentive* to what is true as Kirby or Swammerdam.

Whole zeal of opposers of one uniform; spiritual influence proceeds [not?] from inattention to the strictly divine character of ordinary phenomena. All is miracle, and the mind revolts at representations of two kinds of miracle.

Opus quod Deus operatur a primordio usque ad finem.

Will God work only in Geology and not come
into secret chambers of Spirit? Seek to dwell
with God, O man.[1] . . . Let all the common
duties derive dignity from the dedication to the
Most High. . . .

Live forever *shall* be writ on every thought.
A day will not suffice; but form habits of grand
life, form yourself, your affections, your friend-

[1] In these years it was more and more impressed on Emerson that Nature spoke by parables — the facts that met the
eye of the dullest even at every turn — to man's spirit, and thus
that Religion was revealed to him each hour and not merely
in past centuries. He began to read books on science with
keen interest. Here are some notes written on a loose bit of
paper, shut into this journal: —

"It was a resurrection in miniature," said Cuvier.

Sir James Hall and Gregory Watt set out to see how the
world was made, — basalt and sand stone.

As to burning out coal, we will warm the world with grind-
stones by and by.

A bubble of water, a grain of gunpowder.

A shell may teach more than a range of mountains.

Heat keeps the earth from assuming the shape of a small
crystal.

Expansion of water by freezing.

Man comes in and turns the fishes out. Fishes and their
senses fit for their element.

Atomic theory. Water the mirror, the solvent, the engineer, the presser, the scavenger.

ships, your charities, your talk, your commercial dealings, on principles so vast it will infuse a mighty soul into them all. God will be felt. Cannot a mind thus formed, or reformed, better understand a science or an honest art than another? Can it not acquire such self-subsistence as to give, not take, character from its neighbourhood? The imputation to which priests have always been subjected is that their private and their public discourses differ, that whilst they say one thing formally, they sympathize fully with other men in private, and reason and apprehend or regret the same trivial inconveniences as they. . . .

Now this is the fault of the priest in part, in part the fault of man, and in part the mistake of the censurer. Who expects that the worshipper of God should be wholly grave, overlooks a great part of nature. A grave man is no more a perfect character than a jester. There are many truths manifested by the ridiculous. And in intelligent society, abundance of humour and wit will appear. No one can take sufficiently generous views of Providence, none can go out into the fields and see the rejoicing beauties of morning and of spring, or enter an evening party, without feeling that God never meant that his children should shun each other or should wear a sad countenance.

WRITTEN AT CHARDON ST., BOSTON

Spring of 1831

Dear brother, would you know the life,
Please God, that I would lead?
On the first wheels that quit this weary town
Over yon western bridges I would ride,
And with a cheerful benison forsake
Each street and spire and roof, incontinent.
Then would I seek where God would guide my
    steps
Amid the mountain shires, Hants, Franklin, Berks,
Where down the rock ravine a river roars
Even from a brook, and where old woods,
Not tamed and cleared, cumber the ground
With their centennial wrecks.
Find me a slope where I can feel the sun,
And mark the rising of the early stars.
There will I bring my books,—my household
    gods,
The reliquaries of my dead saint, and dwell
In the sweet odour of her memory.
Then in the uncouth solitude unlock
My stock of art, plant dials in the grass,
Hang in the air a bright thermometer,
And aim a telescope at the inviolate sun.

April 1, 1831.

The spring is wearing into summer, and life is wearing into death; our friends are forsaking us, our hopes are declining; our riches are wasting; our mortifications are increasing, and is the question settled in our minds, what objects we pursue with undivided aim? Have we fixed ourselves by principles? Have we planted our stakes?

April 3.

Trust to that prompting within you. No man ever got above it. Men have transgressed and hated and blasphemed it, but no man ever sinned but he felt it towering above him and threatening him with ruin.

The troubled water reflects no image. When it is calm it shows within it the whole face of heaven.

Our vices even, prove the being of God, as shadows point in (*sic*) the direction of the sun.

It is a luxury to be understood.

Boston, *April* 4.

The days go by, griefs, and simpers, and sloth and disappointments. The dead do not return, and sometimes we are negligent of their image. Not of yours, Ellen. I know too well who is gone from me. And here come on the formal duties which are to be formally discharged, and in our sluggish minds no sentiment rises to quicken them, they seem —

And when the Fast comes, what shall I say? It is forgot and despised. It is remainder of an ancient race, and like old furniture to be dispensed with, it is huddled aside by the upstart generation as if it were a disgrace to their refinement and enlarged views of things. Perhaps there yet remain in the present race so much kindness, so many kindred to the former, as will not like to see their venerable usages trampled upon. Something may be said for those old people, that generous race who delivered two countries, England and America, from tyranny, and founded the institutions by which our fathers and ourselves were reared. It is well to remember the departed. Even savages keep their fathers' bones. . . . The noble love the dead. The Jews were taught in their prosperity to remember the day of small things, to remember the outcast Joseph, and say, " My father was a Syrian and went down a bondman to Egypt." They were taught to remember in their prosperity the stranger, and say, " I was a stranger when the Lord brought me into this land." And happy would be the people of this land, if they never grow unmindful of their stock and stem (for we remember that which is like ourselves) ; if the pride of ancestry from men that loved God and freedom more than worldly good does not fade out of their minds. We may grow so besotted as to think that a disgrace, which is our chiefest ornament, like the stag in the fable. A fop thinks the simple dress and manners of his country-father mean. Let us not be such coxcombs as to dishonour the gray hairs of the Puritans. I think of them as men whom God honoured with great usefulness. That solid sense, that expansion of the inner man, that greater reverence for history, for law, which they had, may compensate for thrift and mechanical improvements and fine houses which they had not.

Seriousness may be forgiven to the redeemers of suffering Liberty, to the defenders of Religion, to the pious men who kept their integrity in an unholy age. Danger is when men will not keep quiet, and grow restless from turning the eye out, instead of inward. When those men had asserted their rights they were appeased and still. We think stillness stagnation, and in a man want of thought. It is want of thought that makes this everlasting inquietude. Great men; great thoughts have they bequeathed to the world. I will honour their institution, if only because it was theirs. Whatever relic precious has come down, I won't spit upon. I will respect this Fast as a connecting link by which the posterity are bound to the fathers; as a trump through which the voice of the fathers speaks.

THE BRIDE OF LAMMERMOOR.[1]

April 9.

Pleasure taken in Ravenswood's grand feudal character great. And why? because the contemplation of somebody that we could depend upon, and should without risk admire and love if we should converse with him, is pleasing. The soul

1 In his speech at the Scott Centennial celebration in Boston, Mr. Emerson said of this novel, " The Bride of Lammermoor almost goes back to Æschylus for a counterpart as a painting of Fate, — leaving on every reader the impression of the highest and purest tragedy." (See *Miscellanies.*)

The last half of this passage in the Journal is used in "History," *Essays II.*

believes in its own immortality and whilst this character floats before it, is already anticipating intercourse with such in other states of being. Is it not too, that by the law of sympathy the soul sees in every great character only a mirror in which its own pinched features are expanded to true dimensions, "the shows of things to the desires of the mind." And does it not find a lesson herein, the suggestion that a mind raised above circumstances may fight this heroic battle day by day; that Sir William Ashton is only another name for a vulgar temptation; that Ravenswood castle is only another name for proud poverty and the "foreign mission of state," only a Bunyan disguise for honest industry; that we may all shoot a wild bull that would toss the good and beautiful, by fighting down the unjust and sensual; that Lucy is another word for fidelity, which is always beautiful and always liable to great suffering in the world, but which is true to itself, and trusts God for success in the abysses of his designs.

April 11, 1831.

The love of novels is the preference of sentiment to the senses. Who are they that love an ideal world and dwell in it? The young, the pure, who believe that love is stronger than lust; who delight in the belief that virtue may prevail over the power of circumstances. . . . If the principles of Jesus could take possession of all breasts, life would not be vile. Society would be pure but not puritanical. 'T is because we are such half-faced friends of God that we have this awkwardness of religion, holiness without beauty. In its source it is the all-fair. A community of Christians would be a field of splendid occasions, exciting recollections, purposes ; grand characters and epical situations that would leave the loftiest fiction, of prose or verse, far beneath it. . . .

What you seek in these novels is the friendships you would form with tempers so true and majestic on which an infinite trust might be reposed. They would act for you across the earth and could not be bribed or scared or cooled. Now in every mind is the material of all this romance and that is the way in which every mind is heir of heaven. Have you not ever felt the pleasure, the tossing, the turmoil of a lofty sentiment? When your pillow would not give rest to your head because of the delight of what you had done or determined. How was life ennobled, and death in that hour lost much of his dread. Is there not living in the world the person for whose advantage you would eagerly have made costliest sacrifices? That sentiment, that occasion, was the beginning of all good to you, if only persevered in ; and if you have left that way, you have wandered; and how have you fared? *Therefore* is life stale and cheap. It is wonderful that men do not learn this lesson from love, so familiar in its lower stages, but seldom carried to any heights.

" All other pleasures are not worth its pains."

Now a greater heroism than has delighted you in Wallace, or Richard, or Ravenswood, is offered to you. In the common sun and air, in the paved street, in all the details trite of vulgar life you may tread with the step of a king. You may not fight down rivals, but you may live like a wise man among silly people. Among gluttons and sycophants you may carry the hand of Franklin and the heart of Paul. And the good *call out* great sentiments, as well as give them out. That which is like you in other minds will start from sleep in your presence.

April 23.

What so fit for man as *trust*? He did not make himself; he has no finger in the opera-

tions of the universe. . . . Let him be calm:
let him assume the port of a resolved mind that
waits an enemy, but does not fear him. This is
the first step. Then let him open his eye and
heart to the good he has received, and put his
finger, if he can, on his title-deed. Are you so
happy? Have you so much? The height of
your fear shows the price of your stake. Well
now, by what right is it yours? It is all received. And, if any cause to complain, it is that
it would be inconsistent with the goodness that
has been shown you not to show you more.
Not with your merits, observe, but with that
grace. Well then, I don't see but you may
trust it still.

Again, man is greater by leaning on the greatest. Nature is commanded by obeying her. God
lends his strength to the good. Thus it is wisest, first, because you cannot help yourself, any
whimpering would be ridiculous; and secondly,
't is wisest, because there's every reason for affectionate trust, for a voluntary act of approval
of God's order. What so sublime and so in-
dicative of a perception of the matchless wisdom that directs as implicit trust?

"One man may lead a horse to water, but
ten canna gar him drink." It is so in the order

of Providence with man. Heaven guards his freedom so carefully that nothing compels him to enter into the spirit of the festival to which he is invited. He may pout in the corner, if he will, and suck his thumbs. But the loss is his own. The company is large and can easily spare him; but he would do more wisely to conform himself to circumstances intended kindly, and carry forward the brilliant game.

April 25.

From our feeble hands we drop the tools. Nobody thinks of the duty and the nobleness of instituting a perfect life. Nobody acts three days on a system. A man rises from a good book or from a good example and the eternal chord in him vibrates to heaven's melody a moment, and then the superincumbent flesh stops its tone. If in some distant world the vision of these weeks we are now so idly spending shall come full on the memory, is it not probable they will be attended with poignant regret? Shan't we think what capabilities, — and what nothings of act! Perhaps we cannot even form steady views of duty; then we are very low indeed and this defect should alarm us. But there is a capacity of virtue in us, and there is capacity of vice to make your blood creep.

*Plotinus pudore quodam affici videbatur quod
anima ejus in corpore esset.*

> "In their distress
> They call a spirit up, and when he comes
> Straight their flesh creeps and quivers, and they dread him
> More than the ills for which they called him up.
> The uncommon, the sublime, must seem and be
> Like things of every day. But in the field,
> Aye, *there*, the Present Being makes itself felt.
> The personal must command, the actual eye
> Examine. If to be the chieftain asks
> All that is great in nature, let it be
> Likewise his privilege to move and act
> In all the correspondencies of greatness.
> The oracle within him, that which *lives*,
> He must invoke and question—not dead books,
> Not ordinances, not mould-rotted papers."

SCHILLER's *Wallenstein*, Coleridge's Translation.

> "In your own bosom are your destiny's stars:
> Confidence in yourself, prompt resolution,
> This is your Venus! and the sole malignant,
> The only one that harmeth you is *Doubt*."

Ibid.

> "At the approach
> Of extreme peril, when a hollow image
> Is found a hollow image, and no more, —
> Then falls the power into the mighty hands

Of nature, of the spirit giant-born
Who listens only to himself."

Ibid.

" Of its own beauty is the mind diseased
And fevers into false creation."

Admiration is a sure mark of a noble mind.
Uncommon boys follow uncommon men. Vulgar minds are too much wrapped up in themselves to mark, much less to estimate, another's merits, though they shine as the sun. But
you admire and you despair; you have no fellowship with what you admire, and it seems to
you that real life is a waste where all your fellows act on low motives, and pour out all the
vessels of ridicule on the innocents who would
hope to act on any better, as unpractical and
romantic. Love even, and high sentiments are
regarded as boarding-school wares. Well now,
what is the lesson God teaches you hereby as
with an angel's trumpet? that you should sternly
conform your life to the dictates of lofty sentiment, that you should be what you admire.
But you say, Nobody can; nobody will estimate me. Very likely, but that is exactly the
scope and occasion of great sentiments, to
prompt right against the voice, it may be, of

the whole world. Every popinjay blows with the wind. The thunder cloud sails against it. . . . Men take counsel in moments of peril of the deceptive face of things and not from themselves. Always listen to yourself, never be tempted to a word of vanity or of pride; persist in the old vulgar road of benevolence: make his good with whom you deal a real omnipresent motive, whilst and whenever you deal with him. Persist, only persist in seeking the truth. Persist in saying you do not know what you do not know, and you do not care for what you do not care. . . .

May 18, 1831.

Went to-night to the Sunday School meeting, but was myself a dumb dog that could not bark. Question was whether the instruction at Sunday School should be exclusively religious. I should have said that in God's goodness this instruction blessed twice, him that gives and him that takes. Teacher must consider it an institution whence he is to derive most essential benefit, and, in order to give and gain the most, he is to aim at the great end with his whole might. If he fill himself with an earnest love of God, all the rest shall be added unto him. The question will answer itself in his practice. It is well known that it is the property of the human mind, when strongly aroused by any sentiment, by any passion, by the love of any science or art, to give its whole knowledge and powers the new force of an arrangement after that principle. And then it acts with as much more efficiency than before, as an organized army acts than a great mob. Whatever passion, whatever love, arrives at a certain heat in a mind, melts away all resistance, fuses all its knowledge, turns everything like fire to its own nature. The poet casts his eyes on no object, how mean soever, not on a tub or shoe, but it grows poetical in his eye. The whole world is a poem to him. The mathematician does not see the dome of a church, or the corner of a house or of a table, but it is a diagram to prove a truth in geometry. The mourner reads his loss in every utensil in his house, in every garment, in the face of every friend. Well now, let the Sunday School teacher dwell fervently alone on the great idea whose servants and worshippers we all are, let him be in heart and soul a worshipper of God, and he will find no need to prescribe rules to direct his instructions into one or another course. He will see the religious face of everything. He will draw precisely that tone and accord of thought he wants from things you would call common and unclean. He will do better than the fable told of the Lydian king whose touch turned everything to gold. He will show everything to be good and from God. But I see the meanness of this illustration : let me offer a better. He will be like the hand of Christ which touched the rolling eyeball, and it saw, which touched the paralytic and he was made whole; yea, and was laid upon dead bones and they started up again into human life, and praised God. He will be a freeman whom the truth has made free, and will put the whole compass of all his reading and all his experience under contribution to convey proofs of God's being and Providence into the mind of his pupil. Nobody doubts, I suppose, that this can be done. Every chip and sea weed contributes its part to the gravity of the system, and every object in the universe, every truth bears testimony to God.

May 20.

Blind men in Rome complained that the streets were dark. To the dull mind all nature is leaden. To the illuminated mind the whole world burns and sparkles with light. You read a poor essayist and you feel humiliated at the poverty of human wit; a few oft repeated saws seem to be all it has attained. You read Burton, or Montaigne, or Sir Thomas Browne — you read Bacon, and you are in wonder at the profusion of wise observations which they seem to have barrelled up from the vast common-places of mankind. The more a man knows, he is the more prepared scholar. The magazine shows more inexhaustible, and the particulars of greater price every moment. Every weed, every atom, discloses its relations. *Mens agitat molem.* "To virtue every day is bright, and every hour propitious to diligence"; and that is the virtue of increased intelligence that it imparts worth to what was counted worthless. The progress of manufactures finds a yellow dye in a crumbling rubbish stone; plants a thistle for its teazel; plucks a whortleberry bush for unwinding silk; saves the coke after the coal is burned, and saves the ashes after the coke is consumed; and so works up into its processes the refuse and dung of the world with the frugality of nature herself.

Mens agitat molem. The whole is instinct with life.

WRITTEN AT WILLIAMSTOWN, VERMONT

June 1, 1831

Why fear to die
And let thy body lie
Under the flowers of June,
 Thy body food
 For the ground worm's brood,
And thy grave smiled on by the visiting
  moon?

Amid great Nature's halls,
Girt in by mountain walls
And washed with waterfalls,
It would please me to die,
 Where every wind that swept my tomb
 Goes loaded with a free perfume
Dealt out with a God's charity.

I should like to lie in sweets,
A hill's leaves for winding-sheets,
And the searching sun to see
That I am laid with decency,
And the commissioned wind to sing
His mighty psalms from fall to spring,
And annual tunes commemorate
Of Nature's child the common fate.

ELLEN

Dust unto dust! and shall no more be said,
Ellen, for thee, and shall a common fate
Blend thy last hour with the last hours of all?
Of thee, my wife, my undefiled, my dear?
The muse thy living beauty could inspire
Shall spare one verse to strew thy urn
Or be forever silent. Ellen is dead,
She who outshone all beauty, yet knew not
That she was beautiful, she who was fair
After another mould than flesh and blood.
Her beauty was of God. The maker's hand
Yet rested on its work,
And cast an atmosphere of sanctity
Around her steps that pleased old age and youth;
Yea, that not won the eye, but did persuade
The soul by realizing human hopes,
Teaching that faith and love were not a dream,
Teaching that purity had yet a shrine,
And that the innocent and affectionate thoughts
That harbour in the bosom of a child
Might live embodied in a riper form,
And dwell with wisdom never bought by sin.
Blessed, sweet singer, were the ears that heard;
To her the eye that saw bare witness . . .

June 15.

After a fortnight's wandering to the Green
Mountains and Lake Champlain, yet finding

you, dear Ellen, nowhere and yet everywhere, I come again to my own place, and would willingly transfer some of the pictures that the eyes saw, in living language to my page ; yea, translate the fair and magnificent symbols into their own sentiments. But this were to antedate knowledge. It grows into us, say rather, we *grow wise*, and not take wisdom ; and only in God's own order, and by my concurrent effort, can I get the abstract sense of which mountains, sunshine, thunders, night, birds and flowers are the sublime alphabet.

June 20.

I suppose it is not wise, not being natural, to belong to any religious party. In the Bible you are not directed to be a Unitarian, or a Calvinist or an Episcopalian. Now if a man is wise, he will not only not profess himself to be a Unitarian, but he will say to himself, I am not a member of that or of any party. I am God's child, a disciple of Christ, or, in the eye of God, a fellow disciple with Christ. Now let a man get into a stage-coach with this distinct understanding of himself, divorcing himself in his heart from every party, and let him meet with religious men of every different sect, and he will find scarce any proposition uttered by them to which he does not assent, and none to the sentiment of which he does not assent, though he may insist on varying the language. As fast as any man becomes great, that is, thinks, he becomes a new party. Socrates, Aristotle, Calvin, Luther, Abelard, what are these but names of parties? Which is to say, As fast as we use our own eyes, we quit these parties or Unthinking Corporations, and join ourselves to God in an unpartaken relation.

A sect or party is an elegant incognito devised to save a man from the vexation of thinking.

Since to govern my passions with absolute sway is the work I have to do, I cannot but think that the sect for the suppression of Intemperance, or a sect for the suppression of loose behaviour to women, would be a more reasonable and useful society than the Orthodox sect, which is a society for the suppression of Unitarianism, or the Unitarian, which is a society for the diffusion of useful knowledge.

Religion is the relation of the soul to God, and therefore the progress of Sectarianism marks the decline of religion. For, looking at God instantly reduces our disposition to dissent from our brother. A man may die by a fever as well as by consumption, and religion is as effectually destroyed by bigotry as by indifference.

The best part of wisdom can never be communicated, as "books never can teach the use of books." And as Bacon said, "the best part of beauty could not be represented in a picture."

To a philosophical infidel the writings of Thomas à Kempis, of Fénelon, of Scougal, should be shown. For the fact that such a new science as this they treat, has been drawn out of the New Testament, — the creation of such a theory as the mind of Thomas à Kempis [evolved] in its very nature claiming authority over all other principles — is a mighty evidence for the divine authority of Scripture.

Wherever goes a man, there goes a great soul. I never more fully possess myself than in slovenly or disagreeable circumstances. When I stamp through the mud in dirty boots, I hug myself with the feeling of my immortality.[1] I then reflect complacently on whatever delicacy is in my taste, of amplitude in my memory. In a university I draw in my horns. On nothing

1 The image was borrowed from Mme. de Staël, quoted by Mr. Emerson in the beginning of the chapter "Literature" in *English Traits*: "I tramp in the mire with wooden shoes whenever they would force me into the clouds."

does a wise man plume himself so much as on independence of circumstances; that in a kitchen, or dirty street, or sweltering stage-coach, he can separate himself from impure contact and em-bosom himself in the sublime society of his recollections, of his hopes and of his affections. Ambassador carries his country with him. So does the mind.

> The days pass over me
> And I am still the same;
> The aroma of my life is gone
> Like the flower with which it came.

FROM BLOTTING BOOK III

June, 1831

Si cum natura sapio et sub Numine,
Id vere plusquam satis est.

GIORDANO BRUNO.

" Our first and third thoughts coincide."
STEWART.

" We know the arduous strife, the eternal laws
To which the triumph of all good is given,
High sacrifice and labour without pause
Even to the death, else wherefore should the eye
Of man converse with immortality?"

WORDSWORTH.

CHARDON ST. [BOSTON], *June* 29, 1831.

Is not the law of compensation perfect? It holds as far as we can see. Different gifts to different individuals, but with a mortgage of responsibility on every one. " The gods *sell* all things." Well, old man, hast got no farther? Why, this was taught thee months and years ago. It was writ on the autumn leaves at Roxbury in keep-school days; it sounded in the blind man's ear at Cambridge.[1] And all the joy and all the sorrow since have added nothing to thy wooden book. I can't help it. Heraclitus grown old complained that all resolved itself into identity. That thought was first his philosophy, and then his melancholy, — the life he lived and the death he died. And I have nothing charactered in my brain that outlives this word Compensation. Old Stubler, the Quaker in the Baltimore steamboat, said to me, that, if a man sacrificed his impurity, purity should be the price with which it would be paid; if a man gave up his hatred, he should be rewarded with love — 't is the same old melody and it sounds through the vast of being. Is it a great

[1] Referring to the failure of his eyes (perhaps *iritis*) with that of his general health, in his damp room in Divinity Hall in 1825.

exertion to you to contain your roving eye, is it very easy to please it, and very hard to forbid it? Well, exactly proportionate is the merit of the self-denial and the power it confers. Is it a great estate that is within your grasp? Will a little servility, a few derelictions, not gross themselves, and such as few can know, suffice to give you an easy subsistence for many years, and do you say it were foolhardy to toss your head with unseasonable virtue that perhaps you will not sustain, and lose the prize? But will you gain nothing by the loss? Consider it well; there's no cheating in nature, not a light halfpenny; not a risk of a doit which is not insured to the total amount on the credit of the king of nature. By that sacrifice of body to soul, of the apparent to the real, have you not given body and fact to a sentiment, which, if it is not recognized on 'Change, is sterling with God and his creation? Have you not been filled, spiritualized, exalted by a delicate, rare magnanimity which constitutes you a nobleman in the kingdom of heaven? Have you not given firmness to your brow, an unquestionable majesty to your eye when you meet other eyes, a serenity to your solitude, — yea, just so much of assured presence of God to your soul? 'T is a noble but a true word of Bacon, — " If once the mind has chosen noble ends, then not virtues but Divinities encompass it — *Si animus semel generosos fines optaverit, statim non modo virtutes circumstant, sed et Numina.*" [1] And so it is, these sentiments are the true native angels of the kingdom, having their lineage written on their faces. The adoption in act of a great sentiment gives you assurance on the faith of *Him that liveth* that you have made exactly that progress which you seem to have made ; but my riches add nothing to me. They make no evidence, but only bewilder my inquiries for truth. In the most barren, echoing solitude, in small, disagreeable circumstances, these thoughts give a ground of assurance most solid. In a hovel, low born and fed on husks, you may think thoughts and act after a manner that you are sure is qualifying you every day for the most exalted enjoyments of *friendship*, though the word may be gibberish or a laughing-stock in that place.

---

1 Probably the correct version is that which occurs a few pages later in this journal: *Animum qui generosos fines semel optaverit, non virtutes solum, sed Numina circumstant.*

> The man who seeks a noble end
> Not angels, but divinities, attend.

See *Poems*, Centenary Ed., Appendix.

The friends exist, and the sympathy is forming, though perhaps years or ages may intervene before the good effects you seek on God's faith shall be fully accomplished, before this union takes place.

What matters it to the mind, as far as concerns the evidence, how one or another fact looks, what may be the aspect of things toward materialism, what may be the impression got from Geology, or the *conatus*, or equivocal generation, or any other humbug? Does not every consciousness contain its own evidence? That consciousness which "cannot ferment its mass of clay," that apprehends death, will die. That which looks death in the face, the master, not the slave, carries therein its own hope and assurance. Now my affections prophesy to me out of heaven, where my angel is, and when I listen to them I do not fear death. I see plainly that the ends to which I live are independent of time and place; and neither the hope nor the fear of conscience profess themselves satisfied with the scanty inches of mortal life.

June 30.

One thought more has occurred to me (if there is no logic by which these thoughts cohere, the mind itself uttering necessary truth must be their *vinculum*), and that is, that God makes us the answerers of our own prayers and so fulfils the cycle and perfection of things, and, as in others, so in the prayer, to be immortal : . . .

IMPERAT PARENDO

Obedience is the eye which reads the laws of the universe. Rejoice when you have not bent your desires to your convenience, but have rested in no good below the level of your desires. Use locks to ascend streams, but never to descend. Go buoyed up as high as sentiments of heaven will, and do not huckster with sense and custom, but treat with princes only, — a sovereign with a sovereign.

July 5.

It is remarkable that we cannot be willing to say, *I do not know.* I am ashamed of my ignorance of history, of science, of languages, daily. "All error," Dr. Johnson said, "is mean." And by this powerful shame doth God wonderfully indicate to us his intention that we should study and learn without end.

July 6, 1831.

All the great and good
And all the fair,
As if in a disdainful mood
Forsake the world, and to the grave repair.

Is there a sage
Needed to curb the unruly times, —
He hastes to quit the stage
And blushing leaves his country to its crimes.

Is there an angel, drest
In weeds of mortal beauty, whom lavish Heaven
With all sweet perfections doth invest, —
It hastes to take what it hath given.

And as the delicate snow
That latest fell, the thieving wind first takes,
So thou, dear wife, must go
As frail, as spotless as those new-fall'n flakes.

Let me not fear to die,
But let me live so well
As to win this mark of death from on high,
That I with God, and thee, dear heart, may dwell.

I write the things that are
Not what appears;

Of things as they are in the eye of God
    Not in the eye of man.

Γνῶθι Σεαυτόν

If thou canst bear
Strong meat of simple truth,
If thou durst my words compare
With what thou thinkest in the soul's free
        youth,
Then take this fact unto thy soul, —
God dwells in thee.
It is no metaphor nor parable,
It is unknown to thousands, and to thee;
Yet there is God.

He is in thy world,
But thy world knows him not.
He is the mighty Heart
From which life's varied pulses part.
Clouded and shrouded there doth sit
The Infinite
Embosomed in a man;
And thou art stranger to thy guest,
And know'st not what thou dost invest.
The clouds that veil his life within
Are thy thick woven webs of sin,
Which his glory struggling through
Darkens to thine evil hue.

Then bear thyself, O man!
Up to the scale and compass of thy guest;
Soul of thy soul.
Be great as doth beseem
The ambassador who bears
The royal presence where he goes.

Give up to thy soul —
Let it have its way —
It is, I tell thee, God himself,
The selfsame One that rules the Whole,
Tho' he speaks thro' thee with a stifled voice,
And looks through thee, shorn of his beams.
But if thou listen to his voice,
If thou obey the royal thought,
It will grow clearer to thine ear,
More glorious to thine eye.
The clouds will burst that veil him now
And thou shalt see the Lord.

Therefore be great,
Not proud, — too great to be proud.
Let not thine eyes rove,
Peep not in corners; let thine eyes
Look straight before thee, as befits
The simplicity of Power.
And in thy closet carry state;
Filled with light, walk therein;
And, as a king

Would do no treason to his own empire,
So do not thou to thine.

This is the reason why thou dost recognize
Things now first revealed,
Because in thee resides
The Spirit that lives in all;
And thou canst learn the laws of nature
Because its author is latent in thy breast.

Therefore, O happy youth,
Happy if thou dost know and love this truth,
Thou art unto thyself a law,
And since the soul of things is in thee,
Thou needest nothing out of thee.
The law, the gospel, and the Providence,
Heaven, Hell, the Judgment, and the stores
Immeasureable of Truth and Good,
All these thou must find
Within thy single mind,
Or never find.

Thou art the *law*;
The *gospel* has no revelation
Of peace or hope until there is response
From the deep chambers of thy mind thereto, —
The rest is straw.
It can reveal no truth unknown before.
The *Providence*

Thou art thyself that doth dispense
Wealth to thy work, want to thy sloth,
Glory to goodness, to neglect, the moth.
Thou sow'st the wind, the whirlwind reapest,
Thou payest the wages
Of thy own work, through all ages.
The almighty energy within
Crowneth virtue, curseth sin.
Virtue sees by its own light;
Stumbleth sin in self-made night.

Who approves thee doing right?
God in thee.
Who condemns thee doing wrong?
God in thee.
Who punishes thine evil deed?
God in thee.
What is thine evil need?
Thy worse mind, with error blind
And more prone to evil
That is, the greater hiding of the God within,

.　　.　　.　　.　　.　　.　　.　　.

And next, the consequence
More faintly, as more distant, wrought
Upon our outward fortunes.

.　　.　　.　　.　　.　　.　　.

There is nothing else but God.
Where'er I look

All things hasten back to him
Light is but his shadow dim.

Shall I ask wealth or power of God, who gave
An image of himself to be my soul?
As well might swilling ocean ask a wave,
Or the starred firmament a dying coal,—
For that which is in me lives in the whole.

July 6, 1831.

President Monroe died on the fourth of
July,—a respectable man, I believe.

RELATION OF MORALS TO INTELLECT

Shaftesbury's maxim, That wisdom comes
more from the heart than the head. "Do
the will, know the doctrines." *Impera parendo.*
Obedience is the eye which reads the laws of
the universe. For the moral sense is the proper
keeper of the doors of knowledge; whom he
will he lets in, and whom he will he shuts out.
A polemic, a partizan, for want of a candid
heart becomes miserably ignorant of the *whole*
question.

The point of view is of more importance
than the sharpness of sight. Fénelon anticipated
Adam Smith. . . . The eye, too near, turns the
fairest proportions of architecture or of sculp-

ture into deformity. Now goodness is the right *place* of the mind.

Make known the law and you can dispense with collecting the particular instances. Kepler's second (?) law was seen at once to contain, and so make useless and ridiculous, all the tables that were made or could be made of falling bodies.

[ADVANTAGE OF THE NINETEENTH CENTURY]

I pay twenty or thirty dollars to the Government of my Country a year. If I had lived before it was discovered that we could do without a court, I should have paid twice as much, and been otherwise troubled. If I had lived earlier, before some moral discoveries were made, I could not have sustained the independent fashion of living I do for less than the support of a garrison of guards. For, plain gentleman as I am, and living no better than a thousand persons in this city, I do believe I live better than any person, not a gentleman or knight, in eleventh, twelfth or thirteenth centuries. If I had lived earlier, I must have been my own guard, and that duty would have taken up all my time, and left me none for speculation, i. e., I should have been a savage. See then what discoveries moral progress has made. . . .

THE RIGHT WORD

July 8.

No man can write well who thinks there is any choice of words for him. The laws of composition are as strict as those of sculpture and architecture. There is always one line that ought to be drawn, or one proportion that should be kept, and every other line or proportion is wrong, and so far wrong as it deviates from this. So in writing, there is always a right word, and every other than that is wrong. There is no beauty in words except in their collocation. The effect of a fanciful word misplaced, is like that of a horn of exquisite polish growing on a human head.

To the same purpose I find at this date in Guesses at Truth, — "In good prose, (says Schlegel) every word should be underlined": "no italics in Plato." In good writing, every word means something. In good writing, words become one with things. I take up a poem; if I find that there is not a single line there nor word but expresses something that is true for me as well as for him . . . it is adamant. Its reputation will be slow, but sure from every caprice of taste. No critic can hurt it, he will only hurt himself by tilting against it. This is the confidence we feel concerning Shakspeare. We know, Charles says, "that his record is true." And this is the ordeal which the new aspirant Wordsworth must undergo. He has writ lines that are like outward nature, so fresh, so simple, so durable; but whether all or half his texture is as firm I doubt, though last evening (27 Oct.) I read with high delight his Sonnets to Liberty.[1]

July 10.

Old English writers are the standards, not because they are old, but simply because they wrote well. They deviated every day from other people, but never from truth, and so we follow them. If we write as well, we may deviate from them and our deviations shall be classical.

"HE INVENTS WHO PROVES"

Every man says a hundred things every day that are capable of much more meaning than he attaches to them. The Declaration of Independence, as Webster intimates, deserves its fame, though every sentence had been somewhere said before. That gave it *flesh* and flower. Not that man is the abolisher of Slavery or Intemperance who calls them evils, but he whose dis-

1 This last clause evidently was written in later.

cerning eye separates between the existence of
society, and these evils, and sees that these may
peel off and the institutions remain whole.

[SOLITUDE OF THE SOUL]

July 14.

One of the arguments with which nature furnishes us for the Immortality of the Soul is, it
always seemed to me, the awful solitude in which
here a soul lives. Few men communicate their
highest thoughts to any person. To many they
cannot, for they are unfit receivers. Perhaps
they cannot to any. Yet are these thoughts as
much made for communication as a sex. Ellen
wondered why dearest friends, even husband
and wife, did so little impart their religious
thoughts. And how rarely do such friends
meet. Here I sit alone from month to month
filled with a deep desire to exchange thoughts
with a friend who does not appear. Yet shall I
find, or refind, that friend. Sampson goes about,
yet never speaks what his soul is full of. Barnes
also; Mrs. Lee; Motte; S. A. R.[1] They can-

1 George Sampson, his young parishioner, a valued friend,
died soon after this time; Barnes and Mrs. Lee were probably friends in his parish. The Rev. Mellish Irving Motte was
a classmate. S. A. R. was Sarah Alden, the wife of his Uncle
Ripley, a remarkable woman, and a dear friend through life.

not discharge this subtle electricity for defect of medium or of receiver.

But was this glorious fabric made for nothing? Will not its day and means and object come? Will not Heaven's matches be made or restored?

July 15.

Nothing more true than the saying, "spiritual things must be spiritually discerned."

God in us worships God.

The things taught in colleges and schools are not an education, but the means of education.

Fable that Love and Death exchanged arrows by mistake.

PHI BETA KAPPA DAY

July 21, 1831.

The feast is pleasant, but its joys have no after life, and seem to be a subtraction from our mortal work-day of so much. Why not follow out the great idolatry, no, the great *penchant*, of the human mind for friendship? Is it not beautiful, this yearning after its mate — its mate, I mean, by spiritual affinities, and not by sex. I never hear of a person of noble feelings but I have the emotion of the *moral sublime*, such as is caused by reading Young's line,

> " Forgive his crimes — forgive his virtues too,
> Those minor faults, half converts to the right,"

or Shakspeare's " *The more angel she*," [1] which Coleridge quotes, — or Bacon's sentence, — *Animum qui generosos fines semel optaverit, non virtutes solum sed et Numina circumstant.* Εἶς οἰωνὸς ἄριστος, *etc.*[2] I put together these with pleasure as two or three specimens of that peculiar and beautiful class of thoughts which set you aglow. *Non verba sed tonitrua audio.* Well, just such a feeling I have in hearing of C. G. L's or J. A's,[3] or anybody else's noble sentiments.

Now if surely I knew there was a mind somewhere thinking and willing, that is a repository of these sentiments, a hive of chosen knowledge, a knower and lover of the golden laws of the intellect and the heart; and that in future I am to

[1] Othello, after smothering Desdemona, says to her waiting-woman, " You heard her say herself it was not I," to which Emilia answers, " O, the more angel she, and you the blacker devil ! "

[2] Hector's speech, " One omen is ever good, — to defend one's country."

[3] Charles Greeley Loring, and John Adams.

meet this mind in connexions of most cheerful and close fellowship, should not I be glad? Yes, indeed: the rainbow, the evening star, day, night, storm, sorrow, death, they would seem preparations, they would seem subjects for this delicious conversation. When I think of you, sweet friend, wife, angel Ellen, on whom the spirit of knowledge and the spirit of hope were poured in equal fulness, when I think of you, I am sure we have not said everlasting farewells.

The impulses of a heart of faultless sentiments would be as much an object of exact calculation as the effects of caloric or azote.

How very thin are the disguises of action! These men that came to-day to Φ B K, came with their purposes writ as legibly on every proposition as if they had said, "I wish an audience when I hold forth"; another, "I hate Everett"; another, "I am an anti-mason"; another, "I love young men"; another, "Truth.". . .

A rich man may lawfully have handsome house and furniture. He is doing better with his money for the world than if he gave it to the beggar. But he must adorn his house with the principle of *love* running through every detail.

" 'Tis use alone which sanctifies expense
  And splendour borrows all its rays from sense."

All possessions that end in self are odious. The
man who shuts himself up in solitary splendour
hath much of the devil in him. . . . Books are
to be read, and every library should be a circu-
lating library. Pictures are to be seen, and are
as if they were not, when unseen, and palaces
have no other use. . . .

[THE REAL POWER]

 . . . Most kings and presidents by title are
merely clerks of some real power which stands
erect at their side and subjugates them. Cromwell and Buonaparte are men in my mind far
more respectable than James I. of England or
George IV. For if they used hypocrisy to rise
by, they rose more by the energy of their own
will, and though thoroughly selfish they scorned
a servile selfishness, — they took off the slave's
cloak when they had got up and tossed it down
in the face of all the mob below. They kicked
the ladder down, crush whom it might. Whilst
these other gentlemen (and wo is me, my Country, many great gentlemen in thy chairs) sit with
it on. If I want a favour of the President of the
United States I need not cultivate his personal

kindness, I will ask it of his President, the bad party in the country, and if they say yea, I shall be sure of Mr. Jackson's bow and smile and sign manual. Whilst I admire Cromwell and Buonaparte, however, for the simplicity and energy of their evil, I lose my reverence the moment I consider their ends. I see they were both wholly mistaken, blind as beetles, . . .

Power is a trust. So also is genius or every degree of wisdom.

Dined with President Adams yesterday at Dr. Parkman's.

[GOD MISREPRESENTED]

Mr. —— said to a woman doubting, — " Do you not fear God? Does not the feeling that your whole future destinies for happiness or misery are in his hands terrify you?" She said, " No, she wished it did." The question was false theology. It does not recognize an immutable God. It was for the woman to become happy or miserable, not for God to make her so.

[GOD'S DOOR]

July 29, 1831.

Suicidal is this distrust of reason; this fear to think; this doctrine that 't is pious to believe on other's words, impious to trust entirely to yourself. To think is to receive. Is a man afraid that the faculties which God made can outsee God, can find more than he made, or different, can bring any report hostile to himself? To reflect is to receive truth immediately from God without any medium. That is living faith. To take on trust certain facts is a dead faith, inoperative. A trust in yourself is the height, not of pride, but of piety, an unwillingness to learn of any but God himself. It will come only to one who feels that he is nothing. It is by yourself without ambassador that God speaks to you. You are as one who has a private door that leads him to the king's chamber. You have learned nothing rightly that *you* have not learned so.

God does not use personal authority. It is the direct effect of all spiritual truth to abrogate, nullify, personal authority, — to make us love the virtue and the person exactly by the measure of his virtues, but not to honour the inherent evils for the sake of any person. He is no respecter of *persons*. And that is the wrong whereby theology has injured Jesus Christ, insisting upon a love to him as a duty. Nobody will ever be loved by compulsion. Love is the reward of loveliness. Tell not me to love my saviour. No, do him not that injustice. But fill me with his goodness and I shall love him, of course. Make me as pure, as meek, as useful, and I shall love him as certainly as a stone falls.

"The progress of custom (*consuetudo*) is arithmetical, of Nature, geometrical."   BACON.

"We think after nature; we speak after rules; we act after custom."   BACON.

"Manifest merits procure reputation, occult ones, fortune."   BACON.

August 15.

The world becomes transparent to wisdom. Everything reveals its reason within itself. The threads of innumerable relations are seen running from part to part and joining remotest points of time and space.

I read verses to-day of Thomas Campbell about the Poles, which are alive. Most of the "Pleasures of Hope" has no life: dead verses.

August 16.

Every composition in prose or verse should contain in itself the reason of its appearance. Thousands of volumes have been written and mould in libraries of which this reason is yet to seek, does not appear. Then comes Adam Smith, Bacon, Burke, Milton; then comes any good sentence, and its apology is its own worth. It makes its pertinence.

[MAN'S REPUTATION]

There is an engine at Waltham to watch the watchmen of the factory. Every hour they must put a ring on to the wheel, or if they fall asleep and do not, the machine will show their neglect and which hour they slept. Such a machine is every man's Reputation.

[THE YOUNGER ADAMS]

August 26.

Yesterday I heard John Quincy Adams deliver an eulogy upon President Monroe. But he held his notes so close to his mouth that he could be ill heard. There was nothing heroic in the subject, and not much in the feelings of the orator, so it proved rather a spectacle than a speech.

September 7.

I think it better to drink water than cider or ale. I think two cups of tea better than three. *Tentandum est.*

[SILENCE. SPEECH. POVERTY]

Loquendi magistros habemus homines, tacendi Deos, apud Jeremy Taylor. And Plutarch said excellently, *Qui generose et regio more instituuntur, primum tacere, deinde loqui discunt.* ("To be taught first to be silent, then to speak well and handsomely, is education fit for a prince.")

Nil habet infelix paupertas durius in se quam quod ridiculos homines facit.

EDUCATION

September 13, 1831.

The things which are taught children are not an education, but the means of education. The grammar and geography and writing do not train up the child in the way it should go, but may be used in the service of the devil.

Education is the drawing out the soul.

[EQUANIMITY]

September 14.

Mr. Walker[1] said in conversation that the information that death must probably take place soon, commonly gave steadiness to the mind and enabled it to do what was fit with more ability. The mind, he said, never plays false. It is always equal to all it is called to meet.

[WHO KNOWETH?]

The first questions still remain to be asked after all the progress of science. What an abyss is my ignorance.

SUNDAY SCHOOLS

September 14, 1831.

Robert Raikes and Mrs. Catherine Cappe the founders of Sunday Schools fifty years ago; Mrs. C. a little the first. Raikes saw the word TRY, as it were, written before him. Now 2,000,000 children attend them, in four continents.

EVERYMAN'S GAUGE

I suppose a skilful judge of character would get some measure of the whole from the smallest actions and from trifling conversation. All would

1 Rev. James Walker, later, President of Harvard College.

be arcs, however small, of the same circle, and from them the whole circumference might be drawn. The swing of his arm, however free and violent, is determined mathematically by the length of the bones. Every motion bears some proportion to the fixed size and form of his whole frame, and so the measure of his mind determines as accurately every word he utters.

MIRACLES

It is impossible that omnipotence should make a ball pass from one point to another point without passing through a space equal to the straight line betwixt them. This necessity the mind perceives. Does not the same necessity make Leibnitz's law of continuity manifest? If we knew more of matter, would not this absurdity strike us as lying against miracles? I think it would in the common understanding of them. Let then a miracle be the effect of far greater knowledge of the laws of nature and so a superior command of nature. *Imperat parendo.*

COMPENSATION

Is it not one of the most thrilling truths of moral science that I write below? The savage of the Sandwich Islands believes that whenever he overcomes and slays an enemy, the strength and prowess of that enemy passes into him.[1] The soul instructed by God, knows, that whenever it overcomes a temptation, it becomes stronger by the strength of that temptation. But for heaven's sake do not (to use the vulgar expression) "treat" your resolution. *Haec est mors mea.*

It is my opinion that, because of the law "that every truth you receive prepares the mind for the reception of unknown truth,"[2] . . .

RHETORIC

September 15.

I often make the criticism on my friend Herbert's diction, that his thought has that heat as actually to fuse the words, so that language is wholly flexible in his hands and his rhyme never stops the progress of the sense. And, in general, according to the elevation of the soul wil' the power over language always be, and lively thoughts will break out into spritely verse. No measure so difficult but will be tractable, so

---

1 This image occurs in "Compensation," in *Essays I.*

2 Here follows in the Journal the passage on the inability of a teacher to hide his own view, printed in "Spiritual Laws," *Essays I*, Centenary Ed., p. 146.

that you only get up the temperature of the thought.

To this point I quote gladly my old gossip Montaigne; "For my part I hold, and Socrates is positive in it, that whoever has in his mind a spritely and clear imagination, he will express it well enough in one kind or another, and, though he were dumb, by sighs."

Verbaque praevisam rem non invita sequentur.

HORACE.

And again Seneca, *Cum res animum occupavere, verba ambiunt.*

And Cicero, *Ipsa res verba rapiunt.*

" Oh how that *name* inspired my style!
The words come skelpin rank and file
Amaist before I ken ! "

BURNS.

I am glad to have these learned Thebans confirm my very thought.

September 21.

Pestalozzi, a venerable name, after witnessing the events of the French Revolution, concluded in 1797, " That the amelioration of outward circumstances will be the effect, but never can be the means of mental and moral improvement," a paralogism to the old words, " Seek ye first the kingdom of God and his righteousness, and all these things shall be added unto you."

[THE LAW INFINITE]

CHARDON ST., *September* 30, 1831.

Pleasant it is to the soul, painful it is to the conscience, to recognize wherever you go the fixed eternity of moral laws. You cannot be too kind, you cannot be too just. There is no excess of observance: be kind in the stage, be kind in the pew, keep your word, be kind in a quarrel. Bear yourself so on all occasions, saith one, that the opposer may beware of thee. Jesus says, so bear yourself as if your trade and business was to serve that man. Don't lose this principle a moment. And your character will be its commentary and exposition. . . . .

> A dull uncertain brain,
> But gifted yet to know
> That God has seraphim who go
> Singing an immortal strain,
> Immortal here below.
> I know the mighty bards,
> I listen when they sing ;
> And more I know
> The secret store
> Which these explore
> When they with torch of genius pierce

The tenfold clouds that cover
The riches of the Universe
From God's adoring lover.
And if to me it is not given
To bring one ingot thence
Of that unfading gold of heaven
His merchants may dispense,
Yet well I know the royal mine,
And know the sparkle of its ore,
Celestial truths from lies that shine [1] —
Explored they teach us to explore.

[NON-RESISTANCE]

October 3.

I wish the Christian principle, the *ultra* principle of non-resistance and returning good for ill, might be tried fairly. William Penn made one trial. The world was not ripe, and yet it did well. An angel stands a poor chance among wild beasts; a better chance among men : but among angels best of all. And so I admit of this system that it is, like the Free Trade, fit for one nation only on condition that all adopt it. Still a man may try it in his own person,

---

[1] A later version printed in the Appendix to the *Poems* gives this line better : —

Know Heaven's truth from lies that shine.

and even his sufferings by reason of it shall be its triumphs. "The more falls it gets, moves faster on." Love is the adamantean shield that makes blows ridiculous. If Edward Everett were a sanguine philanthropist, not a shade would attach to his name from the insults of Platt; but he is thought a selfish man, so by his own law must he be judged ; the Mussulman by the Koran ; the Jew by the Pentateuch.

One thing more; it is said that it strips the good man bare and leaves him to the whip and license of pirates and butchers. But I suppose the exaltation of the general mind by the influence of the principle will be a counteraction of the increased license. Not any influence acts upon the highest man but a proportion of the same gets down to the lowest man. Signboards speak of Titian ; a regular ladder of communicating minds from Webster down to Joe Cash.

CREEDS

People would teach me what they think concerning modes of Justification, and how their supposed offices of Christ are compatible with the Father's dignity, etc. Will they teach me how to resist my temptations ? Will they teach me how to be a good man ? I have nothing to do with their creeds. It is more than I can do now to keep the commandments. Yet they want more than these. I can't keep these. Can they? do they? I think they have no idea how much is contained in them. Yea, Calvinism lays the salve to this very sore, and says, Because you can't keep them, here is Blood to expiate; only give your assent; and it produces no higher level of obedience in the multitude than in the professors of another faith. " All that is simple is enough for all that's good." Don't meddle with others, nor with high beliefs, but strictly keep your own soul. Try to keep the ten commandments a day. You will find they mean enough literally. Well, then take them with the New Testament exposition and keep them from the heart.

BOSTON, *October* 21, 1831.

People . . . talk with a sneer of those who comfort themselves for the evils of life by an imaginary heaven; and they rightly ridicule them who thus do. But Christians do it not. Their heaven is prophesied in their virtuous purpose, and begins in their first deliberate virtuous action, and is established in their virtuous habit. It is not a false or imaginary heaven; . . . Every man, as far as his virtue goes, says it is good; he cleaves to it amidst his wickedness, blasphemy, scoffing and stupidity. He gets credit for it, he loves it, he does not abhor himself because of it, — of this grain of antidote to his evils. Take it out and he would hang himself. . . .

Is it not good to have right opinions; to understand one's self; to know what is and what is not? Men think that instead they are to take religious truth on trust. Impossible; not on the word of God himself. Truth is never crammed down your throat, but is to be understood. Have you not guarantee enough in your own constitution for the discretion of God? . . . Well, this is a part of heaven: to know as we are known, to see what is now hid, to have every secret thing work out its full effect.

" He that made the heart, shall not he understand? "

[LIGHT FROM WITHIN]

Boston, *October* 24, 1831.

" Admiration ennobles and blesses those who feel it. The lover is made happier by his love than his mistress can be. Like the song of the bird, it cheers his own heart. Why are we commanded to give glory to God unless that we ourselves may be made godly."

Guesses at Truth (vol. II, p. 115).

"Glory is a light that shines from us on others and not from others on us."   Landor.
See Quincy's Definition.

"Some minds think about things; others think the things themselves."   Schelling.

Augur cum esset Cato, dicere ausus est, optimis auspiciis ea geri, quae pro reipublicae salute gererentur; quae contra rempublicam ferrentur, contra auspicia ferri.   Cicero, *De Senectute*, 4, 4.

Εἶς οἰωνὸς ἄριστος, etc. And it is like Webster's skill in law, who knows what it is (i. e., what it should be), and Story can tell the authorities.

SHAKSPEARE

[One] thing strikes me in the sonnets, which in their way seem as wonderful as the plays, and perhaps are even more valuable to the analysis of the genius of Shakspeare, and that is the assimilating power of passion that turns all things to its own nature. See sonnet, — "O never say that I was false of heart," etc. and sonnet "Since I left you mine eye is in my mind," or "From you have I been absent in the spring," or "What is your substance, whereof are you made?"

And then see the immortality of the human spirit in them, for who but an eternal creature could so think and express himself as in, " If my dear love were but the child of state," or " No Time," etc. And listen to the stern morality that seems to inform them all and to be present in the eye of the poet, even when contradicted in the expression: but present in spirit and letter in " The expense of spirit in a waste of shame," etc., or " Poor soul!" etc.

THEKLA'S SONG [1]

" The clouds are flying, the woods are sighing,
The maiden is walking the grassy shore,
And as the wave breaks, with might, with might,
She singeth aloud in the darksome night
But a tear is in her troubled eye.

" For the world feels cold, and the heart gets old,
And reflects the bright aspect of nature no more, —
Then take back thy child, Holy Virgin, to thee,
I have plucked the one blossom that hangs on earth's tree,
I have lived, I have loved, and die."

1 Translation from Schiller's *Wallenstein*, *Edinburgh Review*, Oct., 1830. See same number for Geological Article.

THE SOUL'S WORSHIP

October 27.

What we love that shall we seek. . . . The
heart is the sole world, the universe, and if its
wants are satisfied, there is no defect perceived.
But how little love is at the bottom of these
great religious shows; congregations and temples and sermons, — how much sham! Love
built them, to be sure. Yea, they were the
heart's work; but the fervent generation that
built them passed away, things went downward,
and the forms remain, but the soul is well nigh
gone. Calvinism stands, fear I, by pride and
ignorance; and Unitarianism, as a sect, stands
by the opposition of Calvinism. It is cold and
cheerless, the mere creature of the understanding, until controversy makes it warm with fire
got from below. But is there no difference in
the objects which the heart loves? Is there no
truth? Yes. And is there no power in truth to
commend itself? Yes. It alone can satisfy the
heart. Are we asking you to love God as if
there was any arbitrary burden from duty im-
posed, as if we said, Apart from your usual
loves come and cultivate this. It is sour, but it
must be done, for such is the hard law. — No;

THE SECOND CHURCH OF BOSTON

" Old North " in Hanover Street, where Emerson was Pastor

God forbid; we call you to that which all things call you unto with softest persuasion, to that which your whole Reason enjoins with absolute sovereignty. We call you to that which all the future shall teach far more forcibly and simply than we now. These things are true and real and grand and lovely and good.

Is it not all in us, how strangely! Look at this congregation of men;—the words might be spoken,—though now there be none here to speak them,—but the words might be said that would make them stagger and reel like a drunken man. Who doubts it? Were you ever instructed by a wise and eloquent man? Remember then, were not the words that made your blood run cold, that brought the blood to your cheeks, that made you tremble or delighted you,—did they not sound to you as old as yourself? Was it not truth that you knew before, or do you ever expect to be moved from the pulpit or from man by anything but plain truth? Never. It is God in you that responds to God without, or affirms his own words trembling on the lips of another.

November, 1831.

Have been at the Examination of Derry Academy, and had some sad, some pleasant thoughts.[1]

Is it not true that every man has before him in his mind room in one direction to which there is no bound, but in every other direction he runs against a wall in a short time? One course of thought, affection, action is for him — that is his *use*, as the new men say. Let me embark in political economy, in repartee, in fiction, in verse, in practical counsels (as here in the Derry case) and I am soon run aground; but let my bark head its own way toward the law of laws, toward the compensation or action and reaction of the moral universe, and I sweep serenely over God's depths in an infinite sea.

In an unknown wood the traveller gives the reins to his horse, seeks his safety in the instincts of the animal. Trust something to your instincts far more trustworthy. As there is always a subject for life, so there is always a subject for each hour, if only a man has wit enough

1 The occasion of Mr. Emerson's attending the Examination seems to have been that a young kinswoman of his wife, Elizabeth Tucker, lived there, and was one of the scholars. Next year he wrote her a letter of advice as to her reading.

to find what that is. I sit Friday night and note the first thought that rises. Presently another, presently five or six, — of all these I take the *mean*, as the subject for Saturday's sermon.

[WAIT]

November 4.

God is not in a hurry. Don't be impatient of riding in a stage coach and talking less religiously than the orthodox passenger, and wish yourself shown to them doing something, because you would act as a religious being, though it is not in you to talk after their manner. God will provide opportunities. Calmly wait. Now is an opportunity. You can't be true to their principles, but you can to yours now in sitting with them. Your understanding of religion is that it is doing right from a right motive. Stick to that mighty sense. Don't affect the use of an adverb or an epithet more than belongs to the feeling you have.

November 5, *Friday*.

As religious philosophy advances, men will cease to say "the Future State" and will say instead "the whole being." The aim of the wise man will always be to set his tune on such a key as can hold, to bring his life level with the laws of

the mind, not of the body, because those endure.
Third Sunday of December I exchange with Mr.
Barlow. Second Sunday of March Mr. Francis.

ROBERT BURNS

" But fare you weel, auld Nickie-ben !
O wad ye tak' a thought and men' !
Ye aiblins might — I dinna ken —
Still hae a stake.
I 'm wae to think upon yon den,
Ev'n for your sake ! "

If it be comical, yet it belongs to the moral
sublime.

" Thy tuneful flame still careful fan,
Preserve the dignity of man
With soul erect ;
And trust the Universal Plan
Will all protect."

He tells the mouse that he is his " fellow-mor-
tal." The whole mouse piece is capital and this
sublime : —

" Still thou art blest compared with me,
The present only toucheth thee,
But och ! I backward cast my ee
On prospects drear,
An' forward, tho' I canna see,
I guess and fear."

November 18.

As respite from the —— affair, read Wordsworth: *River Duddon; Ode to Duty; Rob Roy*,
excellent, much happier diction than ordinary.
The *Poet's Epitaph*, fine account of the Poet.

> " You must love him ere to you
> He will seem worthy of your love." . . .

But miserable is the last verse, and the intended thought poorly half-conveyed. But sublime is the severe, eternal strain called *Dion*.
What they say of *Laodamia* were better said of
this, i. e., about being read to heroes and demigods. Are not things eternal exactly in the proportion in which they enter inward into nature;
eternal according to their *in*ness?

> " For deathless powers to verse belong,
>   And they like demigods are strong
> On whom the muses smile."

WORDSWORTH.

So also such a line as this [in *Dion*] :

Intent to trace the ideal path of right
More fair than heaven's broad pathway paved with stars
Which Dion learned to measure with delight.

So excellent also is the piece called the *Happy
Warrior*. Come up, William Wordsworth, al-

most I can say Coleridge's compliment, *quem quoties lego, non verba mihi videor audire, sed tonitrua.* His noble distinction is that he seeks the truth and shuns with brave self-denial every image and word that is from the purpose, means to stick close to his own thought and give it in naked simplicity and so make it God's affair, not his own whether it shall succeed. But he fails of executing this purpose fifty times for the sorry purpose of making a rhyme in which he has no skill, or from imbecility of mind losing sight of his thought, or from self-surrender to custom in poetic diction (e. g., the inconsistency with his own principles in the two lines about the Cestus and Thunderer's eye, &c. vol. III, p. 27).

He calls his brother "a *silent* poet."

And almost every moral line in his book might be framed like a picture, or graven on a temple porch, and would gain instead of losing by being pondered.

November 19.

I apologized for his baby pieces to my mother by saying he was Agesilaus, who rode on a cane with his children. She said that *Agesilaus did not ride out of doors.*

November 21.

Spoke with Messrs. Baxter, Foster and Moore at the gate of Mayhew School. They all came into my study. Mr. Foster agreed to meet the committee at the school house at twelve o'clock, but did not appear. While the committee waited there, Mr. Allen came in to inform Mr. —— of the threats, etc. So it was agreed that I should request of the mayor a peace officer, which I did.

November 22.

Marriage of G. L. Emerson.

PRAYER

November 23, 1831.

In connexion with the great doctrines of Compensation or Reaction, we get the best insight into the theory of prayer. It teaches that prayer does not at all consist in words, but wholly is a state of mind. Consider it also in connexion with the doctrine that God is in the soul of man, and we shall make another step towards truth. For it is not to be expected that God should gratify any man in an unreasonable request, only because he asks it violently, but precisely in proportion as a man comes into conformity with God, he asks right things, or things which God wills, and which therefore are done. And when he is wholly godly, or the unfolding God within him has subdued all to himself, then he asks what God wills and nothing else, and all his prayers are granted. In this sense the promises of Christ to his disciples may be understood. Were they not rather admonitions that they should bind, or they should loose, as God would? And I easily believe that Elijah or Peter or John, uplifted in a rapture of devotion, thought with the mind of God for the moment and so the miracle was wrought.

Foede in hunc mundum intravi, anxie vixi, perturbatus egredior. Causa causarum miserere mei!
(Aristotle's reputed death speech.)

It is a curious compensation to be noticed of such as I, that those who talk when everybody else is silent are forced to be silent when everybody else talks.[1]

November 25.

Read Muller, vol. 1, with great pleasure.

1 Compare second verse of " Compensation," *Poems.*

sight. Ignorance is outward sight. The enter-
prising, shrewd, learned, scoffing Ignorant,

> "Whose mind is but the mind of his own eyes,
>   He is a slave."

So love of nature. The soul and the body of
things are harmonized; therefore, the deeper
one knoweth the soul, the more intense is the
love of outward nature in him.

December 10.

Write upon the coincidence of first and third
thoughts, and apply it to affairs; and to religion
and skepticism. I should like to know if any one
ever went up on a mountain so high as that he
overlooked right and wrong and saw them confounded, saw their streams mix, that justice did
not mean anything to his mind.

Unevenness of character. Every man is one-
half of a man, either benevolent and weak, or
firm and unbenevolent; either a speaker and no
doer, or a doer and no speaker, either contem-
plative or practical, and excellence in any one
kind seems to speak defect in the others. This
wisely ordered for the *social* state; and the individual expectation and effort seems to promise
completeness of character in the whole future.

Our very defects are thus shadows of our virtues.

Opposition of first thoughts and common opinion. God has the first word. The devil has the second, but God has the last word. We distrust the first thought because we can't give the reason for it. Abide by it, there is a reason, and by and by, long hence, perhaps it will appear.

How we came out of silence into this sounding world is the wonder of wonders. All other marvels are less.

Charles has gone away to Porto Rico.[1] God preserve and restore him.

1 To visit Edward, who, though his mental balance was restored, was really a broken man. In hope of recovery he had taken some clerical position in a business house at San Juan.

> I see him with superior smile,
> Hunted by Sorrow's grisly train,
> In lands remote, in toil and pain,
> With angel patience labour on
> With the high port he bore ere-while
> When, foremost of the youthful band,
> The prizes in all lists he won,
> Nor bate one jot of heart or hope;
> And least of all the loyal tie
> Which holds to home 'neath every sky.
> "In Memoriam E. B. E," Poems.

When you confer a favour, be very careful how you do it. It must be done with the remembrance of your own squirming when you have received one. And feel that the whole difficulty lies in receiving, not in giving.[1]

Memoranda. Committee of Evangelical Treasury concerning pews of American Unitarian Association. Mr. Thayer, and Kahler; also soliciting subscriptions committee. Pemberton fund for Miss——; ... Tuesday, House of Industry.

Nothing done at random. No accidents in nature. You go out of a city and come to social disorder and wilderness, never get out of God's city. Order, order everywhere, morals paramount, equality of number of the sexes, proportion of vegetable and animal life.

December 14, 1831.

It will not do to indulge myself. Philosopher or Christian, whatever faith you teach, live by it. Who opposes me, who shuts up my mouth, who hinders the flow of my exhortation? Myself,

1 Such was Mr. Emerson's desire to stand on his own feet that it was a little hard for him to receive a favour or gift, all through life.

only myself. Cannot I conform myself to my principles? Set the principles as low, as loose as you please, set the tune not one note higher than the true pitch, but after settling what they shall be, stick to them.

PAROCHIAL VISITS

December 19.

When I talk with the sick they sometimes think I treat death with unbecoming indifference and do not make the case my own, or, if I do, err in my judgment. I do not fear death. I believe those who fear it have borrowed the terrors through which they see it from vulgar opinion, and not from their own minds. My own mind is the direct revelation which I have from God and far least liable to mistake in telling his will of any revelation. Following my own thoughts, especially as sometimes they have moved me in the country (as in the Gulf Road in Vermont), I should lie down in the lap of earth as trustingly as ever on my bed. But the terror to many persons is in the vague notions of what shall follow death. The judgment, an uncertain judgment to be passed upon them, — whether they shall be saved? It ought to be considered by them that there is no uncertainty about it. Already they

may know exactly what is their spiritual condition. . . . He will not suffer his holy one to
see corruption. . . . What are your sources of
satisfaction? If they are meats and drinks, dress,
gossip, revenge, hope of wealth, they must perish with the body. If they are contemplation,
kind affections, admiration of what is admirable,
self-command, self-improvement, then they survive death and will make you as happy then as
now.

December 20.

" Time was his estate." (*Italian Philosopher*,
Johnson, vol. v.) "Daily self-surpast."

Alexander 33 years. 30 years, age of having
done most. Scipio, Hannibal.

Revivals wrought in a moment, great discoveries, great thoughts, great deeds.

It only takes a moment to die, or to kill.
What can't then be done in a year? Life long
enough for any good purpose: a year long
enough.

" Action comes less near to vital truth than
description." Plato, *Republic*, Book v.

" Poetry is something more philosophical and excellent than history."

ARISTOTLE, *Poetica*, ch. 10.

When you throw a stone, the way to hit the mark is to look at the mark and not consider how you swing your arm. When you speak extempore, you must carry your thought to the person opposite and never think of the manner.

TO MISS EMERSON

December 25.

What from the woods, the hills, and the enveloping heaven? What from the interior creation, — if what is within be not the creator? How many changes men ring on these two words *in and out*. It is all our philosophy. Take them away, and what were Wordsworth or Swedenborg? The rough and tumble old fellows, Bacons, Miltons, and Burkes, don't wire-draw. That's why I like Montaigne. No effeminate parlour workman is he, on an idea got at an evening lecture or a young men's debate, but roundly tells what he saw, or what he thought of when he was riding horse-back or entertaining a troop at his chateau. A gross, semisavage indecency debases his book, and ought doubtless to turn it out of doors; but the robustness of his sentiments, the generosity of his judgments, the downright truth without fear or favour, I do embrace with both arms. It is wild and savoury as sweet fern. Henry VIII. loved to see a *man*, and it is exhilarating, once in a while, to come across a genuine Saxon stump, a wild, virtuous man who knows books, but gives them their right place in his mind, lower than his reason. Books are apt to turn reason out of doors. You find men talking everywhere from their memories, instead of from their understanding. If I stole this thought from Montaigne, as is very likely, I don't care. I should have said the same myself.

BOSTON, *December* 28, 1831.

The year hastens to its close. What is it to me? What I am, that is all that affects me. That I am 28, or 8, or 58 years old is as nothing. Should I mourn that the spring flowers are gone, that the summer fruit has ripened, that the harvest is reaped, that the snow has fallen? Should I mourn because so much addition has been made to the capital of human comfort?

In my study my faith is perfect. It breaks, scatters, becomes compounded, in converse with men. Hume doubted in his study, and believed in the world.

Mr. Robert Haskins quoted a significant proverb, That a woman could throw out with a spoon faster than a man could throw in with a shovel.

" Always be sticking a tree, Jock,—it will be growing when ye are sleeping," was the thrifty Scotchman's dying advice. Always be setting a good action to grow, is the advice of a divine thrift. It is bearing you fruit all the time, knitting you to men's hearts, and to men's good and to God, and beyond this it is benefitting others by remembrance, by emulation, by love. The progress of moral nature is geometrical. Celestial economy !

AUTHORS OR BOOKS QUOTED OR REFERRED TO
IN JOURNALS OF 1831

Homer, *Iliad*; Anaxagoras; Socrates; Plato, *Republic* ; Aristotle, *Poetica* ;

Cicero, *De Senectute*; Horace; Plutarch; Plotinus ; Porphyry ; Thomas à Kempis ; Luther ; Montaigne; Calvin; Shakspeare, *Sonnets*; Bacon; Burton; Sir Thomas Browne; Milton; Jeremy

Taylor; Herbert; Lovelace; Swammerdam; Newton; Scougal; Fénelon; Young; Swedenborg;

Abraham Tucker (Edward Search); Samuel Johnson; Adam Smith; Burke; Schlegel, *Guesses at Truth;* Schiller; Wordsworth, *Dion, Rob Roy, Laodamia, Happy Warrior;* Mrs. Barbauld, *The Brook;* Dugald Stewart; Burns, *To the Deil;* Kirby; De Staël; Schelling; Scott; Byron; Campbell, *Pleasures of Hope;* Coleridge; Landor, *Imaginary Conversations;* Müller (Karl Otfried, or Wilhelm?); Webster; Everett.

JOURNAL XXIII

1832

From Ω (Blotting Book III) Ψ and Q

THE GOOD EAR

(From Ω)

BOSTON, *January* 4, 1832.

MORE is understood than is expressed in the most diffuse discourse. It is the unsaid part of every lecture that does the most good. If my poor Tuesday evening lectures (*horresco referens*) were to any auditor the total of his exposition of Christianity, what a beggarly faith were it.

"Death," said you? We die daily. "Death," —the soul never dies.

Theory of agreeable and disagreeable people, alluded to by George Bradford,[1] that reflecting

1 George Partridge Bradford of Duxbury was, like his sister Sarah Alden, wife of Rev. Samuel Ripley of Waltham, through life a close friend of Mr. Emerson. Mr. Bradford was affectionate, refined, a born scholar and a lover of flowers. He prepared himself for the ministry, but was so modest and sensitive that he found himself unfitted for its public offices. He

and self-improving minds are not agreeable company, but that indolent and deceitful, rather.

January 6.

Shall I not write a book on topics such as follow? —

Chapter 1. That the mind is its own place;

Chapter 2. That exact justice is done;

Chapter 3. That good motives are at the bottom of (many) bad actions; e. g. Business before friends;

Chapter 4. That the soul is immortal;

Chapter 5. On prayers;

Chapter 6. That the best is the true;

Chapter 7. That the mind discerns all things;

Chapter 8. That the mind seeks itself in all things.

Chapter 9. That truth is its own warrant.

[Charles?] Sprague, [Rev. Mellish I.] Motte, [Edward] Wigglesworth, [Charles H., later Admiral?] Davis, [George P.] Bradford, [?] Willis, [Rev. George] Ripley, [?] Henry,

was a loyal member of the Brook Farm Community, and after its breaking up, became a teacher of classes of young ladies, an occupation for which his culture and enthusiasm admirably fitted him; also a devoted gardener.

[Cornelius Conway] Felton, [Rev. Frederic H.] Hedge.[1]

[CRYSTALLIZATION]

January 7.

There is a process in the mind very analogous to crystallization in the mineral kingdom. I think of a particular fact of singular beauty and interest. In thinking of it I am led to many more thoughts which show themselves, first partially, and afterwards more fully. But in the multitude of them I see no order. When I would present them to others they have no beginning. There is no method. Leave them now, and return to them again. Domesticate them in your mind, do not force them into arrangement too hastily, and presently you shall find they will take their own order. And the order they assume is divine. It is God's architecture.

[EXCELLENCE IS TRUTH]

January 9.

I cannot help quoting from Mendelssohn's *Phædo* the following rule, "All that which, being admitted as true, would procure the human

1 Very likely a list of the serious-minded and scholarly young men who might meet for conversation or form a literary club.

race a real advantage or a feeble consolation, acquires by that alone a high degree of probability." "When the skeptics," says his Socrates, " object against the belief in God and virtue that it is a simple political invention imagined for the good of society, I reply, ' O, imagine a doctrine as indispensable to man, and I will pledge myself upon its truth.' " This is a true account of our instinctive faith. Why do I believe in a perfect system of compensations, that exact justice is done? Certainly not upon a narrow experience of a score, or a hundred instances. For I boldly affirm and believe the universality of the law. But simply that it is better in the view of the mind than any other way, therefore must be the true way. Whatever is better must be the truer way.

" Little matters it to the simple lover of truth to whom he owes such or such a reasoning."

MENDELSSOHN.

Article " Beauty " in Ree's Encyclopædia written by Flaxman, also " Sculpture."

Mem. Read Treatise on " Commerce " of Lib. Useful Knowledge, and Mr. Lee's " Exposition of Evidence."

DREAMS

Hideous dreams last night, and queried to-day whether they were any more than exaggerations of the sins of the day.[1] . . .

"Regard (not) dreams, since they are but the images of our hopes and fears."

CATO, *apud* Fielding's *Proverbs*.

[MINISTERIAL BONDS]

January 10.

It is the best part of the man, I sometimes think, that revolts most against his being a minister. His good revolts from official goodness. If he never spoke or acted but with the full consent of his understanding, if the whole man acted always, how powerful would be every act and every word. Well then, or ill then, how much power he sacrifices by conforming himself to say and do in other folks' time instead of in his own! The difficulty is that we do not make a world of our own, but fall into institutions already made, and have to accommodate ourselves to them to be useful at all, and this

1 Here follows a long paragraph printed in "Spiritual Laws," *Essays I.*

accommodation is, I say, a loss of so much integrity and, of course, of so much power.

But how shall the droning world get on if all
its *beaux esprits* recalcitrate upon its approved
forms and accepted institutions, and quit them
all in order to be single minded? The double
refiners would produce at the other end the
double damned.

[NATIVE VIGOUR IN SPEECH]

January 11.

People sometimes wonder that persons wholly
uneducated to write, yet eminent in some other
ability, should be able to use language with so
much purity and force. But it is not wonderful.
The manner of using language is surely the most
decisive test of intellectual power, and he who
has intellectual force of any kind will be sure to
show it there. For that is the first and simplest
vehicle of mind, is of all things next to the mind,
and the vigorous Saxon that uses it well is of the
same block as the vigorous Saxon that formed
it, and works after the same manner.

[true philosophy]

January 12.

Diogenes was a true philosopher when he compared his shade and his sunshine to the alternate residence of the Persian king at Susa and Ecbatana. Men live, as it were, upon concentric circles, a king upon a little larger arc, a peasant upon a little less, but the most perfect proportion subsisting between the enjoyments and pains of one and of the other. Set your habits right, as Paley said. Trifles will be occasions of pleasure to a wise man, and of instruction. But nature must be exhausted to furnish one hour's stimulus to John Dart.

The good mind is set to happiness, the evil to pain.

[power]

January 20.

Don't trust children with edge tools. Don't trust man, great God, with more power than he has, until he has learned to use that little better. What a hell should we make of the world if we could do what we would! Put a button on the foil till the young fencers have learned not to put each other's eyes out.

Is it not true that our power does increase exactly in the measure that we learn how to use it?

" O Reason, Reason, art not thou he whom I seek?"   FÉNELON *apud* COUSIN.

January 21.

Write on personal independence. There are men whose language is strong and defying enough, yet their eyes and their actions ask leave of other men to live. A man considers the fashion of his better neighbour's coat and hat, and then condemns his own. The only way to improve the fashion of his own coat and hat is to forget his neighbour and work out his own results; to eat less dinner; to rise earlier; to work harder, do more benefits, and more strictly adhere in his acts to the decisions of his own judgment. So to do will make his own coat and hat very respectable in the eyes of all men. . . .

" Say not then, ' This with that lace will do well ';
But ' This with my discretion will be brave.' "
          HERBERT.

What is the fault of Hotspur's avowal? It seems just.

> " I 'll give thrice so much land
> To any well deserving friend ;
> But in the way of bargain, mark ye me,
> I 'll cavil on the ninth part of a hair." [1]

Be as beneficent as the sun or the sea, but if your rights as a rational being are trenched on, die on the first inch of your territory. It requires circumspection. Else he will be surprised by his good nature into acquiescence in false sentiments uttered by others. Be a Cato, and it will be easier to keep out of sin and shame than in the ease and social habit of Mæcenas.

No man gains credit for his cowardly courtesies. Every one makes allowance for so much bowing and smiling and compliment as he supposes was insincere, and rates the character so much the worse for that heavy subtraction.

The true man of business never brags. He talks simply of extensive commercial operations that embrace years and nations in their completion. A country attorney has much more to say about Washington and the Free Trade and Tariff Conventions than the person whose influence is felt in conventions.

[1] *Henry IV.*, Part I, iii, 1.

DREAMS AND BEASTS

[They] are two keys by which we are to find out the secrets of our own nature. All mystics use them. They are like comparative anatomy. They are test objects ; or we may say, that must be a good theory of the universe, that theory will bring a commanding claim to confidence which explains these phenomena.[1]

TRAVEL

" Here is he who gave away his lands to see those of other men." My friend admires the knowledge and tact of his fellow boarders who have seen the world and know so much more of men then he.[2] They got it however, not by peering about all over the world, but by minding their business. In the steadfast attention to all the details of their profession, they met this information. Let the clergyman attend as steadfastly to his profession, and he will get as much fact, as much commanding knowledge. Let him trust God's order, which supplies every eye which

1 See " Demonology " in *Lectures and Biographical Sketches*, p. 6, Centenary Ed.

2 Probably Mr. Bradford, who enjoyed and valued travel, all through life, as much as Mr. Emerson did little.

keeps its place with its fair share of opportunity, as well as every mouth with its food.

My friend expects with travelling to learn human nature, as if to become acquainted with man it were necessary to know all the individuals upon earth. Were it not wiser to let God judge for us in this matter? He has provided every man with twenty or thirty companions, and two or three hundred acquaintances, by way of specimen of the varieties of human character, and as a large book wherein he may read his own nature *in extenso*.

Consider also that everybody's occasions provide him with much variety of intercourse. He is obliged to see the Statehouse, the college, the almshouse and jail, court, camp, ship, stable, mine, and mountain sometime in his life, to travel many hundred miles by land and water. Keep your eyes open, and God will provide you opportunity. Besides, if you go out to see the moon, it will not please you; but it will brighten and cheer your walk of business. All goes to show that, if you do your duty, wisdom will flow in. . . .

A SUBJECT

Write a sermon upon a house-hero, upon the hero to his *valet de chambre*; the ugly face that obstinate association of true words and good acts has made beautiful.

" Real virtue is most loved where it is most nearly seen, and no respect which it commands from strangers can equal the never ceasing admiration it excites in the daily intercourse of domestic life."   PLUTARCH, *Pericles.*

The stinking philosophy of the utilitarian ! *Nihil magnificum, nihil generosum, sapit,* as Cicero said of that of Epicurus.

Repose of mind we must have, we must not feel pyrrhonistically, however we may speculate. What can comfort us if we think right and wrong are idiosyncrasies?

" Duty subsists. Immutably survive
  For our support the measures and the forms
  Which an abstract intelligence supplies
  Whose kingdom is where time and space are not."

January 27.

Talked with Reed and Worcester last evening about the mutual influence of spirits.[1] Men-

1 Rev. Thomas Worcester was minister of the Swedenborgian Church in Boston for fifty years. He was a little

delssohn's principle, that the desirable is the true, is the best thing which can be alleged in favour of the position. God, we agreed, was the communication between us and other spirits, departed or present. Good wishes of us affect them. What is this more than the stoical precept that "the wise man who lifts his finger in Rome affects all the wise men on the earth."

Indeed, their position is just equivalent, for they suppose that spirit affects spirit, *both unconscious*. Worcester said, God not so much sees as dissolves us.

DR. CHANNING ON WAR

(From Ψ)

BOSTON, *January* 26, 1832.

Heard Dr. Channing last evening at the Peace Society. Very good views. Freedom unfits for war, unchains industry, and so makes property; then men are unwilling to put it at stake; improves men and gives them individuality, do not follow leaders, etc. Only two men ever controlled public opinion in this country, Washington and Jefferson. Efforts of the country in the last war paralysed by the minority, etc.

older than Emerson. He and Sampson Reed, author of *Growth of the Mind*, which Mr. Emerson so valued, married sisters.

January 30, 1832.

Every man hath his use, no doubt, and every-one makes ever the effort according to the energy of his character to suit his external condition to his inward constitution. If his external condition does not admit of such accommodation, he breaks the form of his life, and enters a new one which does. If it will admit of such accommodation, he gradually bends it to his mind. Thus Finney can preach, and so his prayers are short; Parkman can pray, and so his prayers are long; Lowell can visit, and so his church service is less. But what shall poor I do, who can neither visit nor pray nor preach to my mind? Can you not be virtuous? Can you not be temperate? Can you not be charitable? Can you not be chaste? Can you not be industrious? Can you not keep your word, and possibly when you have learned these things you may find the others.

[The following letter, though not in the Journal, seemed to the editors worth while to insert here. It was written by Mr. Emerson to a young cousin of his wife, Miss Elizabeth Tucker (later, Mrs. McGregor), of Derry, N. H.]

Boston, *February* 1, 1832.

My dear Cousin, — If it were not true that it is never too late to do right, I should be quite ashamed to send my list of books at such a long distance behind my promise. When I spent so pleasant a day at your house, I thought it would be very easy and I knew it would be very pleasant for me to make out a scheme of study for your vacation as soon as I got home. But what to select out of so great a company of leather-jackets and so deserving — and then a crowd of things to be done — and withal a Quaker habit of never doing things till their necessary time, in the hope of doing them better, has postponed my letter from day to day and week to week. But so you must never do, my dear Cousin. But for fear you should quite forget your wise adviser, and should be a grown lady and so I should lose the honour of having had any part in your education, I hasten to send you my poor thoughts upon what is good to be read. I make no pretensions to give you a complete course, but only select a few good books of my acquaintance — such as I think you will like, and such as will serve you.

One more preliminary word; Never mind any silly people that try to sneer you out of the love of reading. People are fast outgrowing the old prejudice that a lady ought not to be acquainted with books. It is the display that disgusts; the knowledge that you get from them never disgusts anybody, but is all useful, and has comforted how many hours that would otherwise have been long, dull, and lonely.

First then, you must keep one or two books for the soul always by you for monitors and angels, lest this world of trifles should run away with you. Such a book is Thomas à Kempis's *Imitation of Christ*, written by a German monk near four hundred years ago, and needs only a little allowance for a Roman Catholic's opinions, to make it express the religious sentiment of every good mind. Then there is a little book I value very much, Scougal's *Life of God in the Soul of Man*. Taylor's *Holy Dying* is a good book. Its author was called the 'Shakspear of divines.'

Selections from Fénelon, by Mrs. Follen.

Ware, *On the Formation of the Christian Character*.

Sir Thomas Browne's *Religion of a Physician;* this is a beautiful work lately republished in this town.

Young's *Night Thoughts*. A friend whom I

value very much told Ellen always to keep
Young upon her table.

But I suppose you will think here are Sunday books enough. Now for History. The
'American Society for the Diffusion of Useful
Knowledge' are publishing Müller's *Universal
History* in four duodecimo volumes. It is very
much the best of all the general histories, and is
very easily read. They have only printed the first
volume. The sketch of Rome and of Greece in
it are (*sic*) excellent. Then the most important
modern history to be read perhaps is Robertson's
Charles V., which is an account of Europe in the
most interesting period. I would skip the first
volume, which is a general View of Europe, and
read the two last. Then you might take up Hûme,
say at the reign of Elizabeth, which would continue pretty well the line of events. The best
history of Europe during the French Revolution is Scott's *Life of Napoleon*. For the American history, as you happen to live at Derry,
N. H., I would read Dr. Belknap's *History* of
the State. It is not only a very good book
itself, but will give you a pretty good idea of
all the States, — their story is so much alike.

Morton's *New England's Memorial* is a little
book and a pleasing account of the Forefathers.

Milman's *History of the Jews* in the Family Library is a very good book.

But what is far more soothing, and never painful like the history of man, is Natural History in its various parts. The first Volume of the American Library of Useful Knowledge (and you must make the Social Library of Derry subscribe for that book) contains *Mr. Brougham's Discourse Upon the Advantages and Prospects of Science*, which is excellent, and *Mr. Herschel's*, which is better. The same Mr. Herschel, son of the famous astronomer, is about to publish a *Discourse on Astronomy*, which is expected with great interest. Then there is a beautiful book on American Birds, the *Ornithology* by Mr. Nuttall, that every one who lives in the country ought to read.

I suppose you have read *School Conversations on Chemistry*. *The Conversations on Vegetable Physiology* are just as good. With this class of books is the *Account of Polar Expeditions*, a volume of the Family Library.

I suppose to such a formidable list I must add a novel or two, or you would think me very unkind. So I really hope you will read *De Vere* by the author of *Tremaine*, and as much of Walter Scott and Miss Edgeworth as you please.

For poetry read Milton. If the *Paradise Lost* tires you, it is so stately, try the Minor Poems. *Comus*, if the mythology does not make it sound strange, is a beautiful poem and makes one holy to read it. Read Bryant's Poems; I know you will love them, and Cowper and Thomson, and perhaps (a very large perhaps) Wordsworth. If you do not like poetry, which I suppose you do, the best way to learn is to write some.

Now I do not suppose that you will read all these books in a short time, or perhaps at any time, and some of them very probably you have read. I only wanted to fulfil your command and speak a good word for some valued acquaintance of mine. The best of all ways to make one's reading valuable is to *write* about it, and so I hope my Cousin Elizabeth has a blank-book where she keeps some record of her thoughts.

And if you think my letter very long, why you must bear in mind that once I was a school-master, and I am so proud of my new scholar as to keep her long at my lecture.

Make my respectful remembrances to your mother and father, and my compliments to your sister.

Your affectionate Cousin,

R. W. Emerson.

POVERTY AND RICHES

February 6.

Every man has some facts in his mind which invalidate the common sayings, and incline him to think that the poor are as happy as the rich. The man, not the condition, imports. There are many rich who would be happy if they were poor; many poor who would be unhappy if they were rich. A poem would give me more pleasure than a hundred dollars, and mind does so far vindicate itself that I think the man does not live so base who would exchange the least intellectual power for the wealth of the world. I believe a hundred dollars a year would support me in the enjoyment of what I love best. Why toil I then for twenty times as much? Might I cut and run? Might I dignifiedly walk away, and keep the man nor turn cat? . . .

Take nothing for granted. That strikes you in hearing the discourse of a wise man, that he has brought to the crucible and the analysis all that other people receive without question, as chemists are directed to select what manufacturers throw away.

The words of wise men are heard in quiet more
than the cry of him that ruleth among fools.

Ecclesiasticus ix, 17.

Consider the permanence of the best opinion;
the certainty with which a good book acquires
fame, though a bad book succeeds better at first.
Consider the natural academy which the best
heads of the time constitute, and which, 't is
pleasant to see, act almost as harmoniously and
efficiently, as if they were organized and acted
by vote.

Men appreciate instinctively the measure of
a superior intellect; as if a part of the man acknowledged the messiahship of wisdom, whilst
a part denied it,—an awkward consciousness
that here is merit, here is power, though latent
and wholly inapplicable to my wants and state of
mind. I should say it is the Newton within the
peasant that recognizes Newton as the ornament
of the human race. I met some good sentences,
in Brewster's *Life of Newton*, from Leonardo
da Vinci. I of course take the spiritual sense
of the passage. " In the study of the sciences
which depend on mathematics, those who do
not consult nature, but authors, are not the
children of nature, they are only her grand-

children. Nature alone is the master of true genius."

Adhere to nature, never to accepted opinion. The sermon which I write inquisitive of truth is good a year after, but that which is written because a sermon must be writ is musty the next day. . . .

February 18, 1832.

What can we see, read, acquire, but ourselves. Cousin is a thousand books to a thousand persons. Take the book, my friend, and read your eyes out, you will never find there what I find. If I would have a monopoly of the delight or the wisdom I get, I am as secure now the book is English as if it were imprisoned in Syriac.[1] Judge of the use different persons can make of this book by the use you are able to make of it at different times; sometimes very imperfectly apprehending the author and very little interested; again delighting in a sentence or an argument; another time, ascending to the comprehension of the whole reasoning, but implicitly following him as a disciple; at another, not only understanding his reasoning, but understanding his mind; able not only to discern, but to pre-

---

1 The substance of the last sentences occurs in "Spiritual Laws," *Essays I.*

dict his path and its relation to other paths, to discern his truth and his error.[1] . . .

NOTHING IS NEW

February 19.

Was not all truth always in the world? Even the Lord's Prayer, Grotius represents as a compilation of Jewish petitions, and the German commentators trace almost all the precepts of Christ to Hebrew proverbs. And I learn to-day that the Copernican system, — it is gathered from the writings of Aristotle, — was *maintained by some philosophers before his* (*Aristotle's*) *time.* (Library Useful Knowledge, *Life of Galileo.*) And the new light, brand new, of the Swedenborgians even, is old as thought. I match every saying of theirs with some Greek or Latin proverb, e. g., "the wise man lifting his finger," etc.

GALILEO

February 20, 1832.

One is tempted to write a lecture on the right use of the senses, from having attention called to the fact that Galileo lost his sight in 1636. "The noblest eye is darkened," said Castelli, "which

1 Here follows in this journal the passage, "Introduce a base person among gentlemen," etc. in "Spiritual Laws."

nature ever made, an eye so privileged, and gifted with such rare qualities, that it may with truth be said to have seen more than all of those who are gone, and to have opened the eyes of all who are to come." See also the expressions of Galileo himself, quoted p. 75, *Life of Galileo*, in Library Useful Knowledge. Galileo died in 1642, æt. 78.

So the eye of Milton.

It is idle in us to wonder at the bigotry and violence of the persecution of Galileo. Every man may read the history of it in himself when he is contradicted and silenced in argument by a person whom he had always reckoned his inferior.

[UNANSWERED QUESTIONS]

I wrote one day, after being puzzled by a mechanical alderman, that the first questions remain to be asked. 'T is even so ; and many a profound genius, I suppose, who fills the world with fame of his exploding renowned errors, is yet every day posed by trivial questions at his own supper-table.

[SIN]

It is not permitted to do wrong in the dark. Set out to sin, and the whole cause *will have* a hearing, however brief and mad you be. The best arguments are yet stated by the opposition. The angels are faithful to their post as the devils.

[FROM Q]

CHARDON STREET, BOSTON.

March 10, 1832.

Temperance is an estate. I am richer, the stoic might say, by my self-command than I am by my income. And literally, for his acquaintance spends at the confectioner's what pays the bookseller's bill of the Stoic and makes him rich indeed. Then the sum withholden from the liquor-dealer enables the Stoic to be magnificent in expenses of charity and of taste. To say nothing of the doctor's and apothecary's accounts.

A good way to look at the matter is to see how it figures in the ledger. Bacon says, Best spent in the most permanent ways, such as buying plate. This year I have spent say $20 in wine and liquors which are drunk up, and the drinkers are the worse. It would have bought a beautiful print that would have pleased for a century; or have paid a debt. . . .

But every indulgence weakened the moral fac-

ulty, hurt at least for the time the intellect, low-
ered the man in the estimation of the spectators
though sharers, injured them, and diminished
the means of beneficence.

TU CURA TIBI

March 14, 1832.

Anything not base is desirable to bring about
so good an end as this of personal purity. Be
master of yourself, and for the love of God keep
every inch you gain. No man who has once by
hatred of excess mastered his appetites would be
bought back to his bondage by any possessions.

28 March, my food *per diem* weighed 14 ¼ oz.
29 "   "   "   "   "   "   13   "
 2 April, "   "   "   "   "   12 ½ "

[DISSATISFACTION]

What ails you, gentlemen? said Jupiter. What
ails you, my wo-begone friend? Speak, what
are you? "Bilious." And you? "A slave."
And you? "Hypp'd." And you? "Poor." And
you? "Lame." And you? "A Jew."

March 29.

I visited Ellen's tomb and opened the coffin.

March 30.

I am your debtor, Sir James Mackintosh, for your Ethics, and yet, masterly book as it is, highly as I esteem the first account of the Conscience that has ever been given, yet is it at last only an outline, nor can suffice to my full satisfaction. . . .

Omnis Aristippum docuit color et status et res.
HORACE.

" Be not almighty, let me say,
Against, but for me."
HERBERT.

An ingenious and pleasing account of human nature is Hartley's successive passions as expounded by Mackintosh. Each becomes the parent of a new and higher passion, and itself dies. If the scheme of Necessity must be admitted, then let that doctrine also be the antidote, the gradual glorification of man. . . . Very costly scaffoldings are pulled down when the more costly building is finished. And God has his scaffoldings. The Jewish Law answered its temporary purpose and was then set aside. Christianity is completing its purpose as an aid to educate man. And evil is a scaffolding on which universal good is reared. God shall be all in all. . . .

MOORE TO CRABBE OF CAMPBELL

" True bard ! and simple, as the race
    Of heaven-born poets ever are,
When, stooping from their starry place,
    They 're children, near, though gods afar."

[SUUM CUIQUE]

The world is an academy to the scholar, a
butt to the satirist, a church to the devotee, " the
scaffold of the divine vengeance " to the Calvinist, good society to the fashionist, a market to
the merchant, a conquest to Alexander.

" No one can guess what kind of vision belongs to the fly. There are probably 25,000 hex-
agonal lenses or *menisci* on its surface, or the same
number of distinct visual organs, as some comparative anatomists would lead us to believe."

ABERNETHY, *Lectures.*

" DEUS ANIMA BRUTORUM "

April 2.

Write a sermon upon animals. They are to
man in life what fables about them are in ethics.
Draw the moral then of the bee, ant, fox, hedge-
hog, ermine, swine, roe, woodpecker, pigeon,
worm, moth, mite, a frozen snake.

[MEMORANDA FOR] SERMON ON IDLENESS

" In the sweat of thy face thou shalt eat bread."
Galileo's eye. He that does nothing is poorer
than he that has nothing. " The devil tempts
others, an idle man tempts the devil." "An idle
brain is the devil's shop." "He hath no leisure
who useth it not." The busy man is entirely ignorant of what was doing this morning all over
the city. Working in your calling is half praying. What keeps the world from being a horrid
Poneropolis? What divides and conquers? Necessity of all; Labor; " Poverty is a good which
all hate." Give us no leisure until we are fit
for it.

[THE FORCE WITHIN]

. . . Blundering rhetorician seeking in the
tones or gestures of Chatham or Adams, or in
the circumstances of the parties present or concerned, the electricity that lay only in the breast
of Chatham and Adams ; — *Pectus est disertum
et vis mentis.*[1]

---

[1] Probably a fragment from Quintus Fabius Pictor, the
" Father of Latin History," who lived in the time of the
Third Punic War, and is quoted with respect by Cicero and
Livy.

[NATURE'S TEACHING]

April 6, 1832.

It was the comparing the mechanism of the hand and the foot that led Galen, who, they say, was a skeptic in his youth, to the public declaration of his opinion that intelligence must have operated in ordaining the laws by which living beings are constructed.

"In explaining these things," he says, "I esteem myself as composing a solemn hymn to the great architect of our bodily frame, in which I think there is more true piety than in sacrificing hecatombs of oxen or burning the most costly perfumes, for I first endeavour from his works to know him myself, and afterwards by the same means to show him to others, to inform them how great is his wisdom, his goodness, his Power." GALEN, *apud* ABERNETHY, *Lectures*.

Hunter like Pestalozzi; each lived to an idea which was their guide and genius; but Abernethy is hardly a Niederer. So Jussieu wrote nothing, yet had an idea.

[PERSIAN SCRIPTURES]

April 17.

A strange poem is Zoroastrism. It is a system as separate and harmonious and sublime as Swed-

enborgianism — congruent. One would be glad
to behold the truth which they all shadow forth.
For it cannot but be truth that they typify and
symbolize, as the play of every faculty reveals
an use, a cause and a law to the intelligent. One
sees in this, and in them all, the element of poetry according to Jeffrey's true theory, the effect
produced by making every thing outward only a
sign of something inward: Plato's *forms or ideas*
which seem almost tantamount to the *Ferouers* of
Zoroaster. " Of all the Ferouers of beings that
should exist in the world, the most precious in
the eyes of Ormuzd were that of Law, that of
Iran and that of Zoroaster," *Académie des Inscriptions*, vol. 37, p. 623. But what I would
have quoted just now to illustrate the poetry
theory is this : —

" Fire, the sun of Ormuzd, was also created.
He represented, though imperfectly, the original fire which animates all beings, forms the
relations which exist between them and which in
the beginning was a principle of union between
Ormuzd and Time-*sans-bornes* " (which is the
first name in their Theodicæa).

By the way, I cannot help putting in here an
exquisite specimen of the *vraisemblance* in fiction.
Among the evil persons and things produced by

Ahriman, it is said, — *Ahriman produisit même une espèce de feu ténébreux, dont vient celui de la fièvre,* — p. 628.

Do we not feel in reading these elemental theories that these grotesque fictions are the gallipots of Socrates, that these primeval allegories are globes and diagrams on which the laws of living nature are explained? Do we not seem nearer to divine truth in these fictions than in less pretending prose?

Here is one of the sentences. Goschoroon rejoicing before Ormuzd at the prospect of the creation of Zoroaster, says, "I said to heaven in the beginning when there was no night, that there must be purity of thought, of word and of action," — p. 643.

I am quoting from the *Histoire de l'Académie des Inscriptions,* vol. 37.

Prometheus archaic : "Jupiter an upstart."

The foolish took no oil in their vessels with their lamps. Pestalozzi said, "that no man was either willing or able to help any other man."

CHARDON ST., *April* 29, 1832.

You may chuse for yourself, or let others chuse for you, in things indifferent. You may give the law, or take it. Let a man set down his foot and say, "this or that thing I can't and won't do," and stand it out, it shall be counted to him not only for innocency, but for righteousness; whilst a poor craven stands by, omitting the same thing and apologizing for it, and receives the hearty contempt and round abuse of all observers.

You had better begin small, sail in an eggshell, make a straw your mast, a cobweb all your cloth. Begin and proceed on a settled and not-to-be-shaken conviction that but little is permitted to any man to do or to know, and if he complies with the first grand laws, he shall do well. He had better stick by what he *knows sartain*, that humility and love are always to be practised; but there is no such pressing reason for his asserting his opinions, but he had better be humble and kind and useful to-day and to-morrow and as long as he lasts. Count from yourself in order the persons that have near relation to you up to ten or fifteen, and see if you can consider your whole relation to each without squirming. That will be something. Then, have you paid all your debts? Then, have you paid to the world as much kindness as you received from early benefactors? It were a sort of baseness to die in

the world's debt. Then, can you not, merely for
the very elegancy, the *eruditus luxus* of the thing,
do an unmixed kindness or two?

EXPRESSION

May 3.

Sir J. Mackintosh said well, that every picture, statue and poem was an experiment upon
the human mind. I hunt in Charles's dish of
shells each new form of beauty and new tint, and
seem, as Fontenelle said, " to recognize the thing
the first time I see it." Every knot of every cockle
has expression, that is, is the material symbol of
some cast off thought.

SERMONS

To analyse a foolish sermon may require
much wisdom. Strange that so learned and gifted
a man as my friend should please himself with
drawing for an hour such gingerbread distinctions.

May 7.

Charles says that Porto Rico is a place where
one is never pestered with cold feet and never
needs a pocket-handkerchief, and never is unwilling to get out of bed in the morning.

[A THOUGHT UNDER ANOTHER NAME]

Mutato nomine, de te fabula narratur.

To be at perfect agreement with a man of most opposite conclusions you have only to translate your language into his. The same thought which you call *God* in his nomenclature is called *Christ*. In the language of William Penn, moral sentiment is called *Christ*.

May 11.

There is no country so extensive as a thought. "He who contemplates hath a day without night."

[SYMBOLS]

I suppose an entire cabinet of shells would be an expression of the whole human mind; a Flora of the whole globe would be so likewise; or a history of beasts; or a painting of all the aspects of the clouds. Everything is significant.

[BE MASTER]

. . . Reduce the body to the soul. Make the body the instrument through which that thought is uttered. It is counted disgraceful in the ambassador not to represent in the dignity of his carriage the power of his country. If your manners are false to your theory, cut them off,

as Cranmer burnt the offending hand. Don't
shrink from your work. It will never be an
example *further* than it should be : for no other
man has the same freak. Do not believe that
possibly you can escape the reward of your action. You serve an ungrateful master, — serve
him the more. Be wholly his. Embrace any service, do what you will, and the master of your
master, the Law of laws, will secure your compensation. . . .

He that rides his hobby gently must always
give way to him that rides his hobby hard.

Is it not better to intimate our astonishment
as we pass through the world, if it be only for
a moment ere we are swallowed up in the yest
of the abyss? I will just lift my hands and say,
κόσμος!

[WOMAN]

May 12.

Burns's remark about fine women too true
in my experience. Is not affluence, — or at least
easy circumstances, — essential to the finish of
the female character? Not to its depth and
resources, perhaps, but to the *beauty* of mind
and manners. Is it not because woman is not

yet treated properly, but some taint of Indian barbarity marks yet our civilization? She was made, not to serve, but to be served, and only wealth admits among us of that condition. Or is it that an eye to interest is a fatal blot to the female character, and the poor scarce can help it?

Write a sermon upon Blessed Poverty. Who have done all the good in the world? Poor men. "Poverty is a good hated by all men!"

SPANISH PROVERBS

God comes to see us without a bell.

A wall between both, best preserves friendship.

Whither goest thou, Grief? Where I am used to go.

Make the night night, and the day day.

Working in your calling is half praying.

When you are all agreed upon the time, quoth the curate, I will make it rain.

He counts very unskilfully who leaves God out of his reckoning.[1]

---

[1] Brahma, in Emerson's poem, says: "They reckon ill who leave me out."

A good man is ever at home wherever he chance to be.[1]

[TRUTH COMING]

"Truth never is; always is a-being." Does not that word signify that state in which a man ever finds himself conscious of knowing nothing, but being just now ready to begin to know? He feels like one just born. He is ready to ask the first questions.

Strange how abysmal is our ignorance. Every man who writes a book or pursues a science seems to conceal ambitiously his universal ignorance under this fluency in a particular.

The higher the subjects are, which occupy your thoughts, the more they tax yourself; and the same thoughts have least to do with your individuality, but have equal interest for all men. Things moreover are permanent in proportion to their inwardness in your nature.

SHAKSPEARE

May 16, 1832.

Shakspeare's creations indicate no sort of anxiety to be understood. There is the Cleopatra,

---

1 "Go where he will, the wise man is at home."
Poems, "Woodnotes."

an irregular, unfinished, glorious, sinful character, sink or swim, there she is, and not one in the thousand of his readers apprehends the noble dimensions of the heroine. Then Ariel, Hamlet, and all; all done in sport with the free, daring pencil of a master of the World. He leaves his children with God.

It is a good sign in human nature, the unmixed delight with which we contemplate the genius of Shakspeare, and if it were ten times more, should be glad.

[KNOW, TO LIKE]

May 17.

King James liked old friends best; as he said, his old shoes were easiest to his feet. We are benefitted by coming to an understanding, as it is called, with our fellow men, and with any fellow man. It empties all the ill blood; it ventilates, purifies the whole constitution. And we always feel easiest in the company of a person to whom the whole nature has been so made known. No matter what, but how well known.

[NEW LIGHTS]

The moment you present a man with a new idea, he immediately throws its light back upon

the mass of his thoughts, to see what new relation it will discover. And thus all our knowledge is a perpetually living capital, whose use
cannot be exhausted, as it revives with every
new fact. There is proof for noblest truths in
what we already know, but we have not yet
drawn the distinction which shall methodize our
experience in a particular combination.

ENVY

May 18.

Shall I not write upon Envy? upon the wisdom of Christ which ranks envy with robbery,
which is only envy in act? upon the folly of
envy, which seeks an impossible thing, viz., to
draw another man's good to itself? — In the
sweat of *thy* brow shalt thou eat bread. — Upon
the nobleness which converts all the happiness
of the world into my happiness, and makes Mr.
Davis's house agreeable to me? Pestalozzi's
melancholy paradox, that no man is able or willing to help any other man, should set men right.
Who receive hospitality? the hospitable; who
receive money? the rich. Who receive wisdom?
the wise. To whom do opportunities fall? to
the opportune. Unto him that hath shall be
given.

Malthus coops up indomitable millions ; spiritual world not so. We rejoice unmixedly in Shakspeare's genius. Ardour with which we desire a friend, a teacher of *prima philosophia*. Admiration warms and exalts. The lover is made happier by his love than the object of his affection.

"No revenge is more heroic than that which torments envy by doing good." Would you be revenged ? Live well.

Who hath envy ? I do not envy any one, in the sense of wishing their goods mine. But I am capable, I may easily see, of malevolence to those who have injured me, or before whom I have played the fool. Charles saith, The Jackson Party hath envy, and doubtless the low idle hate the high rich. It is a very low passion, if we have to look so hard to find it. It is as rare as robbery, its bad son.

[CONSTANCY]

May 19.

How has the soldier acquired his formidable courage ? By a rare occasional action, effort ? No ; by eating his daily bread in danger of his life, by having seen a thousand times what resolution and combination can accomplish.

Well, is any other virtue to be gained in any other way? How is a firm, cheerful conversation to be got? Not by one effort, but by spending days and years well, and so having a divine support for such a frail nature to lean upon. A divine support of all the virtue of his life. The bubble of the Present is every moment hardening into the flint of the Past.

What makes the majesty of Brougham, and Webster and Mackintosh? No brass resembles gold. The consciousness of an innocent life, and the cumulative glory of so many witnesses behind.[1] . . .

CONCEALMENT

If you would not be known to do anything, —never do it.[2] . . .

THE PRESENT

The vanishing, volatile froth of the Present which any shadow will alter, any thought blow

1 The journal here gives essentially the passage in "Self Reliance" (p. 59, Century Ed.), with "the heroes of the senate and field" instead of the names here given; and, a few lines later, instead of "the thunder of Chatham's voice," the original has "music of Channing's voice."

2 Here follows a passage differing but slightly from that in "Spiritual Laws" beginning with the same words.

away, any event annihilate, is every moment converted into the Adamantine Record of the Past,—the fragility of the man into the Eternity of God. The Present is always becoming the Past. We walk on molten lava on which the claw of a fly or the fall of a hair makes its impression, which being received, the mass hardens to flint and retains every impression forevermore.

THE POINT OF VIEW

There is a great *parallax* in human nature ascertained by observing it from different states of mind. . . . .

JORTIN

Jortin said in his tracts that they who uphold the orthodox doctrine of the Trinity must be prepared to assert " that Jesus Christ is his own Father and his own Son. The consequence will be so, whether they like it, or whether they like it not." He also said in a letter to Gilbert Wakefield, " There are propositions contained in our liturgy and articles which no man of common sense among us believes." [1]

1 John Jortin, D. D. (1698–1770), author of *Discourses concerning the Truth of the Christian Religion* and *Life of Erasmus.*

[MISSIONARY WORK]

" You send out to the Sandwich Islands one missionary and twenty-five refutations in the crew of the vessel," said Mr. Sturgis.

[THE MIRACLE OF THE UNIVERSE]

Indeed is truth stranger than fiction. For what has imagination created to compare with the science of astronomy? What is there in *Paradise Lost* to elevate and astonish like Herschel or Somerville? The contrast between the magnitude and duration of the things observed and the animalcule observer! It seems a mere eye sailing about space in an egg-shell, and for him to undertake to weigh the formidable masses, to measure the secular periods, and settle the theory of things so vast and long, and out of the little cock-boat of a planet to aim an impertinent telescope at every nebula and pry into the plan and state of every white spec that shines in the inconceivable depths! Not a white spot but is a lump of suns, — the roe, the milt of light and life. Who can be a Calvinist, or who an atheist? God has opened this knowledge to us to correct our theology and educate the mind.

"How many centuries of observations were necessary to render the earth suspected!"

Am. Encyclopædia.

"A good naturalist cannot be a bad man."

Bewick.

Bonus orator, bonus vir.

So Galen, so Abernethy, so Davy.

Has not some astronomer said Young's sentiment of astronomy?

I hope the time will come when there will be a telescope in every street.[1]

DESIGN

Every form is a history of the thing. The comparative anatomist can tell at sight whether a skeleton belonged to a carnivorous or herbivorous animal, a climber, a jumper, a runner, a digger, a builder. The conchologist can tell at sight whether the shell covered an animal that fed on animals or on vegetables, whether it were

[1] "Stars haunt us with their mystery," wrote Mr. Emerson in "The World Soul," and the spectacle of the heavens at night always stirred him; see the opening passage of "Nature." The great astronomers interested him; see the passage in "The Method of Nature" about the stars and star-gazers: also the early verses, "The Poet," in the Appendix to *Poems*.

a river or a sea shell, whether it dwelt in still, or in turbid waters. Everything is a monster till we know what it is for, a ship, a telescope, a surgical instrument, are puzzles and painful to the eye until we have been shown successively the use of every part, and then the thing tells its story at sight and is beautiful. A lobster is monstrous, but when we have been shown the reason of the case and the colour and the tentacula and the proportion of the claws, and seen that he has not a scale nor a bristle nor any quality but fits to some habit and condition of the creature, he then seems as perfect and suitable to his sea-house as a glove to a hand. A man in the rocks under the sea would be a monster, but a lobster is a most handy and happy fellow there.

ASTRONOMY

May 26.

Astronomy hath excellent uses. The first questions it suggests, how pregnant! Do you believe that there is boundless space? Just dwell on that gigantic thought. Does not idealism seem more probable than a space upon whose area what is, the family of being, is a mere dot, and the thought of men or angels can never fathom more than its verge? All is lost in the bosom of its great night.

Next see how it corrects the vaunty speculations of men. It was an old sarcasm, If the triangles had a god, they would paint him with three sides. And men take man, of course, for the type of the highest beings, and suppose whatever is intelligent and great must be like him in nature. Astronomy gives the lie to all this, and shows that whatever beings inhabit Saturn, Jupiter, Herschel, Venus, even in this little neighbourhood of social worlds that so nearly resemble ours, must be of entirely different structure from man. The human race could not breathe in the moon, nor exist in the cold of Saturn, nor move in the gravity of Jupiter.

Well then, it irresistibly modifies all theology.

> " Not to earth's contracted span
> Thy goodness let me bound,
> Nor think thee, Lord, alone of man
> When thousand worlds are round."

Calvinism suited Ptolemaism. The irresistible effect of Copernican Astronomy has been to make the great scheme for the Salvation of man absolutely incredible. Hence great geniuses who studied the mechanism of the heavens became unbelievers in the popular faith. Newton became a Unitarian, Laplace, in a Catholic country, became an infidel, substituting necessity for God; but a self-intelligent necessity is God.

Thus astronomy proves theism, but disproves dogmatic theology. The Sermon on the Mount must be true throughout all the space which the eye sees and the brain imagines, but St. Paul's epistles, the Jewish Christianity would be unintelligible. It operates steadily to establish the moral laws, to disconcert and evaporate temporary systems. At the touch of time errors scatter, in the eye of Eternity, truth prevails.

[THE CRISIS]

June 2, 1832.

Cold, cold. Thermometer says temperate. Yet a week of moral excitement.[1]

Is it years and nations that guide my pen?

I have sometimes thought that, in order to be a good minister, it was necessary to leave the ministry. The profession is antiquated. In an

1 This must have been the week in which Mr. Emerson made known to his people his repugnance to the Communion rite, and proposed its modification, at least to one of Commemoration simply, omitting the use of the elements. The matter was referred to a Committee for consideration. Meanwhile the young minister, following the example of Jesus in all periods of trial and distress, withdrew to the mountains for spiritual renewal.

altered age, we worship in the dead forms of our forefathers. Were not a Socratic paganism better than an effete, superannuated Christianity?

Does not every shade of thought have its own tone, so that wooden voices denote wooden minds?

Whatever there is of Authority in religion is that which the mind does not animate.

CONWAY, N. H., *July* 6.

Here, among the mountains, the pinions of thought should be strong, and one should see the errors of men from a calmer height of love and wisdom. What is the message that is given me to communicate next Sunday?[1] Religion in the mind is not credulity, and in the practice is not form. It is a life. It is the order and soundness of a man. It is not something else *to be got*, to be *added*, but is a new life of those faculties you have. It is to do right. It is to love, it is to serve, it is to think, it is to be humble.

ETHAN ALLEN CRAWFORD'S,
WHITE MOUNTAINS, *July* 14, 1832.

There is nothing to be said. Why take the pencil? I believe something will occur. A slight

1 Probably in the village church.

momentum would send the planet to roll forever, and the laws of thought are not unlike.
A thought, I said, is a country wide enough for
an active mind. It unrolls, it unfolds, it shows
unlimited sense within itself. A few pains, a few
pleasures, — how easily we are amused, how easily
scared. A too benevolent man is at the mercy of
every fop he meets, and every householder. His
willingness to please withdraws him from himself. Sure he ought to please, but not please at
the expense of his own view by accommodation.

"Imitation is a leaning on something foreign;
incompleteness of individual development; defect of free utterance."

Edinburgh Review, no. cx.

"Ah me," said the mourner to me, "how
natural he looked when they had put on his
dickey!"

"It was this that caught him," said the
wife to me, touching her pearl earring.

MEDITATIONS

The golden days of youth are gone,
The hours of sun and hope; And round thee —

How hard to command the soul, or to
solicit the soul. Many of our actions, many of

mine, are done to solicit the soul. Put away your flesh, put on your faculties. I would think, I would feel. I would be the vehicle of that divine principle that lurks within, and of which life has afforded only glimpses enough to assure me of its being. We know little of its laws, but we have observed that a north wind, clear, cold, with its scattered fleet of drifting clouds, braced the body, and seemed to reflect a similar abyss of spiritual heaven between clouds in our minds; or a brisk conversation moved this mighty deep, or a word in a book was made an omen of by the mind and surcharged with meaning, or an oration, or a south wind, or a college, or a cloudy lonely walk, — " striking the electric chain wherewith we are darkly bound." And having this experience, we strive to avail our-selves of it, and propitiate the divine inmate to speak to us again out of clouds and darkness. Truly, whilst it speaketh not, man is a pitiful being. He whistles, eats, sleeps, gets his gun, makes his bargain, lounges, sins, and when all is done is yet wretched. Let the soul speak, and all this drivelling and these toys are thrown aside and man listens like a child.

The good of going into the mountains is that life is reconsidered; it is far from the slav-

ery of your own modes of living, and you have
opportunity of viewing the town at such a distance as may afford you a just view, nor can
you have any such mistaken apprehension as
might be expected from the place you occupy
and the round of customs you run at home.

He who believes in inspiration will come here
to seek it. He who believes in the wood-loving
muses must woo them here, and he who believes
in the reality of his soul will therein find inspiration, and muses, and God, and will come out here
to undress himself of pedantry and judge right-
eous judgment, and worship the First Cause.

The reason why we like simplicity of character, the reason why grown men listen with un-
tiring interest to a lively child is the same, viz.,
it is something more than man, above man, and
we hearken with a curiosity that has something
of awe. We should so listen to every man, if
his soul spake, but it does not; his fears speak,
his senses speak, and he himself seldom.

WHITE MOUNTAINS

July 15, 1832.

A few low mountains, a great many clouds always covering the great peaks, a circle of woods

to the horizon, a peacock on the fence or in the yard, and two travellers no better contented than myself in the plain parlour of this house make up the whole picture of this unsabbatized Sunday. But the hours pass on, creep or fly, and bear me and my fellows to the decision of questions of duty; to the crises of our fate; and to the solution of this mortal problem. Welcome and farewell to them; fair come, fair go. God is, and we in him.

The hour of decision. It seems not worth while for them who charge others with exalting forms above the moon to fear forms themselves with extravagant dislike. I am so placed that my *aliquid ingenii* may be brought into useful action. Let me not bury my talent in the earth in my indignation at this windmill. But though the thing may be useless and even pernicious, do not destroy what is good and useful in a high degree rather than comply with what is hurtful in a small degree. The Communicant celebrates on a foundation either of authority or of tradition an ordinance which has been the occasion to thousands, — I hope to thousands of thousands, — of contrition, of gratitude, of prayer, of faith, of love and of holy living. Far be it from any of my friends, — God forbid it be in my heart, — to interrupt any occasion thus blessed of God's influences upon the human mind. I will not, because we may not all think alike of the means, fight so strenuously against the means, as to miss of the end which we all value alike. I think Jesus did not mean to institute a perpetual celebration, but that a commemoration of him would be useful. Others think that Jesus did establish this one. We are agreed that one is useful, and we are agreed I hope in the way in which it must be made useful, viz., by each one's making it an original Commemoration.

I know very well that it is a bad sign in a man to be too conscientious, and stick at gnats. The most desperate scoundrels have been the over-refiners. Without accommodation society is impracticable. But this ordinance is esteemed the most sacred of religious institutions, and I cannot go habitually to an institution which they esteem holiest with indifference and dislike.

GEORGE FOX

George Fox, born 1624, son of a weaver, was put out to a shoemaker, and for him tended sheep. In [1643–44] he began his wanderings, dressed always in leather clothing for strength's sake, and suffering much from hunger, thirst, want of lodging, imprisonment and abuse. He taught that the Scriptures could not be understood but by the same spirit that gave them forth. Rails had been built about the communion table in churches about ——, and the house in which the Episcopalians worshipped of course was only called "the Church." These things moved George's indignation very much. He called them steeple-houses, and on almost all occasions preferred to preach out of doors. When the church was manifestly the only convenient place, he went in. He told the priests that he was no man-made priest.

"The visible," he said, "covereth the invisible sight in you."

"It pleased the Lord to show him that the natures of those things which were hurtful without were also within in the minds of wicked men, and that the natures of dogs, swine, vipers, etc., and those of Cain, Ishmael, Esau, Pharaoh, etc., were in the hearts of many people. But since this did grieve him, he cried to the Lord saying, —Why should I be thus, seeing I was never addicted to commit those evils? And inwardly it was answered him, That it was needful he should have a sense of all conditions."—"About that time it happened that

walking in the town of Mansfield by the stee-
ple-house side it was inwardly told him, 'That
which people trample upon must be thy food.'
And at the saying of this it was opened to him
that it was the life of Christ people did trample
on, and that they fed one another with words,
without minding that thereby the blood of the
Son of God was trampled under foot." (Sewell, vol. 1.)

Thoroughly consistent he was; how much
more than other reformers. A consistent reformer. The natural growth, by reaction, of a
formal church. " Words, words, ye feed one
another with words,"— he said. He would have
the substance of religion seen and obeyed. All
his prophetic rhapsodies are directed at some
moral offence. They put him in prison. He
saw the evils of the jail " and laid before the
judges what a hurtful thing it was that prison-
ers should lie long in jail, because they learned
wickedness one of another in talking of their
bad deeds; and that therefore speedy justice
ought to be done."

He also wrote to them about the evil of putting to death for stealing. (*Fox's Life.*)

In jail, there was a conjurer who threatened
to raise the devil and break the house down.

But George went to him and said, "Come, let us see what thou canst do, and do thy worst: the devil is raised high enough in thee already; but the power of God chains him down." At the undaunted speech, the fellow slunk away. They gave him liberty to walk a mile from jail, hoping he would escape. Socrates-like, he would not. They offered him bounty if he would serve against Charles. He said his weapons were not carnal. A band of volunteers chose him their captain. Still he refused.

Col. —— threatened to kill the Quakers. "Here's my hair," said G. Fox, "here's my cheek, and here's my shoulder." The colonel and his companions stood amazed, and said, "if this be your principle, as you say, we never saw the like in our lives." To which Fox said, "What I am in words, I am the same in life."

Practical good sense he had, when, at the request of someone, he lay down on a bed to refute the rumour that he never slept in a bed.

A reformer putting ever a thing for a form. "My allegiance," he said, "doth not consist in swearing, but in truth and faithfulness."

Swedenborg "considered the visible world and the relation of its parts as the dial plate of the invisible one." Quoted in *New Jerusalem Magazine* for July, 1832.[1]

GOD

I have complained that the acknowledgment of God's presence halts far behind the fact. What is it intended to be but the tribute to one without whose movings no tribute can be paid, for no tributary can be? One without whom no man or beast or nature subsists; one who is the life of things, and from whose creative will our life and the life of all creatures flows every moment, wave after wave, like the successive beams that every moment issue from the Sun. Such is God, or he is nothing. What is God but the name of the Soul at the centre by which all things are what they are, and so our existence is proof of his? We cannot think of ourselves and how our being is intertwined with his without awe and amazement.

[TRUTH IMMORTAL]

August 11.[2]

The truth is not injured nor touched though thousands of them that love it fall by the way.

1 The *New Jerusalem Magazine* was the Swedenborgian organ.

2 Mr. Emerson was acutely ill in that week. — Ed.

Serene, adorable, eternal it lives, though Goethe, Mackintosh, Cuvier, Bentham, Hegel die in their places, which no living men can fill.

REPAIRS

The errors that the moon and earth make in the heavens in a long period of time, an equal period repairs; the seventh Pleiad was lost and is found; the sweet fern dies, but revives; as much rain as the mountain sheds in forming torrents is replenished by visiting clouds. But these are far-off signs of compensation. Before tea I counted not myself worth a brass farthing, and now I am filled with thoughts and pleasures and am as strong and infinite as an angel. So when, one of these days, I see this body going to ruin like an old cottage, I will remember that after the ruin the resurrection is sure. . . .

The principle of repairs is in us, the remedial principle. Everybody perceives greatest contrasts in his own spirit and powers. To-day he is not worth a brown cent, to-morrow he is better than a million. He kicks at riches and could be honoured and happy with nothing but arrowroot and balm tea. This we call being in good or bad spirits. It is only in the bad fit, that we doubt and deny and do ill, and we know well at that time that sorrow will come for the bad action; and sorrow is repairs, and belief in the powers and perpetuity of man will return, and we shall be magnified by trust in God. When, therefore, I doubt and sin, I will look up at the moon, and, remembering that its errors are all periodical; I will anticipate the return of my own spirits and faith.

Patrick Henry's speech full of religion.

[REAL ANTIQUITY]

Our upstart antiquities hide themselves like little children between the knees of such a fatherly place as London. The bishop of London sits in his cathedral by a regular succession of twelve hundred years. Read Palgrave's account of Saxon religion, vol. 1, p. 55.

God = good. Man = wickedness. They believed in future state.

[A BRITISH PLUTARCH]

August 12.

The British Plutarch and the modern Plutarch is yet to be written. They that have writ the lives of great men have not written them from love and from seeing the beauty that was to be desired in them. But what would operate such gracious motions upon the spirit as the death of Lord Cobham and of Sir Thomas More, and a censure of Bacon, and a picture of George Fox and Hampden, and the chivalrous integrity of Walter Scott, and a true portrait of Sir Harry Vane, and Falkland, and Andrew Marvell? I would draw characters, not write lives. I would evoke the spirit of each, and their relics might rot. Luther, Milton, Newton, Shakspeare, Alfred, a light of the world, — Adams. I would walk among the dry bones, and wherever on the face of the earth I found a living man, I would say, here is life, and life is communicable. Jesus Christ truly said, My flesh is meat indeed. I am the bread, for of his life or character have the nations of the earth been nourished. Socrates I should like well, if I dared to take him. I should repeat Montaigne though. I would n't.

> " Eyes that the beam celestial view
> Which evermore makes all things new."

These I claim as sole qualification, ewe-lamb. I would make Milton shine. I would mourn for Bacon. I would fly in the face of every cockered prejudice, feudal or vulgar, and speak as Christ of their good and evil.

[IDEAL MEN]

When we look at the world of past men, we say, what a host of heroes; but when we come to particularize, it is like counting the stars which we thought innumerable, but which prove few and rare. Bacon, Shakspeare, Cæsar, Scipio, Cicero, Burke, Chatham, Franklin, — none of them will bear examination, or furnish the type of a *Man*.

What we say, however trifling, must have its roots in ourselves, or it will not move others. No speech should be separate from our being like a plume or a nosegay, but like a leaf or a flower or a bud, though the topmost and remotest, yet joined by a continuous line of life to the trunk and the seed.

CHOLERA TIMES

August 17.

It would be good to publish Girard's heroism in yellow fever at Philadelphia, and Dr. Rush's account of his own practice, to stimulate the cowed benevolence of this dismal time.

We are to act doubtless in our care of our own health as if there were no other world. We are to be punctilious in our care. No caution

is unseemly. This is the design of Providence.
But we are to recognize, in every instant of this
creeping solicitude, that happy is the lot of
those to whom the unspeakable secrets of the
other state are disclosed. When our own hour
comes, when every medicine and means has been
exhausted, we are then to say to the angel,
Hail! All Hail! and pass to whatever God
has yet to reveal to the conscious spirit. Why
should we dread to die, when all the good and
the beautiful and the wise have died, and earth
holds nothing so good as that which it has lost.
But oh! let not life be valued, when that which
makes the value of life is lost. It is only a clean
conscience, the knowledge that we are beloved
by our friends, and deserve to be beloved, that
can persuade an honourable mind to pray that
its being may be prolonged an hour; but to
outlive your own respect, to live when your
acquaintance shall shrug their shoulders, and
count it a disgrace to you the breath that is yet
in your nostrils, — I shall be glad to be told
what is the pleasure, what is the profit that is
worth buying at such a price.

August 18.

To be genuine. Goethe, they say, was wholly
so. The difficulty increases with the gifts of the

individual. A plough-boy can be, but a minister, an orator, an ingenious thinker how hardly! George Fox was. "What I am in words," he said, "I am the same in life." Swedenborg was. "My writings will be found," he said, "another self." George Washington was; "the irreproachable Washington." Whoever is genuine, his ambition is exactly proportioned to his powers. The height of the pinnacle determines the breadth of the base.

A SUBJECT FOR A SERMON

August 19.

Reverence man, and not Plato and Cæsar. Wherever there is sense, reflexion, courage, admit it to the same honour, — embrace it, quote it from a truckman as quick as from Webster. If you cannot get the habit of seeing qualities except in the great, if anything new should spring up, it will be lost to you. "Socrates," says Montaigne, "makes his soul move a natural and common motion. 'A country peasant said this; a woman said that.' . . . He has done human nature a great kindness in showing it how much it can do of itself. We are all of us richer than we think we are, but we are taught to borrow and to beg, and brought up more to make use of what is another's than our own."

"He was content to stand by, and let reason argue for him."

Potentissimus est qui se habet in potestate.

Seneca.

The sublime of morals seems ever to be of this kind, frail man intimating this defiance of the universe and gathering himself into his shell. Every grand sentiment of religion, far as it flies, comes back to self. As when you say, "the gods approve the depth, but not the tumult, of the soul," the sublime of it is, that "to the soul itself depth, not tumult, is desireable." When you say, "Jupiter prefers integrity to charity," your finest meaning is, "the soul prefers," etc. When Jesus saith, "he that giveth one of these little ones a cup of cold water shall not lose his reward," is not the best meaning, "the love at which the giver has arrived"? "Every plant which my heavenly Father hath not planted shall be rooted up," "everything is transitory but what hath its life from the interior of the soul," and so on through the New Testament there is not a just or grand thought but is made more round and infinite by applying it to the soul considered as the universe, living from God within. Consider the sense of such propositions as " the pure in heart shall see God."

Is not then all objective theology a discipline, an aid, to the immature intellect until it is equal to the truth, and can poise itself. Yet God forbid that I should one moment lose sight of his real eternal Being, of my own dependence, my nothingness whilst yet I dare hail the present deity at my heart.

The understanding speaks much; the passions much; the soul seldom. The only friend that can persuade the soul to speak is a good and great cause. Out it comes now and then like the lightning from its cloud, and with an effect as prodigious.

September 5.

Hypocrisy is the attendant of false-religion. When people imagine that others can be their priests, they may well fear hypocrisy. Whenever they understand that no religion can do them any more good than they actually taste, they have done fearing hypocrisy.

[On September 9th, Mr. Emerson met his congregation again. In his sermon, he simply and freely stated his opinion, that Jesus did not intend to establish a perpetual observance when he ate the Passover with his disciples; and further, that it was not expedient to celebrate it as was then done in his church. For this opinion he gave his reasons, drawn from the Scriptures. He then stated what seemed to him real objections to the customary observance. Finally, since the changes he had proposed had not recommended themselves to the worshippers at the Second Church, he resigned his pastoral charge, "Because," he said, "it is my desire, in the office of a Christian minister, to do nothing which I cannot do with my whole heart." His people did not wish to part with him. Meetings were held in hopes of arranging some way of keeping him, but at last his resignation was reluctantly accepted, and he and his people parted in peace. (See Sermon on " The Lord's Supper " in *Miscellanies* ; also Cabot's and Holmes's memoirs of Emerson.)]

September 14.

The true doctrine respecting forms is this, is it not? — that Christianity aims to form in a man a critical conscience, and that being formed, he is constituted a judge, the only and absolute judge, of every particular form that the estab-

lished religion presents to him. The discretion
he exercises is like the discretion of the bench,
which hath nothing arbitrary.

Every man feels the strain of duty in a different place; L[owell] in domiciliaries, I in
paræneticks.

"Think of Living."   GOETHE.

Don't tell me to get ready to die. I know
not what shall be. The only preparation I can
make is by fulfilling my present duties. This
is the everlasting life.

To think of mortality makes us queasy, the
flesh creeps at sympathy with its kind. What
is the remedy? to ennoble it by animating it
with love and uses. Give the soul its ends to
pursue, and death becomes indifferent. It saith,
What have I to do with death?

The vice of Calvinism has been to represent
the other world wholly different from this. So
that a preparation to live in this was all lost for
that.

I would very temperately speak of future
delights, employments, . . . solely from the
prophecy of the powers that are immortal. Not
by description to captivate, for the impenetrable

veil, not to be lifted, has been shut down for that reason, to confine us to the present where all duty and excellence for us lies, — " *in seipso totus teres atque rotundus.*

Truth and virtue teach the same thing. It is in being good to wife and children and servants that the kingdom of heaven begins. It is in settling punctually with your tailor, and not holding out false hopes to young men. It is not over-praising your goods, or underrating your debtor's goods. It is in forming your own judgment upon questions of duty. It is in preferring a just act to a kind one, and a kind act to a graceful one. It is in thus trying your powers, and bringing out each one in order, until the whole moral man lives and acts and governs the animal man.

It is no argument against the future state, the ignorance of man, no more than the lifelessness of the egg is a proof that it shall not be a bird, or the want of intelligence in the human embryo a proof that it shall not be a reasoning speaking man.

But this ignorance is argument as significant as a visible finger out of the sky, that we should not fabricate a heaven in our heads, and then square life to that fiction.

These powers, and these powers alone, contain the revelation of what you can do and can become. It is writ in no book. It can never be foretold or imagined. Their's is your secret. They are your heaven, or they are your hell. And their hell shall be whatever part of heaven you miss of: i. e., it is the perversion of a good power that makes your misfortunes.

[SEEK TRUTH]

September 17.

I would gladly preach to the demigods of this age (and why not to the simple people?) concerning the reality of truth, and the greatness of believing in it and seeking after it. It does not shock us when ordinary persons discover no craving for truth, and are content to exist for years exclusively occupied with the secondary objects of house and lands and food and company, and never cast up their eyes to inquire whence it comes and what it is for, wholly occupied with the play, and never ask after the design. But we cannot forgive it in the ——s and ——s that they who have souls to comprehend the magnificent secret should utterly neglect it and seek only huzzas and champagne. My quarrel with the vulgar great men is that they do not generously give themselves to the measures which they meddle with ; they do not espouse the things they would do, live in the life of the cause they would forward and faint in its failure, but they are casting sheep's eyes ever upon their own by-ends ; their pert individuality is ever and anon peeping out to see what way the wind blows, and where this boat will land them, whether it is likely they will dine nicely and sleep warm. That for the *first* thing, that choosing action rather than contemplation, they only half act, they only give their hands or tongues, and not themselves to their works.

My *second* charge against them is, that they lack faith in man's moral nature. They can have no enthusiasm, for the deep and infinite part of man, out of which only sublime thought and emotions can proceed, is hid from them.

Socrates believed in man's moral nature and knew and declared the fact that virtue was the supreme beauty. He was capable therefore of enthusiasm.

Jesus Christ existed for it. He is its Voice to the world. Phocion felt it, recognized it, but was a man of action, true in act to this conviction. Luther, More, Fox, Milton, Burke, every great man, every one with whose character the idea of stability presents itself, had this faith.

The true men are ever following an invisible Leader, and have left the responsibleness of their acts with God. But the artificial men have assumed their own bonds and can fall back on nothing greater than their finite fortunes; . . . empirics with expedients for a few years, reputation instead of character, and fortune instead of wisdom. The true men stand by and let reason argue for them. I talk with Sampson and see it is not him, but a greater than him, " My Father is greater than I." Truth speaks by him. (Can my friend wish a greater eulogy ?)

Whatever I say that is good on the Sundays, I speak with fervour and authority, — surely not feeling that it rests on my word, or has only the warrant of my faulty character, but that I got it from a deeper and common source, and it is as much addressed to me as to those I speak to.

[CARLYLE]

October 1.

I am cheered and instructed by this paper on Corn Law Rhymes in the *Edinburgh* by my Germanick new-light writer, whoever he be. He gives us confidence in our principles. He assures the truth-lover everywhere of sympathy. Blessed art that makes books, and so

joins me to that stranger by this perfect railroad.

[SOVEREIGNTY OF ETHICS]

Has the doctrine ever been fairly preached
of man's moral nature? The whole world holds
on to formal Christianity, and nobody teaches
the essential truth, the heart of Christianity, for
fear of shocking, etc. Every teacher, when once
he finds himself insisting with all his might
upon a great truth, turns up the ends of it at
last with a cautious showing *how* it is agreeable
to the life and teaching of Jesus, as if that was
any recommendation, as if the blessedness of
Jesus' life and teaching were not because they
were agreeable to the truth. Well, this cripples
his teaching. It bereaves the truth he inculcates
of more than half its force, by representing it
as something secondary that can't stand alone.
The truth of truth consists in this, that it is
self-evident, self-subsistent. It is light. You
don't get a candle to see the sun rise.

Instead of making Christianity a vehicle of
truth, you make truth only a horse for Christianity. It is a very operose way of making
people good. You must be humble because
Christ says, " Be humble." " But why must I
obey Christ?" " Because God sent him." But

how do I know God sent him? Because your own heart teaches the same thing he taught. Why then shall I not go to my own heart at first?

THE TERRIBLE FREEDOM

October 2.

It well deserves attention what is said in *New Jerusalem Magazine* concerning External Restraint. It is awful to look into the mind of man and see how free we are, to what frightful excesses our vices may run under the whited wall of a respectable reputation. Outside, among your fellows, among strangers, you must preserve appearances, a hundred things you cannot do; but inside, the terrible freedom![1]

October 9.

"I teach by degrees," says Landor's Epicurus. It is not the will but the necessity of the wise. None are wise enow to teach otherwise. All this pedantry about the peoples not bearing the whole truth,—what else does it mean than that the teacher has not yet arrived at the safe, that is, the *true* statement of the particular doctrine which he would oppose to the ruling error. He knows in general there is an

---

1 Compare the early poem beginning, "How much, protecting God, to thee I owe." *Poems*, Appendix.

error; he has not yet found its boundary lines. . . .

All our art is how to use what the good God provides us. There is water enough; we are only so to shape aqueducts as to bring it to our door. There is air enough; we must only so build as that it shall ventilate our house. So with man's education. There is truth enough; only open the mind's door, and straighten the passages. There are men enough; only so place yourself to them in true position (*en rapport*), i. e., by amity, as to suck the sweetness of society. There is power and happiness enough.

> I will not live out of me.
> I will not see with others' eyes;
> My good is good, my evil ill.
> I would be free; I cannot be
> While I take things as others please to rate them.
> I dare attempt to lay out my own road.
> That which myself delights in shall be Good,
> That which I do not want, indifferent;
> That which I hate is Bad. That 's flat.
>
> Henceforth, please God, forever I forego
> The yoke of men's opinions. I will be
> Light-hearted as a bird and live with God.
> I find him in the bottom of my heart,

I hear continually his Voice therein,
And books, and priests, and worlds, I less es-
teem.
Who says the heart's a blind guide? It is not.
My heart did never counsel me to sin.
I wonder where it got its wisdom,
For in the darkest maze, amid the sweetest baits
Or amid horrid dangers, never once
Did that gentle angel fail of his oracle.
The little needle always knows the north,
The little bird remembereth his note,
And this wise Seer never errs.
I never taught it what it teaches me,
I only follow when I act aright. [1]
Whence then did this omniscient spirit come?
From God it came. It is the Deity.

October 13.

"If thou lovest true glory, thou must trust
her truth." "She followeth him who doth not
turn and gaze after her."   LANDOR.

"Since all transcendent, all true and genuine
greatness must be of a man's own raising and
only on the foundations that the hand of God
has laid, do not let any touch it; keep them off
civilly, but keep them off."   LANDOR.

1 Printed in *Poems*, among *Poems of Youth*: Appendix,
Centenary Ed.

October 13.

Exhortations and examples are better than psalms and sermon.

We have thoughts, but we don't know what to do with them; materials, but we can't manage or dispose. We cannot get high enough above them to see their order in reason. We cannot get warm enough to have them exert their natural affinities and throw themselves into crystal. We see a new sect devoted to certain ideas, and we go to individuals of it to have them explained.[1] Vain expectation! They are possessed with the ideas, but do not possess them.

[THE LIGHT WITHIN]

CHARDON ST., *October* 14, 1832.

The great difficulty is that men do not think enough of themselves, do not consider what it is that they are sacrificing, when they follow in a herd, or when they cater for their establishment. They know not how divine is a man. I know you say, Such a man thinks too much of himself. Alas! he is wholly ignorant. He yet wanders in the outer darkness, in the skirts and shadows of himself, and has not seen his inner light.

1 Probably referring to the Swedenborgians.

Would it not be the text of a useful discourse to young men, *that every man must learn in a different way?* How much is lost by imitation! Our best friends may be our worst enemies. A man should learn to detect and foster that gleam of light which flashes across his mind from within far more than the lustre of [the] whole firmament without. Yet he dismisses without notice his peculiar thought *because* it is peculiar. The time will come when he will postpone all acquired knowledge to this spontaneous wisdom, and will watch for this illumination more than those who watch for the morning. For this is the principle by which the other is to be arranged. This thinking would go to show the significance of self-education; that in reality there is no other; for, all other is nought without this.

A man must teach himself because that which each can do best, none but his maker can teach him. No man yet knows what it is, nor can, till that person has exhibited it. Where is the master that could have taught Shakspeare? Where is the master that could have instructed Franklin, or Washington, or Bacon, or Newton? Every great man is an unique. The Scipionism of Scipio is just that part he could not borrow. . . . Every man comes at the common results with most conviction in his own way. But he only uses a different vocabulary from yours; it comes to the same thing.

An imitation may be pretty, comical, popular, but it never can be great. Buonaparte mimicked Themistocles. If anybody will tell me who it is the great man imitates in the original crisis when he performs a great act, — who Muley Molok imitated, or Falkland, or Scipio, or Aristides, or Phocion, or Fox, or More, or Alfred, or Lafayette, I will tell him who else can teach him than himself. A man has got to learn that he must embrace the truth, or shall never know it; that to be thankful for a little is the way to get more. He is to work himself clear of how much nonsense and mischief. He is to learn, like the Persian, to speak the truth.

[THOUGHT AND SPEECH]

Do you say that a mechanic must attend to language and composition? You are looking the wrong way and seeking the source in the river. Strong thinking makes strong language; correct thinking, correct speech.

[NOTHING WITHIN]

S. gave a sad definition of his friend in saying he resembled a nest of Indian boxes, one
after the other, each a new puzzle, and when
you come to the last there is nothing in it. So
with each man, a splendid barricade of circumstances, the renown of his name, the glitter of
his coach, then his great professional character,
then comes another fine shell of manners and
speech, — but go behind all these and the Man,
the self, is a poor, shrunken, distorted, imperceptible thing.

October 17.

The surveyor goeth about taking positions
to serve as the points of his angles, and thereby
afterwards he finds the place of the mountain.
The philosopher in like manner selects points
whence he can look on his subject from different sides, and by means of many approximate
results he at last obtains an accurate expression
of the truth.

That statement only is fit to be made public
which you have got at in attempting to satisfy
your own curiosity. For himself, a man only
wants to know how the thing is; it is for other

people that he wants to know what may be said about it.

October 19.

Landor said, "The true philosophy is the only true prophet." May I not add, *the whole* Future is in the bottom of the heart. Jung Stilling said of Goethe, "The man's heart, which few know, is as true and noble as his genius, which all know." If Carlyle knew what an interest I have in his persistent goodness, would it not be worth one effort more, one prayer, one meditation? But will he resist the Deluge of bad example in England? One manifestation of goodness in a noble soul brings him in debt to all the beholders that he shall not betray their love and trust which he has awakened. — (*Mem.*) *Fraser's Magazine,* vol. III, March, 1831, Carlyle's notice of Schiller.

Mr. N. K. G. Oliver died on board U. S. ship Potowmac, Commodore Downes. He was Commodore's Secretary. The crew subscribed $2080 for the relief of his destitute family.

The sum raised in Boston for the relief of the Cape de Verde islanders suffering from famine was about $6800.

[MARY MOODY EMERSON]

My aunt had an eye that went through and through you like a needle. "She was endowed," she said, "with the fatal gift of penetration." She disgusted everybody because she knew them too well.

To live in a field of pumpkins, yet eat no pie!

October 28, 1832.

The vote on the question proposed to the proprietors of the Second Church this evening stood thus, Ayes 25; nays 34; blanks 2. On the acceptance of the pastor's letter, ayes 30; nays 20; blanks 4.[1]

"He who would write heroic poems should make his whole life an heroic poem."

MILTON.

SCHILLER

I propose to myself to read Schiller, of whom I hear much. What shall I read? His *Robbers*? Oh no, for that was the crude fruit of his immature mind. He thought little of it himself.

[1] This is the only direct mention in this journal of Mr. Emerson's parting from his church.

What then : his æsthetics ? Oh no, that is only his struggle with Kantean metaphysics. His poetry ? Oh no, for he was a poet only by study. His histories ? — And so with all his productions ; they were the fermentations by which his mind was working itself clear, they were the experiments by which he got his skill, and the fruit, the bright pure gold of all was — Schiller himself.

Carlyle says it was complained of Schiller's *Robbers* that the moral was bad, or it had none, and he saith, "but Schiller's vindication rests on higher grounds than these. His work has on the whole furnished nourishment to the more exalted powers of our nature ; the sentiments and images which he has shaped and uttered, tend, in spite of their alloy, to elevate the soul to a nobler pitch ; and this is a sufficient defence," etc. The writer of a work, which interests and excites the spiritual feelings of men, has as little need to justify himself by showing how it exemplifies some wise saw, or modern instance, as the doer of a generous action has to demonstrate its merit by deducing it from the system of Shaftesbury, or Smith or Paley, or whichever happens to be the favourite system of the age and place. The instructiveness of the one and the virtue of the other exist independently of all systems or saws and in spite of all."

Life of Schiller.

This is tantamount (is it not?) to Aristotle's maxim, "We are purified by pity and terror." And thus is Shakspeare moral, not of set purpose, but by "elevating the soul to a nobler pitch." So too are all great exciters of man moral ; in war and plague and shipwreck greatest virtues appear. Why, but that the inmost soul which lies tranquil every day is moved and speaks ? But the inmost soul is God. The spark passes where the chain is interrupted.

November 6.

Pope is said to have preferred this couplet among his writings : —

" Lo where Mæotis sleeps, and hardly flows
    The freezing Tanais 'mid a waste of snows."

[PUBLIC CONCERN OR PRIVATE?]

A part of our anxiety for the welfare of the State, that the elections should go well, proceeds peradventure from our consciousness of personal defect.

If the soul globe itself up into a perfect integrity — have the absolute command of its desires — it is less dependent on other men, and less solicitous concerning what they do, albeit with no loss of philanthropy. At least, that is my thought from reading Milton's beautiful vindication of himself from the charge of incontinence and intemperance. See vol. 1, p. 239, etc. Yet seemeth it to me that we shall all feel dirty if Jackson is reëlected.

[WASTED LIFE]

November 11.

What is the grief we feel when a man dies? Is it not an uneasiness that nothing can be said? He has done nothing; he has been merely passive to the common influences that act on all men. And now that the great endowments proper to every man have passed away from this flesh, we feel that the nothingness of life and character is sad dispraise, and the affectionate expressions of friendship are apologetic. Certainly the feeling would be very different if the departed man had been an earnest self-cultivator, scattering streams of useful influence on every side of him. Then every tear that flowed would be a tribute of eulogy. Friends would not need to say anything, his acts would speak for him. They would keep a proud silence; a rich consolation would shine in all eyes. But now, let our tears flow for the vanity of man, for the poor issues of a God's charity.

November 13.

We think so little that we are always novices in speculation. We think so little that every new thought presented to us, even every old thought in a new dress of words, takes us by surprise and we are thus at the mercy of Goethe, Kant, Cousin, Mackintosh, and even of Burton. If, from their natural centre, our thoughts had taken a natural arrangement by frequent and free exercise, we should detect the falsehood at sight in whatever was proposed to us on all the primary questions. As it is, we can hardly stand our ground against the ready advocate of a proven lie.

Excellence is always brand new.

A kingdom has the rig of a man-of-war; a republic the rig of a merchantman.

Men in our day consent to war because the antagonists are strangers. I know my neighbour, but the Frenchman, the Maylay, the Buenos Ayrean are no more to me than *dramatis personæ.*

The chief mourner does not always attend the funeral.

A fine day is not a weather-breeder, but a fine day.

The whole future is in the bottom of the heart.

"' What shall I teach you the foremost thing?'
Could'st teach me off my own shadow to spring?"
GOETHE, *apud* CARLYLE.

[SARTOR RESARTUS]

Unconsciously we are furnishing comic examples, to all spectators, of cobwebbed ethical rules. I go to the Atheneum and read that "man is not a clothes-horse," and come out and meet in Park St. my young friend who, I understand, cuts his own clothes, and who little imagines that he points a paragraph for Thomas Carlyle.

Goethe says, "Others will never spare you." So true is it that I am not reminded of my own unfaithfulness when I animadvert upon it in C.

MISS MARGARET TUCKER

Saturday, 11 A. M., *November* 24, 1832, died my sister, Margaret Tucker. Farewell to thee for a little time, my kind and sympathizing sister. Go rejoice with Ellen, so lately lost, in God's free and glorious universe. Tell her, if she needs to be told, how dearly she is remembered, how dearly valued. Rejoice together that you are free of your painful corporeal imprisonment. I may well mourn your loss, for in many sour days I had realized the delicacy and sweetness of a sister's feeling. I had rejoiced too, as always, in the gifts of a true lady, in whom was never anything little or mean seen or suspected, who was all gentleness, purity and sense with a rare elevation of sentiments. God comfort the bitter lonely hours which the sorrowing mother must spend here.

Farewell, dear girl. I have a very narrow acquaintance, and of it you have been a large part. We anchor upon a few, and you have had the character and dignity that promised everything to the esteem and affection of years. Think kindly of me, — I know you will, — but perchance the disembodied can do much more, can elevate the sinking spirit and purify and urge it to generous purposes. Teach me to make trifles, trifles, and work with consistency and in earnest to my true ends. The only sister I ever had, pass on, pure soul! to the opening heaven.

A WINTER'S DAY

November 27.

Instead of lectures on Architecture, I will make a lecture on God's architecture, one of his beautiful works, a Day. I will draw a sketch of a Winter's day. I will trace, as I can, a rude outline of the foundation and far-assembled influences, the contribution of the universe whereon this magical structure rises like an exhalation, the wonder and charm of the immeasurable Deep. The bed of a day is Eternity, the ground plan is Space. The account of its growth is Astronomy. Its nearer phenomena are Chemistry, Optics, Agriculture, Hydrostatics, Animated Nature. It ends again in Astronomy, when it has carried forward by its few rounded hours the immense Beneficence.

This magic lanthorn with fresh pictures, this microcosm, this Bridal of the earth and sky, this God's wonder, we cannot take to pieces like a machine, but we may study its miracles apart, one at a time, and learn how to find the whole world, and every one of its pebbles, a tongue.

The *snow* is a self-weaving blanket with which

the parts of the globe exposed to the cold, cover themselves in pile proportioned to their exposure, what time the animated creation in the same parts whiten and thicken their fleeces. The snow crystal, (*nix columnaris*) hexagon, — *densum vellus tacitarum aquarum.*

Provision for keeping the waters fluid : immense force of crystallizing water, — riving of granite blocks. Powers of the Arctic winter. Beneficent effects upon the animal, vegetable, mineral creation — most unknown ; defence of trees, vegetable heat, e. g., last winter. *Crunching of the snow under the wood-sled.*

Domestic effects : *pump frozen* ; thawed by salt. *Water pitcher cracked* ; leave it empty. *Clock too fast* ; lengthen the pendulum. *Gloves not thick enough* ; exchange them for mittens. *Frost on the windows, wood splits better, and stone worse. Cat's back and flannel vest sparkle.* Flowers, bees, ants, flies, none ; but instead, the social apple, the breakfast honey, the good proverb ; and the flies, plain-suited, we are willing to spare, and their cousins the musquitoes that make men draw up the foot. Ice trade, fur trade, and country trade by means of universal railroad ; and conservative powers of frost. Fuel-wood brought out of the wood-lots ; game easier procured ; lime-kiln burned.

Games : skating, sledding, snow-building, Esquimaux hunting with snow-shoes.

Winter evening. Reading, astronomical observations, electricity.

India-rubber shoes ; Winter less interesting here than in the North or in the South, but beautiful.

(*Memoranda* for " The Winter's Day.") Audubon ; Polar Regions ; Polehampton ; Daniell ; Black.

The cholera cost the city of New York 110,000 dollars, and a vast additional expense to individuals. The Holy days are said to cost Spain £7,000,000 sterling a year.

WORDSWORTH

December 1.

I never read Wordsworth without chagrin ; a man of such great powers and ambition, so near to the *Dii majores*, to fail so meanly in every attempt ! A genius that hath epilepsy, a deranged archangel. The Ode to Duty, conceived and expressed in a certain high, severe style, does yet miss of greatness and of all effect by such falsities or falses as,

"And the most ancient heavens thro' thee are fresh
    and strong,"

which is throwing dust in your eyes, because they have no more to do with duty than a dung-cart has. So that fine promising passage about "the mountain winds being free to blow upon thee," etc., flats out into "*me and my bene-dictions.*" If he had cut in his Dictionary for words, he could hardly have got worse.

[COMPULSORY MATHEMATICS]

Among things to be reformed at college is this miserable practice of leading ingenuous youth blindfold through trigonometry and the other mathematics. The first scholar tells me that 'he can understand a page at a time'; and young Appleton[1] himself suggests the great good of having a preliminary treatise, often re-ferred to in the main body, apprizing the reader what it all drives at. Now he has no idea. There are two sorts of *cui bono*, however. If the

[1] Either Thomas Gold Appleton (class of 1831), the well-known wit of Boston later, or William Channing Apple-ton (class of 1832).

boy sees the truth and beauty of the problem, he may well remain ignorant and indifferent for a time as to its practical applications. But if he discern neither necessary truth nor utility, he has got stone for bread. "Teach me," said the young Syracusan to Archimedes, "the divine art by which you have saved your country." "Divine, do you call it?" said A. "It is indeed divine, but so it was before it saved the city. He that woos the goddess, must forget the woman."

> None spares another, yet it pleases me
> That none to any is indifferent.
> No heart in all this world is separate,
> But all are cisterns of one central sea:
> All are mouthpieces of the Eternal Word.

[POSTSCRIPT TO "A WINTER'S DAY"]

The good earth, the planet on which we are embarked and making our annual voyage in the unharboured Deep, carries in her bosom every good thing her children need on the way, for refreshment, fuel, science, or action. She has coal in the hold, and all meats in the larder, and overhung with showiest awning.

The progress of art is to equalize all places.

Reindeer, caoutchouc, glass windows, anthracite coal, Nott stoves, coffee, and books will give Greenland the air and ease of London. Ice, fruits, baths, refrigerators, linen, will fan the hot forehead of Cuba to the 56th degree.

Dangers. The snow-storm.

Capt. Parry's *frozen men*.

Degree of cold tolerable to man,— 58. Temperature of the Celestial spaces.

Γλώσσης πρὸ τῶν ἄλλων κράτει θεοῖς ἑπόμενος.
PYTHAGORAS.

November 29.

I wrote to George A. Sampson: Are they not two worlds, your solitude and your society? one, heaven, the other, earth; one, real, the other apparent. And that society is best and unobjectionable which does not violate your solitude, but permits you to communicate the very same train of thought. And then will our true heaven be entered when we have learned to be the same manner of person to others that we are alone; say the same things to them, we think alone, and to pass out of solitude into society without any change or effort. When an awkward man is alone, he is graceful, all his motions are natural. When a vain man is alone, his thoughts are wise. It is the presence of other people which embarrasses them by over exciting them, and they do and say ungracious things. The reason is, himself is a pepper-corn: his relations to other people are the whole world in his imagination. The only remedy must be from the growth of his true self, and its mastering predominance over him, so that the men and things which looked so great shall shrink to their true dimensions, as already the house in which we lived and the hills on which we ran in childhood appear smaller than they were.

[MISS MARGARET TUCKER][1]

It is not certainly to gratify any impatience of domestic sorrow by a parade of departed merits that this notice of a worthy woman is offered, but it is offered merely because many wet eyes will look in the obituary and ask if there is no word to be spoken over a dear and honoured benefactress, a most gentle and virtuous lady.

In the death of Miss Margaret Tucker one

1 This notice of Mr. Emerson's loved sister-in-law was probably printed in a Boston newspaper. It was written from Malta, February 2, but it seems best to introduce it here.

who was fit to be an ornament of society has passed away almost unknown to it. A beloved member of a gifted family, to whom uncommon accomplishments and most attractive manners were the ornament and riches of a most delicate frame, she has spent her few years in retirement. But in that family, and in the much larger circle of her acquaintance, she was revered and loved in an uncommon degree, and as she deserved. For she possessed the charm and respect that always attaches to a strong sense, when united with elevated sentiments. Never was anything little or mean either seen or suspected in her. She was the considerate, but most liberal friend of all who needed assistance, and many know how ingeniously sometimes her open hand sought the luxury of beneficence. Her extreme delicacy and sweetness never suffered her to wound the feelings of another, and, though almost all her life the victim of slow but disheartening disease, it is not easy to remember that she ever complained. Few have preserved such dignity and gentleness through so long a term of sickness, or gone out of the world to join the friends she had never forgotten, more affectionately remembered by those whom she has left in it.

[In Mr. Cabot's Memoir (vol. 1, pp. 171–175) are given four interesting letters written at this crisis of Mr. Emerson's life; one by him to his brother William telling him of the schemes he was then revolving for the new life before him, among them one for a new magazine in which his brothers should join,—"Give me my household gods against the world, William, Edward and Charles." (William had been giving literary lectures in New York.) Two letters follow from Charles to his Aunt Mary, telling of the illness of Waldo (he was called so in the family), and his decision to go to Europe, and of his (Charles's) "growing disappointment as I go Sunday after Sunday and hear ordinary preachers, and remember what a torch of kindling eloquence has been snuffed out in such an insignificant fashion." Then follows a letter from Waldo telling William of his resolve to go to Europe instead of visiting Edward in Porto Rico.]

Authors or Books quoted or referred to
in Journal for 1832

Zoroaster, *Zend Avesta*, *apud Histoire de l' Académie des Inscriptions*; Pythagoras; Aristotle;

Quintus Fabius Pictor, *apud* Cicero (?);

Cicero; Horace; St. Paul; Plutarch, *Archimedes, Pericles*; Seneca;

Leonardo da Vinci, *apud* Brewster's *Life of
Newton*;

Montaigne, *Essays*; Shakspeare; Grotius;

Milton, *Comus, Prose Works*; George Herbert;

George Fox, *apud* Sewell's *History of the
Quakers*, also *Life of*; Bishop Patrick, *Parable
of a Pilgrim*;

Fénelon, Fontenelle; Saurin;

Swedenborg; John Jortin;

Fielding, *Proverbs*; Lucas, *On Happiness,
On Holiness*; Joseph Black;

Bentham; Patrick Henry; Moses Mendelssohn, *Phædo*; Herschel, William and John;
Jung Stilling, *Autobiography*;

Goethe, *apud* Carlyle; Schiller; John Flaxman, *Beauty, Sculpture*, apud *Rees' Encyclo-
pedia*;

Laplace; Schlegel, *Guesses at Truth*; Malthus; Burns, *Poems*; Mackintosh, *Ethical Philosophy*; Abernethy, *Lectures*;

Jeffrey; Hegel; Pestalozzi, *apud* Biber; Wordsworth; Landor, *Imaginary Conversations*;

Moore, *Poems*; Daniell, *Meteorological Essays*; Mary Somerville, *Mechanism of the Heavens*;

Parry, *Voyages*; Audubon; Cousin; Channing, *Sermon on War*; Carlyle, *Cornlaw Rhymes*, *Sartor Resartus*, *Life of Schiller*;

Edinburgh Review; *New Jerusalem Magazine*.

END OF VOLUME II

The Riverside Press

CAMBRIDGE . MASSACHUSETTS

U . S . A